Disclaimer

I have changed some names to protect individuals' privacy. These are my memories, from my perspective, and I have tried to represent events as faithfully as possible.

MICHAEL OPYD

For all the Realtors who haven't received
the education you deserve,
I hope this serves as the guidance
you've been seeking.

TABLE OF
CONTENTS

Realtor
A History

You are about to embark on a career in a profession that was founded over a century ago, rooted in an industry dating back to the 1600s in America. This profession was created to bring professionalism and integrity to an industry that once lacked both. As you prepare to uphold these established standards, it's essential to understand the historical events that have shaped where we stand today.

The modern Realtor exists because of these past events. Although Realtors now run their businesses differently, the core role and significance of a Realtor remain unchanged.

In the Beginning

For decades after the Pilgrims landed on Plymouth Rock in 1620, real estate as we know it didn't exist. Most settlers arriving in the New World simply selected a plot of land and "claimed" it as their own.

Land Jobbers: 1700s

By the 1700s, the first version of what would later become Realtors emerged—known as "Land Jobbers." These individuals would acquire small parcels of land, bundle them together, and sell them to farmers or real estate speculators.

Buying and selling land was particularly challenging at that time due to the lack of reliable titles. Often, it was difficult to determine who, if anyone, actually owned a piece of property. Unscrupulous Land Jobbers took advantage of this uncertainty by selling land they didn't own.

The First Multiple Listing Service: 1800s

In the late 1800s, a more organized approach to real estate emerged. Real estate professionals would gather to share information about properties they were selling, agreeing to compensate others who helped complete a sale. This collaboration led to the birth of the first Multiple Listing Service (MLS), based on a principle unique to organized real estate: "Help me sell my inventory, and I'll help you sell yours."

Curbstoners, Open Houses, Code of Ethics, and the Official Realtor Name: 1900s — 1920s

The National Association of Real Estate Exchanges (now the National Association of Realtors® or NAR) was founded in 1908 to unite brokers and agents. Before 1919, however, anyone could call themselves a real estate broker without needing a license or certification. This led to a chaotic market, where so-called "Curbstoners" would place signs in front of homes to compete with licensed brokers. Sellers often had to randomly choose a sign to help sell their property.

In the 1910s, brokers introduced the concept of open houses. These events could last days or even weeks, with homes open for 12 hours a day until a buyer was found. Since brokers needed to spend the entire day at the home, they could only represent one listing at a time.

In 1913, recognizing the need for professional standards, the newly formed association adopted a Code of Ethics. The guiding principle was the Golden Rule: "Do unto others as you would have them do unto you."

The term "Realtor" was officially coined in 1916 to distinguish real estate agents who were members of the National Association of Real Estate Boards and adhered to its strict Code of Ethics. By 1919, states began implementing real estate licensing laws to prevent unqualified individuals from selling homes and to ensure that those in the profession were of high moral character and reputation.

Open Houses, Advertising, and the MLS: 1930s — 1980s

By the 1930s, real estate companies started employing multiple agents, allowing them to handle several listings at once. Agents began using open houses not only to sell homes but also as personal marketing opportunities, leveraging the contacts they made to promote other properties that might suit potential buyers.

After the market slump caused by the Great Depression, the real estate industry surged in the 1940s and 1950s, fueled by the post-World War II demand for new construction as soldiers returned home. Agents and sellers advertised homes on the radio and in newspapers, and with properties selling quickly, agents were able to take on even more listings.

By the 1960s, local multiple listing services (MLS) began emerging state by state, consolidating all available listings in a centralized database.

7

The Internet and Reality TV: 1990s

In the 1990s, property listings became publicly available online, and real estate companies quickly followed this trend. Realtor.com, one of the first real estate websites, was launched in the mid-1990s. Around the same time, reality TV began to enter American living rooms, and the first real estate-themed show, House Hunters, debuted, changing the way people viewed home buying.

Peak Numbers: 2000s

As lending guidelines loosened, nearly anyone could secure a loan to buy real estate. With rapid property price increases, the number of real estate agents swelled, peaking at 1.35 million in 2006. However, this figure declined for six consecutive years, hitting a low of 990,000 Realtors in 2012. The industry then rebounded, with numbers rising every year until 2022 when a record-breaking 1.56 million Realtors were registered. This figure decreased the following year.

Key Dates

- **1908:** The National Association of Real Estate Exchanges (now the National Association of REALTORS®) is founded.

- **1913:** The Code of Ethics is adopted.

- **1916:** The term "Realtor" is coined to distinguish real estate agents who adhere to the National Association's strict Code of Ethics.

- **1919:** States begin enacting real estate licensing laws to regulate who can sell homes.

- **1930s:** Agents start using open houses as personal marketing tools.

- **1960s:** Local multiple listing services (MLS) begin appearing state by state.

- **1990s:** Property listings become publicly available on the Internet.

- **1990s:** House Hunters airs as the first real estate reality show on television.

- **2022:** The highest-ever number of Realtors is recorded in America at 1.56 million.

Introduction
Real Estate School is Not What You Think

On a Monday morning in September 2009, I found myself sitting in my 2003 Honda Civic outside a strip mall on the south side of Chicago, sipping warm coffee from a travel mug borrowed from my parents' house. As I sat there in silence, two thoughts crossed my mind: one of pure excitement for what was about to begin, and the other, a simple yet pressing question: "What the hell am I doing?"

To give you some context, a month earlier, I had quit my comfortable corporate job in Boston, Massachusetts, after two years of working there straight out of college. After my goodbyes on a Friday, I packed everything I owned into my car over the weekend and drove fifteen hours back to my parents' house in the southern suburbs of Chicago.

My parents weren't exactly thrilled with my decision to quit without having another job lined up, especially considering I only had $2,000 to my name and the Great Recession of 2009 was in full swing. Still, they generously let me move back into my old room while I figured things out.

Weeks went by, and I still hadn't found a job. The uncertainty of my decision began to weigh on me, especially during late-night moments of lying in bed, staring at the ceiling, wondering if I had made a huge mistake.

One day, while researching finances, I stumbled upon a tool called a REIT (Real Estate Investment Trust). I had heard of these during my corporate job and decided to call my cousin, whose partner was a Realtor, for more insight. After explaining REITs to me, my cousin passed the phone to her partner, who gave me a lengthy update on the real estate market. My curiosity was piqued, so I asked what it was like to be a Realtor. She explained how Realtors are essentially entrepreneurs: their income reflects their effort, they're their own bosses, no day is the same, and real estate is a lifestyle where you can shape your life however you want. By the time the call ended, I knew with certainty what career I wanted to pursue.

I turned off my car, grabbed my worn-out work bag and lukewarm coffee, and stared at the lone lit-up office space in the otherwise dark strip mall. Taking a deep breath, I got out of the car and headed toward the small office.

Peeking through the glass door before opening it, I saw a handful of people already seated, which reassured me I wouldn't be alone. Inside, the room was simple: two rows of six tables, each with two black plastic folding chairs, separated by an aisle leading to a large, animated projector screen next to a podium at the front.

As I scanned the room, I noticed people of different ages and ethnicities, sitting in random spots. I smiled nervously at those who made eye contact with me as I made my way to an open seat in the second row, on the right side, closest to the wall. I didn't want to disrupt anyone if I needed to leave during class. Sitting down in the uncomfortable plastic chair, I placed my coffee on the table and put my bag on the floor. After taking off my jacket, I glanced at the workbook in front of me. As I flipped through its thick pages, I began to feel overwhelmed. School had never been my strong suit, and seeing all the unfamiliar material made me question my decision to be there. I even wondered if I could get my $200 back, especially since it represented 10% of my current net worth.

I closed the workbook and tried to calm myself by practicing deep breathing exercises I had learned in college sports. Just as I started to relax, I heard footsteps behind me. Turning around, I saw an older gentleman, about six feet tall, with shoulder-length gray hair. He wore tan corduroy pants, a dark blue sweater over a plaid collared shirt, and a worn-out blue blazer. Carrying a stack of papers and the same workbook I had, he made his way to the podium.

Once there, he put everything down, held up the workbook, and said, "Don't worry about all the stuff in this book. Just mark what I tell you, and you'll pass this class with no issues." This was my first day of real estate school.

Over the next few days, we hardly referred to the workbook. The instructor spent most of the time sharing random stories from his experience in the industry and warning us that this was the worst time to start a career in real estate because of the terrible market. Despite these odd lessons, I chalked up my uneasiness to nerves and kept pushing forward.

On the last day, we had to take a 50-question exam, requiring a 75% score to pass. I was anxious. I'd never been good at tests, and I knew I had to pass this one before I could even think about taking the state and national exams. Sitting in my usual seat, I found an answer sheet, a blank piece of paper, and a new yellow number two pencil waiting for me. I frantically skimmed through my workbook, trying to absorb as much information as possible. My heart raced when I realized there were large sections we hadn't covered.

When the instructor told us to put everything away, my stomach dropped. After stashing my book in my bag, I took a deep breath and waited for the exam to be handed out. To my surprise, all the questions were directly from the sections the instructor had told us to mark. A wave of relief washed over me as I recognized the material, and I passed the test easily.

A few weeks later, after successfully passing my state and national exams, I officially became a licensed real estate agent.

Forget (Almost) Everything You Learned in Real Estate School

When I signed up for real estate school, I was so eager to jump into my new career that I chose a class starting just two days later. In the 48 hours leading up to it, I spent most of my time watching House Hunters, browsing properties online, and daydreaming about my future life. By the time the class began, I had convinced myself that once I finished, I'd know everything needed to build a successful real estate business. I even told my girlfriend (now wife) that within a few years, I'd buy my parents the Jaguar convertible they'd always wanted.

Unfortunately, I quickly realized on my first day that the purpose of real estate school isn't to teach you how to build a successful business. Instead, the classes focus on basic real estate elements like common terminology (survey, lien, appraisal) and different types of ownership (fee simple, joint tenancy, tenants in common), but little beyond that.

That first night, I lay in bed, staring at the ceiling, wondering if I'd made another huge mistake. After some reflection, I accepted that while I wouldn't get the education I'd hoped for, I'd focus on passing the class and figure out the rest on my own.

Real estate pre-licensing classes are a bit like high school. Remember when your math teacher spent weeks teaching you the Pythagorean theorem ($a^2+b^2=c^2$)? How many times have you used it since graduation? Real estate school is similar. It teaches you what you need to pass the exams but very little that applies in the real world.

It wasn't until a few months into my first year that I fully grasped that real estate is a business learned through experience, not the classroom. Building a successful business requires constant learning, guidance from mentors, and time—despite what reality TV may suggest.

Reality TV

In 2006, Bravo TV launched Million Dollar Listing, a series following young agents selling high-end properties in Los Angeles. The show aimed to tap into America's real estate obsession during the mid-2000s boom. The first season, six episodes long, showed listings from start to close. After mixed reviews, the format changed in 2008, focusing on specific agents rather than real estate companies. The new version portrayed Realtors living extravagant lifestyles, complete with flashy "Potential Commission" graphics on the screen. It was a hit, leading to spin-offs in New York and Miami, and turning the featured agents into celebrities.

Million Dollar Listing wasn't the first real estate reality show, but it's one of hundreds that have flooded TV screens in recent decades. Most follow a similar formula, showing Realtors with glamorous lives, but this depiction is far from the reality most Realtors face.

It's rare for a Realtor to have a private driver or spend over $100,000 on a party. In truth, most Realtors don't earn anywhere near as much as people think. According to the National Association of Realtors, in 2023, Realtors with 16+ years of experience had a median income of $92,500, while those with less than two years earned just $8,100.[1]

87% Fail Within 5 Years

Starting a real estate business is as easy as becoming an Airbnb host or a dog walker. With a few hundred dollars, a GED or higher, and an internet connection, you can get a real estate license. But building a successful real estate business? That's one of the hardest things to do. In fact, 87% of Realtors fail within their first five years in the industry.[2]

Why is that?

Time

Real estate is a slow-moving industry, far removed from the fast-paced world of tech, where people buy a new iPhone every few years. On average, people buy a new home every 10 years and only a few times in their lifetime. That's a huge gap between sales, and there's no guarantee clients will use the same agent again. Realtors must nurture relationships over long periods, hoping that when clients are ready to buy or sell, they'll be top of mind. At the same time, they need to provide such excellent service that clients refer them to others.

Buying real estate is also much more time-consuming than making a purchase on Amazon or TikTok. Instead of an instant purchase, buying a home takes 30-60 days from contract acceptance. And that's after the home viewings, paperwork, inspections, and listing preparations. Realtors only get paid when the deal closes, making it challenging to wait months for a paycheck.

In my experience, most Realtors don't see their careers take off until after five years. Around this time, they start receiving regular referrals, and their marketing efforts pay off as clients come from outside their immediate network. While five years may seem like a blip in hindsight, it can feel like an eternity when you're in the thick of it, struggling. That's why so many Realtors give up before hitting their stride.

No Patience

A study by Microsoft found that the average attention span has dropped from 12 seconds in 2000 to just 8 seconds today.[3] The digital revolution has made us expect instant gratification in every part of our lives. Real estate is no exception. I've seen agents jump from company to company, hoping the next one will offer something—a different CRM system, lead generation—that will magically accelerate their business. But often, I see those same Realtors later, with their businesses still stagnant or having left the industry altogether.

100% Commission-Based

Another reason many Realtors leave the industry is the inconsistency of income. Unlike a corporate job where you get paid every two weeks, real estate agents are 100% commission-based. Realtors only earn money when a sale closes, so a steady paycheck requires a steady stream of clients. As I mentioned earlier, it takes time to build that consistency. It's not uncommon for months to go by without a paycheck, which makes paying personal and business expenses stressful.

Realtors also don't keep the full commission. The brokerage takes a percentage, leaving the agent with less than the original amount. And deals can fall apart at any time. For example, I once spent five months working with a buyer, only for the sale to collapse at the closing table because the seller didn't leave the home in agreed-upon condition. It took another three months before I finally got paid.

No Passion

Building a successful real estate business requires passion. Without it, you'll quit at the first sign of difficulty. Real estate is full of peaks and valleys, and if you don't have a strong desire to succeed, you'll detour at the first roadblock instead of finding a way through it. Throughout my career, I've seen many Realtors leave the industry because they lacked genuine passion for it. They came in full of excitement, thinking they'd get rich quickly, only to discover how challenging the business really is. To succeed in real estate, you need to know why it matters to you and let that drive you forward, no matter what obstacles come your way.

With all that in mind, it's easy to see why only 13% of Realtors make it past the five-year mark. Real estate is a tough business that takes time, patience, and a plan for how to sustain yourself financially. But for those who stick with it, the rewards can be life-changing.

Why I Wrote This Book

Like many people entering the real estate industry, I started with a false sense of what being a Realtor is really like. Knowing how easy it was to get a license, I expected to learn a few things quickly and start making large sums of money right away. But the only thing I learned quickly was that real estate is nothing like what's shown on TV, and to succeed, I needed a major mindset shift.

When reality hit me like a New Year's hangover, I started taking my career seriously. I spent a lot of time educating myself and learning how the real estate industry truly works. I began asking more questions—about what I should be doing each day, where to spend my money, who to market to, and how to generate business. I shadowed successful agents, attended every educational event I could afford, and devoured everything I could read on real estate. Along the way, I realized that the education offered to new agents didn't equip them with the tools they needed to succeed from day one.

The unfortunate truth is that there are no standardized education requirements for Realtors. Education falls to each brokerage, and they can offer as much or as little training as they want. Most brokerages earn their income by taking a percentage of each agent's commission, so their training is often focused on increasing sales rather than teaching new agents the essentials of building a sustainable business. This leaves many new agents to fend for themselves, learning to swim without a life preserver.

As I gained experience, I began to understand the uneasy feeling I had during real estate school. New agents, who are still learning, are entrusted with guiding consumers through what is often the biggest financial decision of their lives. Many of these agents don't yet have the knowledge to offer the guidance their clients need.

So, why did I write this book? I want to transform the real estate industry by giving Realtors practical, actionable knowledge from day one. I also want to shift the public's perception of Realtors. By providing new agents with the tools to build a successful business and better serve their clients, both the Realtors and their customers will benefit. Over time, this will help change the narrative around Realtors and elevate the profession, moving it beyond the stereotypes portrayed in movies, GIFs, and memes.

Throughout this book, I'll share personal stories of my own mistakes, lessons I've learned, and the experiences I've had along the way. You'll find practical advice on how to start and grow a real estate business, with relatable examples to simplify complex concepts and help you apply them more quickly.

This book is the result of years of trial and error, hard work, research, and self-discovery. My hope is that you'll take what I've learned and use it not only to become a better Realtor but also to improve as a person. With the right mindset and work ethic, everything you dream of is possible.

As Steve Jobs once said, "Those people who are crazy enough to think they can change the world, are the ones who actually do."

How to use
This Book

As I mentioned earlier, I wrote this book to provide Realtors with practical knowledge that can be applied immediately. To ensure the information is easy to absorb and put into action, I've structured the book in a specific way to help you avoid the steep learning curve that many new agents face.

Three Sections

The book is divided into three parts: Start, Build, and Succeed. **Start** includes chapters designed to prepare you for the challenges of entering the industry and building your business. **Build** focuses on helping you generate business and start earning income. **Grow** offers advice to take your business to the next level, reaching heights that few agents achieve.

Each part builds upon the previous one, allowing you to avoid the common mistake of skipping crucial foundational steps early in your career. It's important to focus on each chapter, take your time, and ensure you fully understand the material before moving on.

Chapters

Each chapter begins with a story about a mistake I or another agent made, followed by the lessons learned. These stories reflect common missteps many agents face, and by sharing them, I hope to help you avoid the same traps. The rest of each chapter is organized by importance and in a logical, step-by-step order, with tips, notes, and examples to clarify key points.

Tips and Notes

Throughout the book, you'll find **TIPS** and **NOTES** designed to complement the main content:

- **TIPS** include useful tools I've used in my business, practical advice, and suggestions to incorporate into your own practice.

- **NOTES** provide additional clarity and insight into specific topics.

While these aren't the main focus, they are essential for enhancing your understanding. Pay close attention to them.

Examples

Each chapter includes recognizable examples to make the material easier to grasp. These examples are specifically chosen to help you quickly understand and remember the content.

Important to Remember

At the end of each chapter, you'll find a summary of key points. This "Cliff Notes" section offers a brief overview of the chapter's main takeaways for easy reference. However, I encourage you not to rely solely on these summaries; you'll miss important details if you do.

End of Chapter Notes

At the end of each chapter, there's space for you to take notes. While the book is designed to be absorbed quickly, it's impossible to remember everything the first time through. Writing down key points will help reinforce your understanding and accelerate your learning.

Summary

No book can guarantee success, but I believe that if you apply the knowledge in these pages and approach your career with a strong desire to succeed, a solid work ethic, and patience, you will be among the rare 13% of Realtors who thrive beyond their first five years in the industry.

PART
01
Start »

Chapter 1
Becoming a Realtor

It was a beautiful spring morning in April 2018, and I had just finished an initial buyer consultation with my new clients from India. I was ecstatic—these clients were every Realtor's dream: cash buyers with a large budget, a clear idea of what they wanted, and a well-defined area of the city where they were looking to buy. They also needed to purchase quickly, as the property was for their two kids who would be starting school at a university downtown over the summer. Knowing their tight timeline, we scheduled a single day of showings for the following Sunday, with the goal of selecting a property that day.

Starting on Thursday, I began requesting showings for the eight properties they were interested in. By Sunday morning, I had secured appointments for seven of the eight, but the one they were most interested in still hadn't been confirmed. Since Thursday, I had been trying to reach the listing agent for that property without success. I was growing worried that we wouldn't be able to view it, despite multiple attempts that morning to contact her.

Realizing I had to meet my clients soon, I tried calling the agent again, hoping for a last-minute miracle. As the phone rang, I dejectedly lowered my head, expecting another disappointment. Just as I was about to end the call, I heard a voice say, "Hello?" Surprised, I quickly explained that I had been trying to schedule a showing for the last few days. The agent responded, "Oh, sorry. I've been swamped at my full-time job and forgot to get back to you. The property is vacant. Go ahead and get the keys from the doorman in the lobby. Feel free to show it whenever you like."

Relieved, I continued with the showings, taking my clients from building to building over the next few hours. After seeing the last unit, we sat in the lobby and discussed everything we had viewed over the past three hours. Even before we sat down, I knew which property they wanted to make an offer on—the one that had been difficult to schedule. We talked through the offer terms, and after saying our goodbyes, I rushed back to my office to submit the offer to the listing agent.

Our offer was a full-price cash offer with a closing date set for two weeks—a listing agent's dream. After emailing the offer, I immediately called the agent to inform her and discuss the terms. Once again, I couldn't get hold of her, so I sent a text to make sure she was aware of what was in her inbox.

Two days passed, and I still hadn't heard anything from the agent. I called, texted, and emailed again, but received no response. Finally, I got an email from her saying the sellers had decided to accept our offer. Excited, I called my clients to share the good news and let them know we should receive the signed paperwork within 24 hours (as is customary in my market). However, days went by, and I still hadn't received anything.

Three days after the initial acceptance email, the signed contract finally arrived. By this time, most of the first week of our two-week timeline had passed, and we still needed to schedule the property inspection. Fortunately, the property was vacant, so it was easy to schedule the inspection for two days later. After reviewing the inspection report, my clients had only a few minor requests for the sellers to address. As Illinois is an attorney state, I asked our attorney to include those requests in the letter he was preparing for the seller's attorney, alongside the necessary legal documentation for the purchase.

Three more days passed with no word from the seller's attorney. Our attorney's office followed up daily, but we had no luck. I even reached out to the listing agent again, hoping she could help, but got no response. Finally, after four days, the seller's attorney replied, apologizing for the delay. He explained that he didn't practice real estate law—his expertise was in civil law—so he had to consult a colleague who specialized in real estate transactions before responding.

With all the delays on the seller's side, we were now in the third week of the transaction, well past the originally agreed-upon closing date. Once the seller's attorney handed the file over to his colleague, things began moving more smoothly, and we were able to schedule the closing for a few days later. After receiving the closing confirmation email from my attorney, I contacted the listing agent to arrange the final walkthrough before the closing, so my clients could see the property one last time.

This time, the agent picked up immediately but informed me that we couldn't close on the scheduled date. Her clients had requested that she be present for the walkthrough, but due to her full-time job, she wasn't available on that day—or any day before. Dumbfounded but left with no choice, we reluctantly pushed the closing to the end of the week.

Thankfully, the final walkthrough went smoothly, and my clients and I planned to meet at the title company to finalize the purchase. After my clients signed all the paperwork, the title company representative asked me to send the commission statement (a document detailing the commission splits between the buyer's and seller's brokerages) so she could process the payments. This document is typically submitted by the listing agent, so I called her again to ask about it. She admitted she didn't know she needed to submit one and would have to get help from someone at her office on how to prepare it.

Three and a half hours later, we finally closed. What should have taken 14 days, with a quick 30-minute closing, ended up taking 20 days, with an additional 3.5 hours at closing.

Lesson Learned

There is a big difference between having a real estate license and being a committed Realtor. Just because someone has a license doesn't mean their main focus is practicing real estate. The industry is well-known for having many part-time agents, and chances are, you'll encounter some who are not as dedicated as you. After working with part-time agents a few times, I quickly realized that to ensure my transactions went smoothly, I needed to be heavily involved from start to finish. This meant keeping everyone on the same page and ensuring communication lines stayed open for all parties. I never assumed that anyone would automatically do their job (or even know how to), so my hands-on approach kept everything moving forward, minimizing the risk of anything getting lost in the process.

Examples

It's no secret that getting a real estate license is one of the easiest professional licenses to obtain. Compared to other industries, the required training hours aren't even close.

Average Training Hours Required Before Licensing Exam :

- ☑ **Cosmetologist:** 1,000 - 1,500 hours (varies by state)*

- ☑ **Truck Driver (CDL License):** 200 hours (combined classroom and driving)

- ☑ **Electrician:** 4,000 - 8,000 hours (varies by state)

- ☑ **Realtor:** 80 hours (average across all 50 states)

While there's absolutely nothing wrong with becoming a cosmetologist, the key difference is that hair grows back. But if someone makes a poor financial decision on a property they shouldn't have purchased because they were represented by an undertrained Realtor, it could have long-lasting effects on their family's finances for years, or even generations.

Because the requirements to get a real estate license are minimal, the industry is saturated with people holding a license. According to InboundREM, an inbound marketing lead generation company focused on SEO, there are roughly 1.5 million active real estate licensees in the U.S. at the time of writing.[1] With about 341 million people living in the U.S., that means approximately 0.4% of the population holds a real estate license. By comparison, the financial planning industry, which also deals with people's finances, has around 100,000 licensees.

Even though there are many licensed agents, most don't transact much business. In October–November 2023, Inman (a leading real estate news site) conducted a study of 100 randomly selected agents from five major brokerages in four urban areas:

---

*The average time to complete cosmetology training and licensing is four to five years, compared to just a few weeks or months for a Realtor.

Central Pennsylvania; Orlando, Florida; Tucson, Arizona; and Minneapolis, Minnesota. The study found that 49% of agents in these areas sold either zero homes or just one in the previous year.[2]

So while many people claim to be Realtors, most simply hold a license. It's like a 14-year-old with a fake driver's license—just because they have one doesn't mean they know how to drive.

Pre-Licensing (Real Estate School)

To obtain a real estate license, you must first complete a pre-licensing course. These courses teach the basics of real estate, including ethics, fair housing laws, agency law, and different types of home ownership.

The number of hours and classes required will vary by state, and you can easily find your state's requirements with a quick Google search. Many of these courses can be completed online, although some states may require in-person attendance.

After completing the course, you'll need to pass a final exam. Typically, you must answer 75% of the questions correctly to pass (though this can vary by state). Once you've passed, you'll be eligible to take your state and national licensing exams.

✔ The cost of a pre-licensing course varies, but it's usually between $300 and $600.

State and National Exams

To officially obtain your license, you'll need to pass both state and national exams. These exams are often combined, with state-specific and national questions mixed.

The state portion tests your knowledge of the laws, regulations, and practices specific to real estate in your state. The national portion covers general real estate knowledge and skills, based on a job analysis conducted by Pearson VUE, a company that designs exams for real estate professionals. The number of questions and the passing score required vary by state.

✔ The cost to take the state and national exams typically averages around $50 per attempt.

> **NOTE:**
> Each state has a limit on the number of attempts you can make to pass the exam. If you exceed that limit, you'll have to retake the pre-licensing course before trying again.

After passing the state and national exams, there are a few additional costs to consider, such as the license application fee, background check, fingerprints, and the cost of the license itself. These fees vary by state and service provider, but average costs are:

- ✅ **Application Fee:** $25–$30
- ✅ **Fingerprints & Background Check:** $100–$125
- ✅ **Real Estate License:** $150
- ✅ **Estimated total cost:** to obtain a real estate license, including pre-licensing, exams, and additional fees: $625–$955.

Compared to other industries, obtaining a real estate license is relatively inexpensive. Many professions require significant financial investment to get started, often running into the thousands of dollars. In some industries, financial aid is available to offset these costs. For example, famed cosmetologist Paul Mitchell's beauty school provides resources to help students find financial aid to support their training.

Cost Comparison to Other Industries

- ✅ **Cosmetologist:** The average cost of attending a cosmetology school is around $16,000, including tuition, student kits, and state licensing fees.
- ✅ **Truck Driver (CDL License):** The average cost to obtain a CDL license ranges from $4,000 to $12,000, covering training and fees.
- ✅ **Electrician:** The average cost is between $4,000 and $12,000, plus the cost of books and materials.

❘ Anyone Can Hold a License

Getting your real estate license is the first step to becoming a full-time Realtor, but it doesn't mean you can start advertising your services right away. Before making any announcements on social media, you must be sponsored by a brokerage to begin selling.

Joining a Brokerage

After passing your state and national exams, you are not eligible to sell real estate until you join a brokerage. Joining a brokerage means "hanging" your license with a company, where they will act as your sponsoring broker. Since every brokerage offers different options and benefits, it's important to take your time and interview multiple brokerages to find the one that best fits you and your business goals.

Having switched brokerages multiple times throughout my career, I understand how crucial it is to choose the right one, especially for a new Realtor. This is why I've dedicated an entire chapter (Chapter 7: Joining a Brokerage) to help you with this decision.

> **NOTE:**
> After passing your state and national exams, you have one year to join a brokerage. If you don't, you will have to go through the entire pre-licensing process again.

Commissions

One of the most challenging aspects of selling real estate full-time is that you only get paid when a property closes. Once all the paperwork is signed, and the title company confirms the closing, they will issue a check for the commission. However, the check won't be made out to you directly—it will be made out to your brokerage. Since commission checks are payable to the brokerage, you'll need to bring the check to your office for processing. During processing, your brokerage will deduct their fees, and then cut you a check based on your commission split (the percentage you earn versus what the brokerage keeps).

For example, if you bring a $5,000 commission check to your brokerage, the breakdown might look like this:

- **Commission Check:** $5,000
- **Transaction Fee:** $250 (brokerage fee)
- **Processing Fee:** $200 (brokerage fee)
- **Total Commission After Brokerage Fees:** $4,550
- **Your Split With Brokerage:** 60%
- **Your Total Commission:** $2,730 (60% of $4,550)

> **NOTE:**
> Brokerages have different fees and commission plans. I will cover commissions in more detail in Chapter 7.

Expenses

As a real estate licensee, you are considered an independent contractor. This means you are responsible for all your business expenses, from buying a client's coffee to investing in marketing and advertising. In addition to the day-to-day costs of running your business, there are also annual expenses you need to account for.
Common annual costs include:

- Local Realtor association fees
- National Association of Realtors fees

- ✅ MLS access fees
- ✅ Brokerage fees
- ✅ Errors and omissions insurance

The total cost of maintaining a real estate license varies based on several factors, but new agents can expect to spend between $2,000 and $5,000 annually on these expenses.

NOTE:

I will cover expenses in more detail in Chapter 5: Expenses and Budgeting.

Continuing Education

Throughout your career, you'll need to take continuing education courses to maintain your license. These courses are similar to pre-licensing classes but are updated to reflect any new laws or practices. You typically have the option of taking courses online or in person.

The cost of continuing education depends on your state's requirements, but it typically ranges from $100 to $300+ per year.

| Not Everyone Can Be a Realtor

Early in my career, I attended an event with a panel of industry professionals. When the moderator asked the panelists what had surprised them most about the industry, the first panelist—a mortgage lender—mentioned that most Realtors she worked with had little to no knowledge about how buyers qualify for loans. The second panelist, a real estate coach, added that statistically, everyone knows at least three Realtors.

While I haven't found hard data to back up that claim, the coach's comment has stuck with me over the years. While many people can name someone with a real estate license, how many can name three people who practice real estate full-time as their main career?

Having been a Realtor for almost two decades and owning a brokerage for nearly a decade, I know firsthand how challenging this job can be and how it takes a certain type of person to succeed. Over the years, I've observed key fundamentals that separate full-time Realtors from those who just hold a license.

Mindset

On January 1st, there's a phenomenon where people believe the new year will wipe the slate clean and bring a "new and better" version of themselves. They make resolutions like "getting into shape" and sign up for gym memberships, but studies show that 90% of New Year's resolutions fail. The main reason? People set overly ambitious goals without being mentally prepared to achieve them.

The same goes for new real estate agents. Many enter the industry with grand expectations, only to discover that their vision was unrealistic. When things don't go as planned, they give up—just like those who quit their New Year's resolutions. Successful Realtors understand that real estate is a marathon, not a sprint, and they mentally prepare themselves to persevere through the inevitable challenges.

> **NOTE:**
> Mindset is such an important part of building a lasting real estate business that I've dedicated the entire next chapter to it.

It's a Lifestyle

If you've watched any of the Million Dollar Listing shows on Bravo TV, you've probably heard Realtors say that real estate isn't just a job—it's a lifestyle. Unlike many other careers, to be successful as a Realtor, you need to treat it as a part of who you are. Let me explain.

Most employees view their job as a separate part of their lives. They clock in, work for eight hours, and then clock out, returning to their personal life. They need permission to take time off during regular hours, which keeps work compartmentalized.

Realtors, on the other hand, don't have set hours. Their schedule is flexible and self-determined, allowing them to mix personal and professional activities. It's common for a Realtor to spend the morning at the office, run errands in the afternoon, and show properties in the evening. On weekends, they might host open houses, attend family events, and squeeze in more showings later in the day.

The most successful Realtors embrace this lifestyle. They blend personal and business tasks seamlessly, ensuring they handle everything in real-time.

> **NOTE:**
> Buyers typically want to see properties after work or on weekends.

Prospecting

Prospecting in real estate differs from other industries because Realtors aren't selling a product—they're offering a personal service. This requires a unique approach. For instance, when Apple launches a new iPhone, they use billboards to highlight the product's benefits, making it easy for consumers to decide whether to upgrade. Buying a home, however, is a much bigger decision with lasting financial consequences, and a billboard won't build the trust necessary for such a purchase.

Buying real estate is deeply personal. It's about choosing where to live, a significant financial decision that most people make only a few times in their lives. To make such an important choice, buyers seek guidance from someone they trust. Trust is built through relationships, not advertising. Realtors create trust by consistently cultivating connections over time.

A mentor once told me, "If you wait for business to come to you, you'll be waiting forever." I took that advice to heart, ensuring that prospecting became part of my daily routine. Every day, I'd call, text, email, and message potential clients. The most successful Realtors know that prospecting is their top priority—and they never miss a day.

> **NOTE:**
> I dedicate an entire chapter to prospecting (Chapter 11: Prospecting), where I explain how to prospect like a top Realtor.

Marketing

On February 11, 2024, the Kansas City Chiefs faced the San Francisco 49ers in Super Bowl LVIII. While the game itself was thrilling, can you guess what three-quarters of viewers were most excited about? The commercials. Companies spent $7 million for just 30 seconds of ad time during the Super Bowl, understanding that the massive viewership—over 124 million in 2023—makes it worth every penny for brand exposure.

While Realtors don't spend millions on ads, the successful ones understand the importance of marketing to build brand recognition. They allocate part of their budget to items like yard signs, postcards, flyers, and client appreciation events. These Realtors have a marketing plan they execute each year with precision.

> **NOTE:**
> Throughout this book, I'll share various ways Realtors market themselves to help you create your own plan.

Expenses

In January 2019, WeWork was valued at $47 billion and operated nearly 50 million square feet of office space globally. It had all the makings of a unicorn startup: major investors, an in-demand concept, and a charismatic CEO. However, none of this prevented the company from losing staggering amounts of money.

WeWork's rapid expansion and unchecked spending led to its downfall. By 2017, the company's financial strain was evident, exacerbated by excessive spending on ventures like luxury health clubs, co-working acquisitions, and even a private school in New York. When WeWork attempted to go public in 2019, due diligence revealed critical flaws in its financials, leading to a downward spiral.

As a cautionary tale, WeWork teaches us the importance of controlling business expenses. The most successful Realtors are diligent about managing their costs, tracking every dollar spent on both business and personal expenses.

TIP:

Save enough money to cover 6-12 months of both business and personal expenses before becoming a full-time Realtor.

Important to Remember

Anyone Can Get a License

- It's relatively easy to obtain a real estate license. On average, it requires 80 hours of pre-licensing education before you can sit for your state and national exams.
- To earn your license, you must first pass a pre-licensing course, with a minimum score of 75% on the final exam.

Anyone Can Hold a License

- After completing the pre-licensing course, you must pass your state and national exams (requirements vary by state).
- Once you pass the exams, you must join a brokerage to sell real estate, as you need a sponsoring broker to operate.
- Realtors are independent contractors, not employees:
  - You earn a commission only when you sell or lease a property; there's no salary.
  - You are responsible for covering all your own expenses.
  - Co ntinuing education is required for all Realtors (specific requirements vary by state and association).

Not Everyone Can Be a Successful Realtor

- Success requires a strong mindset. Real estate is a long-term career, more like a marathon than a sprint.
- Being a Realtor is a lifestyle, not just a job. It doesn't end at 5 PM; it becomes part of your daily life.
- Consistent prospecting for new business is essential for long-term success.
- You must market yourself continuously to build brand recognition and become the go-to Realtor for clients.
- Controlling expenses is crucial. Successful Realtors account for every dollar spent, both in their business and personal lives, to avoid financial pitfalls.

NOTES

Chapter 2
Mindset

The sun was beginning to cast a golden hue as it set on the horizon, its glow spilling over the ocean. I sat at a table in a local seafood restaurant in Venice, Florida, surrounded by my mother's side of the family. Laughter filled the air as we took turns sharing stories about the wonderful man my grandfather had been. Earlier that day, we had spread his ashes in the Gulf of Mexico, as he had wished, and now we were enjoying each other's company, reminiscing.

The waitress had just taken our dinner orders when my phone buzzed in my front jeans pocket. I glanced at the screen and, seeing who was calling, excused myself from the table to step outside and take the call. A few hours earlier, before leaving my grandmother's house, I had countered an offer for one of my buyer clients. Now, the agent on the other end was calling to let me know that the sellers had accepted our counteroffer.

Excitement welled up inside me as I ended the call. I quickly called my clients to share the good news. As I was about to head back inside, I received a text from another agent I had been negotiating with for the past week. The message stopped me in my tracks: "WE HAVE A DEAL!"

I was speechless. In the span of five minutes, I had two offers accepted—the highest price-point transactions I had ever worked on. Until that moment, I had only closed a few smaller sales. This felt like a turning point. After years of hard work and struggling to make ends meet, things were finally starting to pay off.

After letting my other clients know the news, I took a moment to compose myself before walking back into the restaurant to rejoin my family. A few hours later, after we had finished dinner, we all walked out together. The excitement of my two big sales finally boiled over, and I couldn't keep it in anymore. I jumped onto my father's back, much to his surprise, and yelled, "I just sold $550,000 in real estate!" while pumping my fist in the air.

But two weeks later, I found myself sitting at a table in Starbucks, my head down, once again questioning whether real estate was the right career for me.

After returning from Florida, I had scheduled both of my buyer clients' property inspections for the following day. I attended each one and felt positive about the results—both inspectors had only found minor issues. The next day, we received the inspection reports and set up calls to discuss them. Despite my confidence, both sets of buyers decided they didn't feel comfortable moving forward with their purchases.

Just as quickly as I had celebrated selling $550,000 in real estate, I had lost both sales. I was back to square one with my clients. I sat there for a moment, feeling the weight of *the setbacks. Then, I lifted my head, took a deep breath, and opened the Multiple Listing Service to start searching for new properties for each of my buyers.*

Lesson Learned

Coming from the corporate world, I was used to consistency. My days followed a predictable pattern: I'd arrive at 8:00 AM, work through my tasks, and leave by 5:00 PM. Rarely did I feel mentally drained at the end of the day, and when I did, it was usually because something had gone wrong with a project I was working on.

Real estate, on the other hand, is a mental battle every single day. One day, everything can go right, and you'll feel like you're on top of the world; the next day, it could all come crashing down, leaving you wondering what just happened. Throughout my career, I've experienced numerous days where the highs and lows were so extreme, they were hard to comprehend. I vividly recall one day that began with a massive low when a client I had worked with for six months walked away from a deal at the closing table. Later that same day, I was on a huge high after landing a $700,000 listing during an interview.

These swings are common in real estate because the only thing consistent about this industry is its inconsistency. No two days are ever the same, and things can change instantly. Anyone considering real estate as a career needs to understand this and mentally prepare themselves for whatever the job throws at them. While many factors contribute to a successful career in real estate, having the right mindset is by far the most important.

| What is Mental Strength?

Mental strength refers to how effectively someone deals with challenges, pressures, and stressors. Being mentally strong doesn't mean you never feel doubt, frustration, or sadness. Instead, it's about developing long-term coping skills—emotional resilience, self-awareness, and adaptability in the face of changing circumstances.

Mental strength is the bridge between you and your goals, giving you the extra push to overcome obstacles. For instance, when a long-awaited sale falls apart at the closing table, mental strength helps you see the setback as a learning experience rather than a reason to quit.

Being mentally strong allows you to navigate both personal and professional stress with confidence. It enables you to roll with the punches, view obstacles as opportunities, and stay focused on long-term success. For most people, mental strength isn't something they're born with—it's developed through experiences that shape their mindset.

Take Oprah Winfrey, for example. She's one of the most successful people in the world, but few people know that she was born in rural Mississippi to a single teenage mother, raised in poverty, and suffered abuse and neglect as a child. Oprah overcame her difficult upbringing by developing the mental strength to rise above her circumstances, eventually becoming one of the most influential people in the world.

While your experiences might not mirror Oprah's, her story illustrates that anything is possible when you don't let external circumstances control your internal mindset. Becoming mentally strong is a process—it doesn't happen overnight. It involves cultivating healthy mental habits through various methods.

Stay Positive

Traits of a Positive Person

- Confident
- Accepting
- Focused
- Optimistic
- Trusting

When I was younger, I had a saying I'd repeat whenever something didn't go my way: "Why do bad things always happen to me?" I'd say it no matter how big or small the setback was. I started this habit as a high school freshman and carried it into adulthood, even into the early days of my real estate career. I'd get frustrated nearly every day and use this saying to justify any negative situation that came up.

Then one day, while I had an hour to kill before an appointment, I stopped by a Barnes & Noble. As I walked into the store, the first book I saw on the front table was Unlimited Power by Tony Robbins. I had heard of Tony but had never read any of his books, so I picked it up and began flipping through. Eventually, I landed on page eight, where my eyes settled on the last paragraph:

"Your level of communication mastery in the external world will determine your level of success with others—personally, emotionally, socially, and financially. More importantly, the level of success you experience internally—the happiness, joy, ecstasy, love, or anything else you desire—is the direct result of how you communicate with yourself. How you feel is not the result of what is happening in your life—it is your interpretation of what is happening. Successful people's lives have shown us over and over again that the quality of our lives is determined not by what happens to us, but rather by what we do about what happens."

After reading that paragraph, it hit me: what I had been saying to myself all those years was affecting me far more than I realized. From that day forward, I made a conscious decision to change my mindset. I stopped repeating that old phrase and focused on staying positive instead.

The benefits of having a positive mindset are remarkable. Studies show that positive thinking can lead to lower risks of depression, lower blood pressure, and a stronger immune system. It also improves problem-solving, adaptability, and creativity—all of which contribute to a successful career and a better life.

Real estate is a career filled with ups and downs, and to excel, you must always look at things through a positive lens. If something negative happens, take a moment to digest it, then move on. The longer you dwell on it, the more it will affect both your business and your life.

TIP:

When I get frustrated, I remind myself that the past cannot be changed. I reflect on what happened, learn from it, and focus on the next steps to move forward.

Regardless of what happens, stay positive, and success will follow!

NOTE:

If you carry a negative event with you, it will spill into other parts of your day and may cause you to miss out on future opportunities. For example, if you walk into a listing consultation with a negative mindset, you won't be able to think clearly or sell yourself effectively. Not being at the top of your game could cost you the listing—and any future business that might come from that relationship.

Have Perspective

Traits of a Person with Perspective

- Empathetic
- Grateful
- Self-aware
- Curious
- Unbiased

After moving back from Boston and starting my real estate career, I split my time between Chicago and my parents' house in the south suburbs. I was determined to sell in the city, so I spent as much time there as possible, learning the ins and outs of every neighborhood. However, since I didn't have a consistent place to stay, I often had to drive all the way back to my parents' house at night.

At my parents' home, I spent most of my time at the desk in my room, working on different aspects of my business. One day, to my surprise, my mother walked in unannounced. I turned around to see her standing there with an expression that told me she wasn't happy. We stared at each other for a few moments as I racked my brain, trying to figure out what I had done wrong. After what felt like an eternity, she finally asked, "Are you going to get a job?"

Even more confused, I blurted out, "I have a job, I'm a Realtor." But I could instantly tell this wasn't the response she was looking for. After a pause, she leaned in and said, "You don't have a job—you don't have a salary." With that, she turned and walked out, closing the door behind her with a bang.

That moment, in the early days of my new career, lit a fire under me. I used her words as motivation, determined to prove her wrong. Every day, I thought about what she said, and for the longest time, I couldn't let it go. This drive stayed with me for years—until my perspective shifted.

By early 2021, I had achieved everything I wanted in real estate sales and had shifted my focus to growing my company. Although I had proven my mother wrong, my mindset around that moment remained unchanged. Then, one morning, while sipping coffee in my office, I stumbled upon a podcast called On Purpose with Jay Shetty. I clicked on a random episode and started listening while working on my to-do list. At some point, Jay said something that made me stop in my tracks. I turned the volume up, and though I don't remember his exact words, the message was clear: Every person in our life plays a role, just as we play roles in the lives of others. These roles can be big or small, but their impact can be enormous.

I paused the podcast, reflecting on what I had just heard. In that moment, I realized that my mother wasn't being critical that day—she was playing the role she needed to play at that point in my life. She was concerned about me because I was her son, and she wanted the best for me. By putting myself in her shoes, I gained a new perspective on that experience and developed a deeper appreciation for what she did for me.

Perspective shapes how we view and interpret the world. It influences our thoughts, emotions, and actions, and it can have a profound effect on our well-being. It allows us to see things from others' points of view, taking into account their beliefs, intentions, and motivations. As a Realtor, your role is to guide clients through one of the biggest financial decisions of their lives. To do this effectively, you need to put yourself in their shoes and offer advice that's truly in their best interest. Only with a clear perspective can you do this successfully.

Embrace Failure

Traits of Someone Who Embraces Failure

- Resilient
- Accountable
- Resourceful
- Purposeful
- Optimistic

In 1978, James Dyson, dissatisfied with the performance of his new Hoover Junior vacuum, had a breakthrough idea. He noticed how a local sawmill used cyclone technology to separate sawdust from the air and wondered if this could work in a vacuum. Dyson removed the vacuum's bag and replaced it with a crude cardboard prototype of his cyclone design—and it worked.

From that point on, Dyson devoted himself to perfecting his invention. Supported by his wife's salary as an art teacher, Dyson worked tirelessly for five years, creating around 5,127 prototypes before finally launching the "G-Force" cleaner in 1983. However, no manufacturer or distributor in the UK wanted to produce his vacuum, fearing it would disrupt the replacement dust bag market. Undeterred, Dyson launched his product in Japan, where it became a commercial success and even won a design prize in 1991.

Fast-forward two decades: Dyson's company has grown into a global technology enterprise with over 10,000 employees. Nearly half of them are engineers, solving problems others overlook. Reflecting on his journey, Dyson stated in a 2007 interview with Fast Company, "I made 5,127 prototypes of my vacuum before I got it right. There were 5,126 failures. But I learned from each one. That's how I came up with a solution."

In your real estate career, you will face numerous failures. Transactions will fall apart, and clients may choose not to work with you again. Failure is inevitable, and that's okay. The key is how you respond to failure. To succeed as a Realtor, you must embrace failure as a learning tool and ensure that you never repeat the same mistakes.

Be Adaptable

Traits of Someone Adaptable

- Flexible
- Creative
- Open-minded
- Resourceful
- Inquisitive

In the fall of 2001, the Oakland Athletics were competing against the New York Yankees in the playoffs. The Yankees had a payroll of $125 million, while the Athletics operated with only $42 million. Athletics General Manager Billy Beane had built a competitive team using undervalued players, knowing this was their best chance to win the World Series. However, after losing the playoff series, Beane watched as his top players signed huge contracts with rival teams in the offseason.

Desperate to replicate his past success, Beane sought solutions. During a meeting with the Cleveland Indians, he encountered Peter Brand, a young analyst with a revolutionary philosophy. Brand explained that instead of paying for players, Beane should pay for wins—and to pay for wins, he needed to pay for runs. Intrigued, Beane brought Brand to the Athletics, and together they built a team based on analytics, defying traditional scouting methods.

Their strategy worked. The Athletics, a team composed of mostly overlooked players, set an American League record by winning 20 consecutive games and finished the season with a 103-59 record—one win more than the previous year. Although they lost in the playoffs again, their success sparked a revolution in baseball, with the Boston Red Sox adopting similar analytics to win their first World Series in 86 years, and the Chicago Cubs following suit in 2016, ending their 108-year championship drought.

In real estate, adaptability is just as crucial. As a full-time Realtor, your career is a lifestyle choice that requires you to seamlessly blend work and personal life. Being adaptable means thinking creatively and being resourceful in finding solutions to serve your clients and run your business effectively.

For example, if your buyers want to view a property they've fallen in love with online, but you have to pick up your kids from school, what do you do? Do you push the showing to a later date, or do you find a colleague to help? An adaptable Realtor will find a way to make the showing happen, knowing that quick action could be the difference between securing an accepted offer or losing a client. Even if the buyers decide not to pursue the property, your effort demonstrates your commitment to their needs and reinforces your value as their agent.

Tools

Early in my career, I attended a training session designed to help Realtors generate more business. One speaker emphasized the power of visualization to achieve desires, specifically through creating a vision board. The idea was that by seeing your goals daily, your mind would focus on them, and eventually, you'd manifest those desires.

Inspired by the speaker's advice, I went home that night and crafted a vision board filled with everything I thought I wanted: a powder blue Lamborghini convertible, an oversized beach house, a Rolex watch, a closet of colorful suits, and even a private ice rink. Proud of my creation, I hung it in my room at my parents' house. For the first week, I diligently followed the speaker's advice, looking at the board every morning and evening. But as time passed, I started forgetting to look at it, and a few months later, I didn't even notice it was there anymore. Unsurprisingly, none of the things on the board came into my life, and when I eventually moved out, I tossed it in the recycling bin without a second thought.

Nearly a decade later, I realized the speaker had left out a crucial element: to make a vision board work, you must genuinely desire the things on it. The items I pasted onto mine weren't things I truly wanted—they were just symbols of what I thought I should want.

While tools like vision boards, self-talk, and others can be powerful, they only work if you understand how to use them properly and if they align with your true desires.

Self-talk

The thoughts running through your mind drive your emotions and mood. These one-sided conversations you have with yourself can be either damaging or helpful. Regardless, they influence how you feel about yourself and how you react to the world around you.

Self-talk is something we naturally do every day. As we go through our day, we're constantly talking to ourselves about whatever occupies our minds at that moment. Yet, most people don't realize that the words they use can steer them in the wrong direction. To understand the power of self-talk and its impact, let's first explore how our minds work.

Think of your mind as a computer. A computer has two essential components: hardware and software. The hardware includes the physical parts you can see, like the keyboard, mouse, and the CPU (Central Processing Unit) inside. Software, on the other hand, is the collection of programs you can't see, which tell the computer how to operate. This includes the operating system—such as Microsoft Windows for a PC or macOS for a Mac. If you're reading this on your iPad, it's because your tablet's operating system, iOS, is functioning behind the scenes to perform the tasks you ask it to. Without software, your computer, phone, or tablet would be nothing more than an expensive paperweight. The software allows these devices to do everything we need, and we can also update it to make them more efficient.

Your mind operates similarly. We're all born with a built-in CPU that handles basic functions, and throughout our lives, we're constantly downloading new "software"— updating our thoughts, experiences, and perspectives. It's like getting new updates on your phone every second. At the same time, just as you can control your phone's settings and apps, you can control how your brain functions through what you think and say.

For instance, when I couldn't figure something out or had a tough day, I often said, "I'm struggling." You've probably heard this before, maybe in phrases like "I'm on the struggle bus" or "The struggle is real." Saying "struggle" became my default, and I found myself repeating it several times a day. What I didn't realize then was that by using this word, I was instructing my mind to search for reasons to justify the struggle. This made every task feel more difficult than it needed to be.

It wasn't until one day, while driving to work, that I understood just how powerful the words we use can be. I was listening to a random motivational playlist on Spotify, and a speaker mentioned that by simply changing the words we say to ourselves, we can change our lives. She shared how she identified her negative self-talk and flipped those words into more positive ones, which helped her mind focus on finding better outcomes. This idea clicked with me, and I began to think about the opposite of "struggle." The word "challenge" came to mind. From that day forward, I stopped saying, "I'm struggling" and replaced it with, "This is challenging." This small change allowed my mind to become more creative in finding solutions, instead of justifying the struggle.

Our brains focus on what we tell them to focus on. So, pay attention to the negative words you regularly use and try flipping them to positive ones. By doing so, you'll allow your brain to help you move forward, instead of holding you back.

Affirmations

When I was running my brokerage, my partner and I developed a custom mentorship program designed to shorten the learning curve for new Realtors. Over six weeks, we aimed to provide them with as much knowledge and as many tools as possible.

NOTE:

Everything we taught in the mentorship program is featured throughout this book.

By the time we sold the brokerage, nearly 50 agents had completed the program, with an average sales volume of $1.5 to $2 million in the 12 months that followed. However, the program was challenging, and agents often shared their negative thoughts as they faced difficulties. We heard things like:

"I'm never going to be able to sell a house."

"I'm just not meant to be a Realtor."

"Why am I so stupid?"

Many of us experience similar negative thoughts, sometimes frequently. When we think this way, our confidence, mood, and outlook can take a negative turn as well.

The problem with negative thoughts is that they can become self-fulfilling prophecies. We convince ourselves we're not good enough, and soon these thoughts begin to drag down our personal lives, relationships, and careers.

While it's common to have negative thoughts, they don't have to be permanent. Since we have control over our minds, we can flip these negative thoughts into positive ones. By using affirmations, we can combat and overcome these destructive patterns.

Affirmations are a form of self-talk. However, instead of changing just one word, you repeat a positive phrase to yourself daily—one that counters your regular negative thoughts or one that you design specifically for your situation. For example, instead of saying, "I'm never going to be able to sell a house," you might change it to, "I will do everything possible to sell this house for my sellers and will not quit until I do!" Repeating this to yourself over and over stimulates the parts of your brain that make positive change more likely.

TIP:

To get the most out of your affirmations, say them with passion and emotion. Studies show that emotions play a crucial role in helping us recall memories when we try to revisit them.[1]

This is just one example of an affirmation. You can create as many as you need and use them in a way that suits you best. I repeat my affirmations in the morning while I exercise. I wake up before everyone else in my house, so I have quiet time to focus. I typically repeat four to five affirmations between sets or while I'm running. I've found this method works best for me, but everyone is different—find what works for you and choose the best time of day to say them.

NOTE:

Life changes often, and it's perfectly fine to adjust your affirmations to match your current circumstances. Don't hesitate to make adjustments when necessary.

Vision Boards

I found myself staring at different colors of poster boards for over half an hour, trying to decide which one would be best for the background of my new vision board. Should I choose a bright yellow so it would catch my eye on the wall, or go with black to make the pictures pop? The internal debate went on as I stood in the arts and crafts store, blankly staring at the shelf. After weighing all my options, I finally chose yellow—and grabbed three, just in case I made a mistake.

Creating a new vision board wasn't something I had initially planned after my first one didn't go so well. But one day, I happened to hear Oprah Winfrey talking on a podcast about how she used vision boards to manifest her desires in life. I was a bit surprised, considering I didn't have much faith in them myself. However, hearing someone I deeply respected like Oprah discuss her use of vision boards made me reconsider. I decided it wouldn't hurt to follow her lead and dig a little deeper into how to make one properly.

A vision board is a visual representation of your goals. It's typically a poster-sized display filled with images and text that symbolize what you want to accomplish. Neuroscientist Dr. Tara Swart explains, "Looking at images on a vision board primes the brain to grasp opportunities that may otherwise go unnoticed. That's because the brain has a process called 'value-tagging,' which imprints important things onto your subconscious and filters out unnecessary information."[2]

For example, let's say you want to take a two-week trip to Europe, visiting several destinations. This dream trip might cost thousands of dollars, so you'll need to save up for it. To manifest this goal, you could cut out pictures of the places you want to visit and create a dedicated section on your vision board. By looking at your board daily, you train your mind to recognize opportunities that align with your goal—opportunities that might have otherwise slipped past unnoticed because your focus wasn't on them. I'll delve further into how focusing on what you truly desire opens your mind to possibilities in the next chapter.

TIP:

To bring your vision board to life, write a specific date next to each item for when you want to achieve it. Having a deadline makes the goal feel more tangible, reduces procrastination, and increases your accountability.

There are no strict rules for creating a vision board—it's about designing something that inspires you to pursue your dreams and goals. Some vision boards focus on a single idea, while others capture the bigger picture of what you envision for the future. Before rushing into making yours, take some time to reflect and write down what you truly want. Then, dive in!

How to Make a Vision Board

1.   Reflect on What Matters Most to You
Take a moment for self-reflection and figure out what's truly important.

2.   Gather Pictures That Represent Your Goals
Look through magazines, Pinterest, Instagram, or Google, and paste them onto your board.

3.   Place Your Board Somewhere You'll See it Often
For example, your bedroom, bathroom, or even as a background on your phone or computer.

Mind Movies

During my first few months in real estate, I was completely lost when it came to structuring my days. I had spent the previous two years working an 8-5 job with a consistent Monday through Friday routine. Every day, I would wake up at 6:45 AM, get ready, and leave my apartment by 7:20 AM to catch the T train downtown. By 8:00 AM, I was at my desk, working until 5:00 PM. After work, I'd take the train home, hit the gym, shower, eat dinner while watching TV, and stay on the couch until about 10:30 PM, when I would read a bit before falling asleep. On weekends, I followed a similar routine, minus the work, which meant spending a lot of time watching TV. Naturally, when I transitioned into real estate, I fell back into these familiar patterns, especially on weekends. Working on Saturdays and Sundays felt completely foreign to me.

Everything changed one random weekday evening. I was watching Wedding Crashers for the third time that month when I realized my old routine wasn't going to work for my new career. There's a scene in the movie where John Beckwith (Owen Wilson) and Jeremy Grey (Vince Vaughn) are sitting on the steps of the Lincoln Memorial, the morning after crashing a wedding. Jeremy hands John a bottle of champagne as they watch the sunrise. John, clearly lost in thought, asks, "Are we being irresponsible?" Jeremy laughs it off, replying,

"No, one day you'll look back and laugh, saying we were young and stupid." He playfully nudges John, but John's expression remains contemplative.

The scene continues with Jeremy trying to justify their actions, but John quietly responds, "We're not that young." The camera lingers on their awkward silence before Jeremy lightens the mood with a comment about it being a great wedding season.

This time, the scene hit me differently. After it ended, I paused the movie and reflected on the past few months of my life. It became clear that trying to force my old routine into my new real estate career wasn't working. I knew I had to change how I approached my days. So, I made some immediate adjustments—limiting TV time to only watching movies on the weekends to avoid getting sucked into binge-watching, shifting my workouts to the morning, and dedicating time each day to educating myself.

Over the years, I've continuously refined my daily structure, adding multiple routines (which I'll dive into in Chapter 4: Routines) and dedicating time to personal and professional growth. Part of this journey involved recreating my vision board. It gave me something visual to remind me daily of my goals. But then, I discovered something that elevated the concept of vision boards to a whole new level—*mind movies.*

In 2023, I set a goal to read as many books as possible on unlocking the mind's full potential. One book that kept coming up in my searches was Becoming Supernatural by Dr. Joe Dispenza. Around June, I finally bought it, and while the entire book is packed with incredible insights, Chapter 8 really stood out. In this chapter, Dispenza introduces the concept of mind movies—a next-level version of vision boards.

A mind movie is essentially a vision board in video format, set to music. Imagine it as an Instagram reel or TikTok post—a 30 to 60-second clip of everything you want in life, backed by music you love. What sets a mind movie apart from a vision board is the music. As Dr. Joe Dispenza explains, "Music has a way of calling up the memory of a specific time and place in our life." Think about a favorite song—doesn't it conjure memories of a time when that song was a key part of your life?

For example, in 2017, my wife and I vacationed in the Dominican Republic. Every night, the resort put on a show featuring Justin Bieber's song Sorry. Every afternoon, the staff would rehearse to that song, blasting it over the speakers by the pool. Now, every time I hear the intro to Sorry, I instantly picture myself lounging by the pool, feeling the warmth of the sun on my skin.

A mind movie uses the powerful combination of visual images and music to keep you focused on your goals. After watching your mind movie for a few days, you'll start to associate the images of your goals with the song, and just hearing it will bring those visions to mind.

As with vision boards, there are no strict rules for creating a mind movie. The key is to craft something that inspires you to achieve your dreams. Take your time and plan it out. Rushing the process won't yield the results you're hoping for.

How to Make a Mind Movie

1. **Gather Your Digital Images**

Collect all the pictures or any other elements you want to include in your mind movie.

2. **Use a Program or Site**

Add the images to a program like iMovie or a site like Canva.com.

3. **Choose Your Music**

Download the song you want to associate with your mind movie and add it to the program.

4. **Save Your Mind Movie**

Download the finished product and save it somewhere easily accessible, like on your phone, so you can watch it daily.

> **TIP:**
>
> To elevate your mind movie, include your affirmations between images in word format.

Journaling

In my early 20s, I had a friend who was 10 years older and significantly more established. He had the house, the career, and the stability that I aspired to achieve. While spending time with him, I soaked up his wisdom and noticed he was always well-informed about various topics. I once asked how he knew so much, and he told me about a simple practice that became pivotal in my life—he signed up for every newsletter on topics that interested him. This allowed him to gather a wide range of knowledge directly to his inbox, helping him stay informed about the world.

From that point on, I made it a habit to subscribe to newsletters on subjects I was passionate about, and it broadened my understanding of the world. This routine became one of my most valuable daily habits, allowing me to engage in conversations with anyone about current events or emerging trends.

> **TIP:**
>
> Reading your newsletters in the morning is a great way to start the day with fresh knowledge to carry with you.

The Power of Journaling

In 2023, I stumbled across a story in one of my newsletters about a father who created a digital scrapbook for his son by writing emails to him while he grew up. The idea struck me, especially since I have two boys of my own. I began thinking about the benefits of journaling—not just as a way to pass down wisdom but as a tool for mental clarity and stress reduction.

Research shows that journaling has countless benefits, from reducing stress to processing emotions and eliminating negative thoughts. It's a therapeutic practice that helps you figure out your next steps in life, and it's also a way to reflect on what's happened. There are many forms of journaling, whether for depression, stress management, self-reflection, or simply sharing wisdom.

For me, I chose to journal as a way to pass on lessons to my boys. Every night at 10:00 PM, I sit down and write what I learned that day. This process not only gives me an opportunity to share insights that my sons can use later in life but also helps me process my emotions from the day so I can reset for tomorrow.

In the real estate industry, where the emotional highs and lows are constant, journaling has been a valuable way to release my thoughts and clear my mind. It's a daily activity that I highly recommend to anyone in a high-stress career, or to anyone who simply wants a space for reflection.

How to Start Journaling

1.   Pick the Type of Journaling That Works for You
Whether it's reflective journaling, gratitude journaling, or simply recording daily events, choose the type that resonates with you and your goals.

2.   Select a Platform
Decide where you want to journal—whether in a notebook, email, a dedicated journaling program, or a Google Doc.

3.   Decide When You Will Write
Some people prefer to journal first thing in the morning to set their intentions for the day. Others, like me, prefer the quiet reflection of the evening. Choose a time that works for you.

4.   Set a Reminder
Place a daily reminder on your phone or calendar to ensure journaling becomes a habit.

5.   Write Freely
Allow yourself to write whatever comes to mind. There are no rules for how long or short your entries need to be. Write as much or as little as you feel in the moment.

Journaling is a highly personal experience, but the benefits it offers—both mentally and emotionally—can have a transformative effect on your life. Whether you're processing the daily grind or recording lessons for future generations, journaling is a tool that can help you navigate life's complexities with greater clarity.

| Support System

When I was younger, I developed a huge chip on my shoulder. This mindset came from constantly being overlooked in athletics, despite my performance. In gym class, I was always one of the last picked, no matter how well I played. In youth baseball, I was regularly passed over for all-star teams, even though I ranked among the best players. And in high school hockey, despite being considered one of the top defensemen in the state, I was never named to the all-state team or all-star rosters.

These moments were difficult, but the final straw came when I was invited to try out for a junior hockey team in Canada—the same developmental league where many National Hockey League (NHL) players start their professional journey.

To earn that invite, I first had to attend a camp in Ann Arbor, Michigan, the weekend before. I had an incredible camp, and afterward, the assistant coach invited me to the main tryout in Port Hope, Ontario, the following weekend. I was thrilled. My father and I packed up our 1994 Ford Explorer and made the 10-hour drive to this small Canadian town. Over the next few days, I played some of the best hockey of my life. My decision-making was sharp, my skating was top-notch compared to the other players—many of whom were older—and I was constantly making plays and scoring goals.

By the end of the weekend, my confidence was sky-high. I was sure I had made the team, especially after a brief conversation with the assistant coach that felt like a confirmation of my spot. But the true test came on when all 50 players trying out were called one by one into a small room to meet with the head coach. I was in the second group of 10.

Waiting in the hallway, I was holding back my smile, playing out how the conversation would go. When it was finally my turn, I walked into a small, dimly lit room painted red, where the head coach sat behind a small table. The setup was simple: a plastic chair for me to sit in across from him, and a sheet of paper on the table—presumably my scouting report.

After taking a seat, the coach, a burly man in his mid-50s wearing the team's warmup gear, gave me a long look before glancing down at the paper. He spent 30 seconds praising my skating, my shot, my positioning—telling me I was everything they were looking for in a player. As he spoke, it felt like the scene I had envisioned while waiting outside. But then he added, "You're just three inches too short."

And just like that, it was over.

There was no discussion, no opportunity to argue my case. He thanked me for coming, called for the next player, and that was it.

After grabbing a quick meal, my father and I drove the 10 hours back home in near silence. The disappointment was crushing. During that long drive, I made a decision that would shape my approach to competition for years to come: I vowed to be the most competitive person in every aspect of my life, seeing everyone as competition so that I would never feel this kind of disappointment again.

▌ The Lesson in Competition and Support

That moment sparked a fiercely competitive mindset within me, but looking back, it also highlighted something equally important—my need for support and perspective. My father was there for me, quietly sitting through the long drive home. While I focused on internalizing my disappointment and turning it into a competitive drive, his presence reminded me that support systems are critical in navigating life's toughest moments. The chip on my shoulder may have driven me forward, but it was my support system, starting with my father, that kept me grounded.

Competition can be healthy, but it's also essential to balance it with strong relationships, empathy, and a sense of perspective.

Fast forward to the start of my real estate career almost a decade later, and I still carried that same competitive mindset. Every Realtor I met was someone I wanted to beat, and beat badly. I didn't see them as peers or potential collaborators, but purely as competition. I wasn't interested in building friendships or even speaking to them. I took this mindset to an extreme: isolating myself in the office conference room with the door closed. I'd avoid any interaction, even when I had to get coffee or use the bathroom, always looking straight ahead, making a beeline back to my conference room. My routine for the first few months was to get to the office early, set up shop in the conference room before anyone else arrived, and leave only when I could be sure I wouldn't have to talk to anyone.

One day, my isolation plan backfired. After drinking way too much coffee, I couldn't wait any longer to use the bathroom. I turned around to check if the coast was clear, but a veteran agent had arrived and set up at the desk right outside the conference room. I tried to wait it out, hoping he'd leave, but eventually realized that wasn't going to happen. So I made a quick dash past his desk, avoiding eye contact as best I could.

On my way back from the bathroom, I overheard the agent talking on the phone about an offer. Curious, I ducked behind some tall desks and listened in. He was discussing the terms of a transaction, but what surprised me most was how friendly and relaxed he sounded. He was joking with the other agent, laughing, and seemed to genuinely enjoy the conversation. It was nothing like the combative negotiations I envisioned real estate agents having.

After the call ended, I couldn't resist approaching him to ask, "Why were you so friendly with the agent you were negotiating with?"

His response changed the course of my career: "People like to do business with people they like."

That short, simple statement was one of the biggest wake-up calls I'd ever had. In my quest to be the best and outdo everyone, I had missed a fundamental truth about the business: you can't succeed in isolation. Realizing my goals wasn't going to happen if I tried to do everything myself.

In real estate, relationships are key. To be a successful Realtor, you need others. You rely on mentors for advice, you collaborate with other agents to negotiate deals, and you spend time with family and friends to take mental breaks and maintain balance. The support system you build around yourself has a profound impact on your career's trajectory.

❚ The Importance of Connection

From that moment on, I began to change my approach. I realized that success isn't just about outcompeting others—it's about building relationships, earning trust, and creating a network of people who can help you grow. Instead of seeing my peers as rivals, I started viewing them as potential allies and sources of knowledge.

That veteran agent's wisdom stuck with me: "People like to do business with people they like." It's a truth that transcends real estate and applies to nearly every profession. Building rapport, being genuine, and fostering connections with others not only makes business more enjoyable, but it also opens doors you didn't even know were there.

Surrounding yourself with a strong support system, whether through colleagues, mentors, or loved ones, is a powerful resource. It keeps you grounded during the ups and downs, helps you learn from others' experiences, and allows you to celebrate successes together.

Mentors

When we hear the word mentor, it often brings to mind images from movies where an older, wiser person passes life advice down to a younger individual who reminds them of themselves. These plots tend to follow a familiar arc: a young person, heading down a dark path, crosses paths with a seasoned mentor who has already traveled that same road and wants to prevent the younger person from making the same mistakes. Initially, the younger person resists the guidance, but eventually, they come to realize just how valuable the mentor's wisdom truly is.

One of my all-time favorite movies, Good Will Hunting, captures this dynamic perfectly. Will Hunting, played by Matt Damon, is a brilliant young man in his early 20s who doesn't know what he wants to do with his life. He lacks the motivation to do anything beyond sticking with his friends, working manual labor jobs, getting into fights, and trying to impress girls. Despite this, Will craves intellectual challenges, which leads him to take a janitorial job at the Massachusetts Institute of Technology (MIT), surrounding himself with brilliant minds. After solving a nearly impossible mathematical problem posted on a blackboard outside a classroom, he catches the attention of Professor Gerald Lambeau, played by Stellan Skarsgård. Intrigued by Will's genius, the professor asks his colleague, Sean Maguire (Robin Williams), to mentor Will after he gets into legal trouble.

(SPOILER ALERT) The rest of the movie unfolds with Sean meeting Will regularly as part of his probation. Will resists Sean's efforts at first, but things take a turn when the two sit on a bench by a pond, where Sean delivers a pivotal message: as smart as Will is, he is naive to think he fully understands life and can navigate it alone. By the end of the movie, Will finally acknowledges Sean's wisdom and leaves to reunite with a girl he had pushed away earlier in the story, realizing he was afraid of letting her change his life.

While Good Will Hunting is a scripted film, the mentor-mentee dynamic it portrays plays out in real life all the time. When studying many of the most famous entrepreneurs, past and present, one common thread I found is that each of them has benefited from the mentorship of someone who came before them. For instance, Facebook founder and CEO Mark Zuckerberg was mentored by Steve Jobs, the chairman, CEO, and co-founder of Apple, during a rough patch in Facebook's early days. After Jobs passed away in 2011, the 27-year-old Zuckerberg shared how Jobs had advised him on building a management team that was "focused on building as high-quality and good things as you are."

While you may not be building a social media platform, you are building a complex business that requires knowledge often gained through experience. A mentor can be instrumental in speeding up your learning curve and guiding you as you find your footing in the industry. In my own career, I've had several mentors to whom I owe much of my early success. Each one played a crucial role in helping me navigate this challenging field, and without their support, I don't believe I would have achieved what I have.

When seeking a mentor, focus on finding someone who can help you reach your goals. A good mentor will listen and offer guidance when you need it, taking pride in helping you grow. However, once you find the right mentor, remember not to rely on them to do everything for you. Make the effort to solve problems on your own first, and then turn to your mentor for a second opinion or when you've reached a point where you can't move forward alone.

Colleagues

After my encounter with the veteran agent, I walked back into my conference room, replaying his words in my head. In just nine words, my entire belief system was turned upside down, and I didn't know what to make of it. It felt as though someone had told my three-year-old self that Santa Claus wasn't real. Even though I had just witnessed the truth in what the agent said, part of me still didn't fully believe it. I'm a fact-driven person, and I needed more evidence to determine whether the conversation I overheard was an anomaly or if it truly reflected how things worked.

To gather more facts, I called the few agents I knew in the industry. My plan was simple: I would ask them how they viewed other Realtors, without providing any context, so I could hear their honest opinions. I started with my cousin, who quickly pointed out that most of her colleagues were friends, and the ones who weren't were simply people she hadn't spent enough time with yet. Then, I reached out to an agent I had met through my cousin. He explained that while the real estate industry is large, the number of agents who regularly do business is relatively small—and those agents tend to be in regular communication with each other.

As I continued down my list, I kept hearing the same thing: agents viewed each other as colleagues and friends. But even after making my final call, I still wasn't 100% convinced. I rationalized this by telling myself that I didn't know enough Realtors yet, and the sample size was too small to be certain. Unsure of how else to prove it, I decided to take a different approach. I made a list of 25 Realtors—some were the ones I had just spoken to, some were agents from my office, and I added a few random agents as well. Then, I dove into each person's Facebook friends list to see who they were connected with. My thinking was that if they were friends with other Realtors, it would be "Facebook official," and they would likely interact with each other on social media.

For the next hour, I scrolled through all 25 agents' friends lists and browsed their Facebook walls to see if other Realtors were commenting on their posts and vice versa. What I found was not what I expected. Not only did every agent have numerous Realtor friends, but those same Realtors were actively commenting on and liking each other's posts. Seeing this unfold in front of me, I finally realized that the veteran agent had been 100% correct: people really do like to do business with people they like.

This revelation completely changed how I viewed my fellow Realtors, and I am forever grateful to the veteran agent for taking a few seconds of his time to share that wisdom with me. Since then, I've experienced the benefits of building relationships with other Realtors countless times. From being tipped off about off-market listings, to getting my buyers in the door before anyone else, to having my offers accepted in competitive situations, the advantages of these connections have been clear. We've shared resources to help each other grow our businesses, and I've even received referral business from agents who don't work in my market.

I firmly believe my career would not have reached the level it has without the support and camaraderie of the colleagues around me.

Family/Friends

In 2023, I hit a point where I felt completely lost, with no clear view of my future. I had taken my brokerage as far as I wanted, shut down my Realtor education company due to a lack of time, and my personal real estate business had completely dried up. It was a feeling I had never experienced before, and I wasn't sure how to redirect myself onto a more stable path.

This sense of being lost actually started about six months earlier when I couldn't figure out how to spend my birthday. Normally, I reserve that day for something new—trying a restaurant, tackling a physical challenge, or exploring a nature park. But this year, nothing sounded appealing. As the day approached, I was still undecided, and by the afternoon, feeling the pressure to do something, I reluctantly visited a museum exhibit that seemed somewhat interesting (it wasn't).

Later that evening, sensing that something was off, my wife asked me what was bothering me. After I explained how I had been feeling, she suggested I speak to a therapist—someone who could serve as a sounding board. Thinking I could work through this "funk" on my own, I brushed off her suggestion and tried to figure it out myself. But over time, the feeling persisted. After months of struggling, I finally asked my wife if she could ask her colleagues (my wife is a psychologist) for a recommendation. A few weeks later, I had my first virtual session with Frank. While our initial meeting went well, and we agreed to meet weekly, I still had doubts that therapy was something I needed.

Over the next few weeks, Frank and I explored various topics, mostly related to work. Despite my initial skepticism, I found it helpful to vent to an unbiased third party. During our first few sessions, Frank mostly listened, letting me talk through my thoughts. Then one week, out of the blue, he asked me how much time I spent with my brother, parents, and non-work friends. The question caught me completely off guard. After thinking for a few seconds, I realized I didn't know. As I said those words out loud, the realization hit me hard. I tried to come up with an answer, but my most recent memories of spending time with my family were limited to family events. As for non-work friends, I couldn't recall a single recent experience.

Sensing my growing frustration, Frank interjected, explaining that while work is important, so is spending time with the people I love. He emphasized that socializing stimulates attention and memory, and strengthens cognitive processing. Given how unsuccessful my attempts to get out of this funk had been, I agreed to follow his advice and spend more time with my family and non-work friends.

True to my word, in the following weeks, I went to a Chicago Cubs game with my parents and brother, and I had dinner and drinks with two of my best friends. During these experiences, I had a great time and barely thought about work. Spending time with family and friends gave me the mental reset I had been searching for. It must have been noticeable, too, because my wife remarked that I seemed more refreshed and in a better place. I agreed with her.

As I mentioned earlier, being a Realtor is a lifestyle choice, and you get to decide how to spend your time. While focusing on your business is crucial for achieving your goals, you can't do so effectively without a clear mind—and social interactions are essential for mental clarity. According to the Centers for Disease Control and Prevention (CDC), social connections can help improve your ability to recover from stress, anxiety, and depression. They also promote healthy eating, physical activity, better sleep, and overall quality of life.[3]

Don't wait until you feel lost like I did. Make the effort to spend time with those close to you and foster new connections along the way. Your business—and your well-being—will benefit from it!

Important to Remember

✓ **What is mental strength?**

Mental strength is the ability to effectively manage challenges, pressures, and stressors in life.

✓ **Stay Positive**

- Traits of a Positive Person:
  - Confident
  - Accepting
  - Focused
  - Optimistic
  - Trusting

✓ **Have Perspective**

- Traits of a Person with Perspective:
  - Empathetic
  - Grateful
  - Self-aware
  - Curious
  - Unbiased

✓ **Embrace Failure**

- Traits of Someone Who Embraces Failure:
  - Resilient
  - Accountable
  - Resourceful
  - Purposeful
  - Optimistic

✓ **Be Adaptable**

- Traits of Someone Adaptable:
  - Flexible
  - Creative
  - Open-minded
  - Resourceful
  - Inquisitive

✓ **Tools**

- Self-talk:
  - Our brains focus on what we tell them to focus on. Pay attention to the negative words you frequently use and consciously flip them into positive terms.

- Affirmations:
  - Use positive affirmations (short, empowering phrases) to counter negative thoughts. Repeating them regularly can help improve your mindset.

- Vision Boards:
  - Create a vision board as a visual representation of your goals. Display it somewhere visible to remind yourself daily of what you're working toward.

- Mind Movies:
  - Make a mind movie by compiling images (similar to a vision board) into a video format, set to music. This combination of visuals and sound creates a powerful tool for staying focused on your goals.

- Journaling:
  - Writing daily can help release emotions, allowing you to process the ups and downs of a Realtor's life. Journaling provides a mental reset.

✓ Support System

- Mentors:
  - Seek mentors who listen, guide, and take pride in helping you grow. A good mentor can accelerate your learning and provide valuable insight as you navigate the real estate industry.

- Colleagues:
  - Although other Realtors are your competition, view them as allies, not adversaries. People prefer to do business with those they like. Building friendships with other Realtors can open doors to new opportunities.

- Family/Friends:
  - Social connections with family and friends help you unwind and maintain a balanced life. The mind needs social interaction to perform at its best, so take time to nurture these relationships.

NOTES

Chapter 3
Goals

as she lay on the hospital bed, waiting for the nurse to start the scan. The nurse grabbed a device that resembled a Nintendo Switch remote, applied some jelly, and placed it on my wife's stomach. I focused on the black-and-white monitor hanging above the foot of the bed. After 15 to 20 seconds, the nurse announced, "OK, here is baby A." Then, after another 10 seconds of searching, she added, "And here is baby B." We were having twins.

The rest of 2017 became a blur. Between trying to get my brokerage off the ground and attending countless doctor's appointments—because my wife was considered high-risk— life became chaotic. We had been preparing for one baby, but now we had to double our efforts. By the end of the year, my production was about the same as in 2016, and once again, I didn't have enough to win. As the clock struck midnight on December 31st, 2017, with my extremely pregnant wife beside me on the couch watching the local fireworks on TV, I made a promise to myself: no matter what happens this year, I will win a top producer award.

My twin boys were born on a snowy day in early January. When we finally brought them home a week later, reality hit me—this year was going to be much harder than I had imagined. Sleep was scarce, and because they were born premature, we had a long list of doctor appointments. At the same time, I was in my second year of running my brokerage, which had grown to include six agents and a marketing director. I did my best to balance my responsibilities at home and at work while serving as many clients as I could. Days blurred into one another as I operated on minimal sleep and excessive caffeine, juggling everything just to stay afloat.

As the year drew to a close, I could barely remember most of it. It had all become a fog. I thought I had done fairly well with sales, and when I reviewed my total production, I saw it was higher than the previous two years. Still, I doubted it was enough to win. The thought of missing out again after such a challenging year was hard to accept. But real estate doesn't sleep, so I kept moving forward into the new year.

A few months into 2019, I was sitting in the lobby of a high-rise building, waiting to show a new listing. Relaxing in a leather chair in the waiting area, I was scrolling through Facebook when an email notification popped up from my association. I tapped on it, and the email opened, informing me that I was being recognized as a 2018 top producer for both production and the number of units sold.

Lesson Learned

To succeed in anything, especially real estate, you need something that drives you— something to turn to when things get tough. This career is full of highs and lows. One day everything is going great, and the next, things can flip, taking you in a completely different direction. One minute your clients are ready to close, and the next, the deal falls apart at the closing table. Or maybe a client you've worked with multiple times lists their property with another broker just a month after asking for your valuation.

I've experienced all of this in my career, but one thing I've learned: when you have something that fuels your motivation, nothing can stop you from achieving your goals. 2018 was one of the hardest years of my life. I was hit with challenges from all directions, but I kept my goals front and center. Those sleepless nights where I still performed at my best? It was all possible because I knew exactly what I was working toward. Without that clear goal, there's no way I would have accomplished what I did that year.

Life will always test you, especially when you least expect it. The key is to stay focused, no matter what comes your way. The most successful people in our industry, and in the world, share one thing in common: an unwavering drive to achieve their goals.

Now that you know the secret to success, let's explore how you can harness it.

▌ The New Car Principle

In early 2023, I started thinking about my next car as my lease was about to expire. I was driving a 2019 Tesla Model 3, but with my boys growing fast, I knew I needed something bigger. I set my sights on the Tesla Model Y, partly because I wanted a larger car and partly because I was seeing Model 3s everywhere and wanted something a bit different. After customizing it on Tesla's website, I decided on a white Model Y with 20" black turbine rims—a version I hadn't seen much of.

I placed my order in January, knowing it would take a few months. Finally, in late May, I got the call that my car was ready for pickup. After finalizing the paperwork, I climbed into my new car, adjusted everything, and took off for my first drive. I was excited, feeling like one of the first people to own this car—or so I thought.

Minutes later, I pulled up to a busy intersection. To my surprise, I saw three other white Model Ys at different points in the intersection. I brushed it off as a coincidence and kept driving, but the more I drove, the more I started seeing my car everywhere. How was this possible? How did everyone suddenly have the same car?

I was puzzled until I came across a Tony Robbins video on YouTube. In it, Tony explained how our brains are like supercomputers, programmed to focus on whatever we tell them to. Hearing this, everything clicked. Those Model Ys had been there all along, but I hadn't noticed them before because I wasn't focused on seeing them. It wasn't until I was driving one myself that my brain started filtering for them.

Our brains are incredible at processing information. Every second, they take in about 11 million pieces of data, but we can only consciously process about 40 of those pieces.[1] It's like having the most advanced filtering system ever created, and it filters based on what we focus on. That's why I started seeing all the Model Ys—my brain was now primed to notice them.

The same principle applies to goals. When you know exactly what you want to focus on, your mind will reveal paths and opportunities that were always around you, but that you hadn't noticed before. The key is clarity: you must know what you truly want in order to see the way forward.

| Paths and Doors

Yvon Chouinard, born on November 9th, 1938, in Maine to a French-Canadian mechanic, didn't set out to become a business mogul. At age nine, his family moved to Southern California, where he took up falconry, a hobby that led him to rock climbing. By the age of 14, to save money and adapt his climbing tools, Chouinard taught himself blacksmithing. His first creation was a set of steel pitons (metal clips climbers use to thread ropes and prevent falls), crafted from an old harvester blade for climbing in Yosemite National Park. Word spread quickly, and soon, his friends wanted Chouinard's pitons too. He found himself running a small business, forging two pitons per hour in his parents' backyard and selling them for $1.50 each. But as competitors began to copy his designs, Chouinard's small venture fizzled out.

In 1970, on a winter climbing trip to Scotland, Chouinard bought a rugby shirt to wear while climbing. The shirt, built tough to withstand the rigors of the sport, had a collar that protected his neck from climbing hardware slings. Back in the States, Chouinard wore the shirt around his climbing buddies, who immediately wanted one for themselves. Seeing another opportunity, he took his first step into climbing apparel. He began selling the shirt, which eventually led him to develop other clothing items that climbers needed but couldn't find on the market.

On May 9th, 1973, after successfully selling clothing, Chouinard launched Patagonia. The first store opened in Ventura, California, and over time, Patagonia expanded its product line to include gear for other sports like surfing, as well as products such as camping food. By 2015, Patagonia's profits had grown to $750 million, and by the late 2010s, the brand's fleece vests became iconic in the corporate world. Chouinard's entrepreneurial journey, driven by a series of discoveries, made him one of the world's most successful businesspeople.

Chouinard's story mirrors the paths of many successful individuals. It begins with a passion, followed by intense focus. That focus reveals opportunities—like the lack of quality climbing equipment—and pursuing those opportunities opens more doors. This cycle repeats until they reach levels of success that few achieve.

To become a successful Realtor, you must first discover what truly drives you. Ask yourself: why do you want to be a Realtor? Is it to prove someone wrong, to provide a better life for your child, or to show yourself that you are more than a product of your environment? Only you can answer this question, but it's one you should confront early in your career to help guide you through inevitable challenges.

| Science Doesn't Lie

Knowing the core reason you want to be a Realtor is just the first step. Achieving that desire takes time and requires setting goals that keep you on the path. Desires don't materialize overnight; they take careful planning.

Research consistently demonstrates the power of goal-setting. A simple Google search will yield countless articles, research papers, and videos on the topic. The central theme across the research is that goal-setting alters how your brain works—it rewires your brain to make it more efficient. This happens because of neuroplasticity, the brain's ability to reorganize itself by forming new neural connections, which goal-setting activates.

Interestingly, studies show that highly emotional goals—those that carry deep personal meaning—cause the brain to downplay obstacles. When people are intensely motivated, their brains view hurdles as less significant. Moreover, researchers have found that challenging goals lead to the most dramatic changes in brain structure.

| Make Them Difficult

In 2001, Elon Musk, then a board member of the Mars Society, first presented his goal of enabling Mars colonization. At that point, space travel was mostly limited to sending astronauts to the International Space Station or launching satellites—both incredibly costly and typically government-run initiatives.

The following year, Musk founded SpaceX with the ambitious goal of creating more affordable, reliable rockets. This was no easy feat. Between 2006 and 2008, SpaceX faced three failed launches, bringing the company to the brink of bankruptcy. However, on September 28, 2008, the company's fourth attempt succeeded, earning them a $1.6 billion contract with NASA.

Since then, SpaceX has continued to push the boundaries of space travel, developing reusable rockets that land safely back on Earth—a technology crucial for the company's Mars colonization goal. While SpaceX hasn't yet achieved its ultimate goal, the pursuit continues to drive innovation, pushing the company to create technologies that might one day make it a reality.

SpaceX is a prime example of how difficult goals push people to maximize their potential. The company's team is working toward something that has never been done before, and the magnitude of the challenge forces them to stretch their abilities to the limit.

When setting your own goals, aim high. Easy, comfortable goals may be more achievable, but difficult goals are more energizing and rewarding. Plus, in pursuing a grand, challenging goal, you'll likely achieve the smaller ones along the way.

| Be Specific

In his book Atomic Habits, author James Clear highlights a 2001 study conducted by British researchers. They divided 248 individuals, all with the goal of working out and getting fit, into three groups to see who would build better exercise habits over two weeks.

The first group, the control group, was simply asked to track how often they exercised.

The second group, called the "motivation" group, was also asked to track their workouts but was given additional reading materials on the benefits of exercise. Researchers explained how exercise could reduce the risk of coronary heart disease and improve heart health.

The third group received the same presentation as the second group, ensuring they were equally motivated. However, this group was also asked to create a detailed plan for when and where they would exercise in the coming weeks. Specifically, each person completed the following sentence: "During the next week, I will partake in at least 20 minutes of vigorous exercise on [DAY] at [TIME] in [PLACE]."

The results were striking. In the first and second groups, only 35% to 38% of participants exercised at least once a week. In contrast, a staggering 91% of the third group exercised at least once a week—more than double the other groups.

This result echoes what happens every year on January 1st. Millions of people set New Year's resolutions without a concrete plan. They sign up for a gym membership, but after two weeks, they stop going. They declare, "This is the year I finally [fill in the blank]," but after the initial excitement fades, they return to their old habits. A study by the University of Scranton found that 92% of people who set New Year's goals fail to achieve them.[2]

For a goal to be achieved, it must be specific and time-bound. Specific, timed goals provide direction and guidance, helping you understand what needs to be done and when. These goals also prevent distractions, keeping you focused on tasks that contribute to your desired outcome.

| Write Them Down

Jim Carrey, growing up in blue-collar factory towns in Ontario, Canada, faced financial struggles throughout his youth. At one point, his family was forced to live in their Volkswagen van on a relative's lawn.

At age eight, Jim discovered his talent for doing impressions by making faces in front of a mirror. By age 15, in 1977, he performed his first stand-up routine in downtown Toronto. Unfortunately, he bombed, which led him to question his future as an entertainer. But he didn't give up. Two years later, he returned to the stage with a more refined act, landing his first paid gig. Soon, the 17-year-old progressed from open-mic nights to regular paid shows, building a reputation in the comedy circuit.

After an article about his stand-up routine appeared in the *Toronto Star,* his popularity grew across the country. This led to him securing a lead role in a made-for-TV movie, which achieved high viewership and solidified his comedic status.

Despite his growing success in Canada, Jim had bigger dreams. In 1983, he moved to Hollywood, where he began performing regularly at The Comedy Store. However, he struggled to replicate the success he had enjoyed in Toronto.

A firm believer in the law of attraction, Jim famously drove his old Toyota to the top of a hill overlooking Los Angeles. While sitting there, broke and frustrated, he wrote himself a check for $10 million with the memo "for acting services rendered" and dated it for Thanksgiving 1995. He tucked the check into his wallet as a symbol of his goal. Remarkably, just before Thanksgiving in 1995, Jim learned that he would earn $10 million for starring in the movie Dumb and Dumber.

A study by Dr. Gail Matthews, a psychology professor at Dominican University in California, found that people are 42% more likely to achieve their goals simply by writing them down. Writing down your goals forces you to clarify what you want, motivating you to take action.

When you write down your goals, create a realistic timeframe and include measurable details, so you know when you've achieved them. While writing them down doesn't guarantee success, it significantly increases your chances.

PUT YOUR GOALS ON PAPER

PEOPLE WHO WRITE DOWN THEIR GOALS ARE

30 TIMES MORE SUCCESSFUL THAN THOSE

WHO DON'T SET GOALS AT ALL.

-HARVARD BUSINESS STUDY

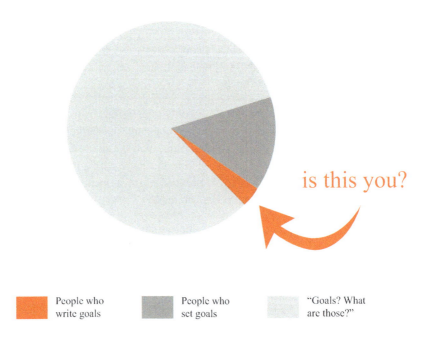

is this you?

People who write goals   People who set goals   "Goals? What are those?"

▍ Visualize Them

Like many successful individuals, Sara Blakely faced numerous challenges early in life. At 16, she witnessed a close friend get hit and run over by a car. Around the same time, her parents separated, leaving her to navigate life between two homes. Blakely had a goal of attending law school but was unable to pass the entrance exam. Needing a job, she spent three months working at Walt Disney World while also performing stand-up comedy. Eventually, she landed a position as a salesperson and later became a national sales trainer for the office supply company Danka.

One evening, while still working at Danka, Blakely was preparing to attend a party. She realized she didn't have an undergarment that would be invisible under the white pants she planned to wear. That's when she had the idea to cut the feet off a pair of pantyhose, accidentally creating a garment that both she and many other women would find useful.

Realizing the potential of her invention, Blakely invested $5,000 of her savings to start her business. She worked at Danka during the day and spent her nights researching fabric types, patents, and trademark designs. Knowing she couldn't manufacture the product herself, she found a hosiery factory willing to produce her footless pantyhose. After writing her own patent application, choosing the playful name "Spanx," and designing a logo, she was officially in business.

With limited funds for marketing, Blakely traveled the country, selling her product to stores like Neiman Marcus. Her big break came when Oprah Winfrey named Spanx one of her "Favorite Things." This skyrocketed the brand's popularity, enabling Blakely to resign from Danka and focus entirely on her company. Spanx became a multi-billion-dollar business, and in 2012, Blakely appeared on the cover of Forbes as the youngest self-made female billionaire in the world.

During the challenging periods of her life, Sara Blakely turned to visualization, a technique she learned from motivational speaker Wayne Dyer's cassette tapes, which her father gave her. She also listened to Tony Robbins, Zig Ziglar, and others, putting visualization into practice. One notable example was when Blakely imagined herself being on *The Oprah Winfrey Show*. She saw herself sitting on Oprah's couch, having an exciting conversation. Fifteen years later, that exact scenario became a reality.

Visualization is a powerful tool where you mentally imagine in detail what you want to achieve. It helps create a clear mental picture of your goals, allowing your mind to figure out ways to bring them to life. Visualization crowds out negative self-talk by generating positive thoughts and emotions, making success more likely.

NOTE:

Your brain doesn't know the difference between what is real and what you visualize, so it treats them the same.

Once you know what you want to achieve, set aside time each day to visualize it. Picture everything down to the smallest details. The more vividly you can imagine your goals, the more real they will feel—and become.

TIP:

Find a quiet, distraction-free space to do your visualizations, so you can focus fully.

| Find Your "Why"

A significant part of running a brokerage involves recruiting agents. Since brokerages earn the bulk of their income from agent commissions, bringing in new talent is crucial to increasing the bottom line. My brokerage focused on newer agents, which led to frequent interviews with people eager to enter the real estate industry. Since it costs money to keep a new agent on board until they start earning commissions, we had to be selective about whom we accepted. One of the main criteria we used to determine this was understanding their deep motivation for becoming a Realtor.

For example, one prospective agent who applied to join my brokerage felt lost. She had worked in other industries but believed real estate might be her true calling. After getting her license and interviewing at several brokerages, she found that building a real estate business was much harder than she anticipated. By the time we spoke, she was discouraged and unsure if the industry was the right fit for her. I asked her a simple question: "Deep down, why do you want to be a Realtor?"

At first, she responded with surface-level answers like "I want to help people," "I want to make a lot of money," and "I like looking at houses." Sensing that these responses didn't truly address her motivation, I pressed her to dig deeper. After a few rounds of questioning, she realized her real reason: she wanted to prove her parents wrong. They had urged her to pursue a career in law or medicine, like her siblings, but she wanted to demonstrate that she could succeed in real estate.

Once she uncovered this deeper motivation, her entire mindset shifted. She now understood why becoming a Realtor was important to her—it wasn't about money or houses, but about proving her capabilities to her parents.

When setting long-term goals, start by understanding why you want to be a Realtor. Is it to prove someone wrong? To provide a better life for your children? Or perhaps to show that you're capable of success despite obstacles? In my experience, those with a deep, personal reason for pursuing their goals are the ones who ultimately achieve them.

> **TIP:**
>
> If you're struggling to uncover your "why," keep asking yourself "why" until you get to the core reason. For instance, if you want to win a top producer award, ask yourself why that's important. Then, ask again about the reason behind that answer. Keep digging until you find your true motivation.

| Start Long

In today's world, we've grown accustomed to getting things instantly. If we're hungry, we can tap an app and have food delivered in minutes. If we need toothpaste, we can order it on Amazon and receive it later that same day. Instant gratification surrounds us, and while it's convenient for satisfying hunger or keeping our teeth clean, it fosters the expectation that everything should happen immediately. This expectation can lead real estate agents to the common mistake of focusing solely on short-term goals.

When I owned my brokerage, my partner and I made it a priority to discuss goals with every new agent. We wanted to understand why they wanted to build a real estate business and see if their goals aligned with their ambitions. More often than not, when we asked agents about their goals, they could readily share their short-term plans. However, when we pushed them to think about their long-term goals, many struggled to respond. This tendency is something I've noticed repeatedly: most people are so focused on instant gratification that they fail to think far ahead.

This approach to goal-setting is backward. If you don't know your ultimate destination, you're setting goals without any real direction. To set goals properly, you must start with the end in mind and work backward.

Take Jim Carrey's famous example: when he wrote a $10 million check to himself, he set a future date for cashing it because he knew the money wouldn't come instantly. He envisioned the end goal, aware that it would require years of hard work to achieve. With a target in sight, Carrey knew exactly what he was working towards each day.

Make It Personal

A common mistake I see agents make when setting long-term goals is focusing solely on business objectives. While there's nothing wrong with setting business-related goals, I've found that personal goals are often more powerful and motivating. Personal goals carry more emotional weight, which pushes you harder to achieve them. Moreover, these personal ambitions often align with your business objectives.

For instance, if your parents supported you throughout your life, you might set a goal to take them on an all-expenses-paid vacation as a way to thank them. Or if you have a young child, you might aim to pay for their college education. Both of these personal goals require a certain level of financial success, which can be tied to specific business milestones—like selling a certain number of homes by a particular date.

Personal goals reflect what you truly wish to achieve. They motivate you on a deeper level, shape your decisions, and give you a sense of purpose. These goals are not just about where you want to go in life, but about who you want to become along the way.

Once you understand why you want to be a Realtor and have clarified your long-term personal and professional goals, the next step is to create a plan to achieve them. This is where short-term goals come into play.

| End Short

If you look at successful people or companies in any field, they all had a grand vision for their future and accomplished many smaller goals to make that vision a reality. Earlier in the chapter, I mentioned SpaceX's goal of colonizing Mars. They can't simply build one massive rocket to achieve this goal—technology isn't advanced enough yet. Instead, they must develop smaller rockets through trial and error, gradually working toward a larger one. In other words, they achieve a series of smaller goals that lead them toward their larger objective.

We've seen this play out in SpaceX's history. They began with three rockets that failed before the fourth succeeded. That success led to more successful launches, which paved the way for larger rocket designs. Today, they are testing the Starship rocket they plan to use for Mars missions. By accomplishing smaller goals, they've steadily moved closer to their ultimate target.

Short-term goals are objectives typically set for weeks, months, or a few years into the future. These goals help you make progress toward larger, long-term goals.

TIP:

Before writing out your short-term goals, break down your main goal as much as possible so you know which smaller steps you need to take. For instance, if your long-term goal is to send your parents on an all-expenses-paid vacation, research all aspects of the trip and estimate the total cost. Knowing this amount will help you set short-term goals, such as saving a specific sum each year.

Short-term goals serve as a roadmap, keeping you focused and motivated. A large goal can feel overwhelming, but breaking it down into smaller steps makes the larger goal feel more attainable.

NOTE:

If your long-term goal is more than ten years away, consider setting medium-term goals that are three to five years out.

Be SMART

A popular method for setting short-term goals is the SMART framework (Specific, Measurable, Achievable, Relevant, and Time-bound). This method transforms vague intentions into clear, actionable plans. Here's how the SMART method works:

- ✅ **Specific:** Your goals should be clear and concise.

- ✅ **Measurable:** You need a way to track your progress.

- ✅ **Achievable:** The goals should be realistic and within reach.

- ✅ **Relevant:** They should align with your values and long-term objectives.

- ✅ **Time-bound:** Set a deadline for completion.

Each element of the SMART method ensures that your objectives are easy to understand and offers a clear path for achieving them. For example, if your long-term goal is to send your parents on an all-expenses-paid vacation, a SMART short-term goal could be: "Save $1,000 over the next 12 months to contribute toward my parents' trip."

By using the SMART method, you can keep track of time, hold yourself accountable, and consistently monitor your progress toward your ultimate goal.

Short-term goals are just as important—if not more so—than long-term goals. Use them as a guide to keep yourself on track, and let them bring you back to the right path quickly if you veer off course.

Review Often

Long before Daymond John became known as "The People's Shark" on Shark Tank, he was a young boy in Queens, NY, hustling to make money. He started working at age 10, handing out flyers for $2 an hour. By high school, he was participating in a program that allowed him to work full-time while attending school on alternating weeks. After high school, he started a commuter van service while waiting tables at Red Lobster.

In 1992, John had the idea to start a clothing company for young men and began selling wool ski hats from his mother's house. The hats' success led to the creation of other clothing items, and before long, FUBU was born. Today, FUBU has earned over $6 billion in global sales.

John, like many successful people, understands the power of setting and reviewing goals. At age 16, after reading Think and Grow Rich by Napoleon Hill, he began writing down his goals. Knowing he needed constant reminders, he made a habit of writing and reading his goals every night before bed and every morning when he woke up—a practice he continues to this day.

Our lives are filled with distractions, and it's easy to lose sight of what we're working toward. Once you've written out your goals, put them somewhere visible so you can review them often. The more you read them, the more they'll begin to shape your reality.

TIP:

Reassess your goals at the end of every year (between Christmas and New Year's) to ensure they're still relevant. Life changes constantly, and you may need to adjust your goals to reflect new priorities.

Important to Remember

☑ **The New Car inciple**

When you clearly know what you desire, your mind naturally starts revealing paths and opportunities (doors) that may have always been there but were previously unnoticed, helping you achieve those desires.

☑ **Paths and Doors**

To succeed as a Realtor, you need a genuine desire for success. That desire opens up paths and doors, guiding you toward your goals.

☑ **Science Doesn't Lie**

Setting goals changes the structure of your brain, optimizing it for success.

☑ **Make Them Difficult**

Challenging yourself with big goals pushes your brain to its full potential, encouraging creative solutions.

☑ **Be Specific**

Goals need clear deadlines and specific details. Specific goals provide direction and keep you focused.

☑ **Write Them Down**

You are 42% more likely to achieve your goals by writing them down. This process helps clarify your desires and motivates you to take action.

☑ **Visualize Them**

Visualizing your goals helps your mind identify ways to turn those dreams into reality.

☑ **Find Your "Why"**

The most successful people, especially in real estate, have a deep, personal reason driving their ambition.

☑ **Start Long**

To set effective goals, begin with the end in mind and work your way backward.

✅ Make It Personal

Personal goals carry more weight and meaning than business goals and can be even more motivating.

✅ End Short

Short-term goals act as stepping stones, keeping you motivated and on track toward your larger objectives.

✅ Be SMART

Use the SMART method for goal-setting:

- Specific – Clear, concise goals.
- Measurable – Track your progress.
- Achievable – Realistic goals.
- Relevant – Goals that align with your long-term objectives.
- Time-bound – Set deadlines.

✅ Review Often

Keep your goals visible. Regularly reviewing them helps turn them into reality.

NOTES

Chapter 4
Routines

One random evening in September 2009, I found myself zoned out on the couch in my parents' living room, watching something mindless on TV. A glance at the clock by the television jolted me back to reality. It was 11:35 PM—much later than I had realized. Shaking off the daze, I turned off the TV and headed to my room, setting my alarm for 6:30 AM with every intention of waking up early. I switched off the light and quickly drifted to sleep.

I was in the middle of a pleasant dream when a piercing noise yanked me awake. It took me a moment to gather my thoughts before I realized it was my alarm clock, screeching obnoxiously. Groggy and annoyed, I silenced it and stared at the ceiling, contemplating whether to get up or indulge in a few more minutes of sleep. After a brief internal debate, I told myself, "What's a few more minutes?" and shut my eyes.

The warmth of the morning sun streamed through my window, making it hard to stay comfortable. Reluctantly, I opened my eyes again, only to find it was much later than I intended. I rolled over to check the time—9:47 AM. Blinking in disbelief, I hoped the time would somehow change, but of course, it didn't. Shocked, I stumbled out of bed and walked toward the kitchen, silently praying my parents wouldn't be there.

Unfortunately, both of them were sitting at the kitchen table as if waiting for me. Startled by their presence, I awkwardly muttered, "Good morning," and made a beeline for the coffee pot. They greeted me in return, but their tone made it clear they were trying hard not to comment on the fact that I was up long after most people had already started their workday.

After an awkward silence while I poured my coffee, I hurriedly made my way back to my room, grateful to escape the situation. Sipping my coffee, I sat at my desk and opened my laptop, hoping for something exciting in my inbox. But to my disappointment, all I found were a few spam emails. Unsure of what to do next, I distracted myself by browsing ESPN and reading whatever caught my eye. I repeated this routine with a few other sites, killing time until my stomach began to growl.

 I tried ignoring the hunger for as long as I could, but eventually, I gave in and ventured back to the kitchen. Once again, my parents were there, and this time I knew I couldn't avoid them. For the next ten minutes, while I hastily made a sandwich, I fielded their questions, doing everything in my power to steer clear of any mention of real estate. As soon as I could, I smiled awkwardly, grabbed my lunch, and retreated back to my room.

Sitting at my desk, guilt gnawed at me as I replayed the brief conversation with my parents. I tried to distract myself by eating, but the guilt wouldn't go away. Determined to do *something productive, I reopened my laptop and typed, "What should a new Realtor do?" into Google. The search engine delivered hundreds of results, but after clicking through a few links, I felt completely overwhelmed. I closed the laptop, pushed my lunch aside, and stared blankly at the wall.*

It was only my second week as a Realtor, and I had no idea what I was supposed to be doing.

Lesson Learned

Being a Realtor means you are an independent contractor, not an employee. You're your own boss. No one tells you where to be or when. There's no fixed time you have to wake up, and no one expects you to clock in at a specific hour. Each day is yours to structure however you see fit. While this freedom may sound appealing, it can also be a downfall for those who don't understand how to create a productive routine.

The concept of not having to wake up at a set time was new to me, and I wasn't prepared for it. For years, while working in corporate America, I had a strict schedule. I knew when to wake up and when I needed to be at work. But in my new career, the only person I had to answer to was myself. This meant I had to take control and build the necessary structure into my day to stay productive. To do this, I realized I needed daily routines and had to commit to them without fail. Throughout my career, I've found that every agent should implement three essential routines, starting with the most important: the nighttime routine.

| Night time Routine

Your morning success is often determined by how well you prepare the night before. A solid nighttime routine ensures that you're set up for a productive next day. This routine consists of a handful of things you do before turning off the lights and laying your head on the pillow, putting your mind in the right place to attack the coming day with focus and intensity.

Everyone's nighttime routine will vary, but I suggest incorporating a few essential tasks that have helped me throughout my career.

Pick Out Your Clothes

This might sound trivial, but choosing your clothes the night before can save time and mental energy in the morning. Knowing what you're going to wear eliminates the need to waste time and brainpower on this simple task, freeing up more time for important things like spending time with family or getting an early start on work.

> **NOTE:**
>
> Think of your brain like a battery. When you wake up, your battery is fully charged after a night's sleep. As the day progresses, that charge depletes—just like an cell phone's battery. The more trivial decisions you make early in the day, the faster that battery drains. By saving energy in the morning, you reserve brainpower for more complex tasks later.

Organize Your To-Do List

The next important task is organizing your to-do list for the following day. Write down everything you need to accomplish, both business-related and personal. No matter how small the task may seem—whether it's following up with a client or picking up the dry cleaning—include it on your list. This ensures nothing gets overlooked.

> **TIP:**
>
> I divide my tasks into two categories: 20% (high-priority tasks) and 80% (less important tasks). By focusing on the 20% list, I tackle the most important items first, ensuring I get the most impactful work done.

Once your list is written, arrange it so that the most challenging tasks come first. Research shows that tackling difficult tasks when your brain is fully charged leads to better results. Additionally, it reduces the temptation to procrastinate.

> **TIP:**
>
> I use Google Keep to manage my to-do list. It's easy to add, delete, and rearrange tasks, and I can access it across all my devices.

Read

It's no secret that many of the most successful people, both past and present, dedicate time each day to reading. For instance, Bill Gates, Microsoft's founder and former CEO, takes two weeks every year to retreat to a cabin in the woods, completely unplugged from technology, just to read! Success leaves clues, and if the visionaries who've shaped our world recognize the value of reading, we should follow their example.

> **TIP:**
> Make reading the last thing you do before bed and put your technology aside. Research shows that our brains are highly sensitive to light, especially the blue light emitted by phones and electronic devices, which delays melatonin production. A reduction in melatonin can make it harder to fall asleep and, over time, lead to insomnia and fatigue.

However, successful people don't just read anything—they're intentional about their choices. They focus on books that will benefit them both personally and professionally. When selecting your next read, look for books that will have a meaningful impact on your business and life. No offense to Harry Potter, but you can't build a business with wizardry.

> **NOTE:**
> If you're looking for book recommendations, I've included a section at the end of this book listing the books that have had the greatest impact on my career.

| Morning Routine

A well-structured morning routine can be the deciding factor in how productive your day will be. Research shows that a consistent routine in the morning can lower stress levels, increase energy, and boost motivation, all of which keep you on track toward success.
A morning routine is what you do before diving into emails, calls, texts, or social media. It's a set of activities designed to prepare your mind and body for the day ahead, starting the moment you wake up.

> **NOTE:**
> It's incredibly tempting to reach for your phone and dive into notifications as soon as you wake up. Those red circles on your apps scream for attention. However, try to resist the urge until after you've completed your morning routine. The more you resist, the more control you'll have over your morning, setting yourself up for success throughout the day. One way to manage this is by adjusting your phone settings so you don't see notifications until a designated time, such as 9:00 AM. Without the visual triggers, you'll feel less tempted to check them.

Rehydrate

During an eight-hour night of sleep, it's estimated that the body loses about 0.5 to 1 liter of water, which translates to roughly one to two pounds of water weight. Given that water is essential for our bodies to function properly, it's crucial to rehydrate as soon as you wake up. Before doing anything else, drink a full glass of water to replenish what was lost and kickstart your body's systems.

Exercise

Morning exercise not only improves focus and mental clarity, but it also boosts your energy levels throughout the day. Exercising in the morning helps regulate your circadian rhythm, making you more alert and productive. Those who commit to morning exercise often accomplish more than those who don't.

That said, exercise isn't for everyone. If you're not inclined to work out, consider taking a short walk instead. Studies show that walking for just 30 minutes a day can improve cardiovascular fitness, strengthen bones, reduce body fat, and increase muscle power and endurance. Regular walking can also lower your risk of conditions like heart disease, type 2 diabetes, osteoporosis, and certain cancers.

Meditate

Meditation is one of the most powerful practices for clearing the mind, reducing stress, and preparing for the day ahead. Studies show that meditation enhances concentration, resilience, and emotional regulation.

Jack Dorsey, co-founder of Twitter, is a well-known advocate of meditation. Every morning at 6:15 AM, as part of his routine, he meditates for one hour. While you may not have a full hour to spare like Jack, you can still experience many of meditation's benefits by dedicating just 15-20 minutes to sitting in silence and letting your mind wander.

> **TIP:**
>
> To get into the right mindset and prepare my body for meditation, I start each session with box breathing. This simple technique involves breathing in for four seconds, holding for four seconds, exhaling for four seconds, and pausing for another four seconds before repeating the process. I find that doing this five times helps me center myself before meditating.

Office Routine

While your nighttime and morning routines are essential for preparing your mind and body to be productive, it's your office routine where the real work happens to push your business forward. Successful Realtors prioritize their office routine every day, while those who struggle often overlook it. Why is it overlooked? Many Realtors confuse being busy with having a routine. They think that answering emails, calls, and texts as soon as they arrive at the office is part of their routine, but that's not the case.

An office routine consists of the essential business tasks that must be completed each day before moving on to anything else. These are the activities that keep your business on track and help you stay focused. Office routine tasks are different from the to-do list items you plan the night before. Your office routine includes static tasks you complete every day, only changing them when you need to make adjustments.

> **TIP:**
>
> I use Evernote for my office routine to-do list. The app allows me to check and uncheck boxes without deleting or moving tasks, which keeps my list consistent and easy to manage. This way, I don't have to recreate the list daily—it stays organized, allowing me to adjust only when necessary.

Prospecting

Prospecting for new business is the cornerstone of any successful office routine. In real estate, sales drive the business, and without sales, there is no business. To make sales, you need clients. And to get clients, you must prospect. Realtors who commit to prospecting daily are often the most successful and consistent in their work.

However, prospecting doesn't always mean cold calling. It can involve reaching out to past clients, connecting with people in your database, contacting new acquaintances, or following up with leads. There are countless ways to prospect, but the key is finding a method that you enjoy and committing to it daily. Doing something you enjoy makes all the difference because you're more likely to stick with it.

> **NOTE:**
>
> In Chapter 11: Prospecting, I will dive deeper into different prospecting techniques and how to effectively use them.

Market Research

Today's buyers are more informed than ever. With advances in technology, they have access to vast amounts of information, making them savvier than buyers of the past. This means you need to know your market inside and out—more than your clients do—or they'll find an agent who does. Your goal should be to become a market expert, knowing the finer details that most buyers overlook, such as the best coffee spots, the most desirable neighborhoods, and upcoming developments in the area.

> **NOTE:**
>
> To accelerate your market knowledge, set aside time each week to explore. Spend time in the neighborhoods where you want to work and attend open houses to familiarize yourself with the types of properties available.

In addition to knowing the neighborhoods, it's crucial to stay on top of what's happening with the properties in your market. Every morning, I spend time reviewing the MLS to see which properties are new, which have accepted offers, and which have recently closed. Most active buyers have access to this information, so it's vital that you stay up to date to maintain your expertise.

If you come across any properties you think your clients would be interested in, send them the details. This not only shows you're proactive but also demonstrates that you're actively working to find them a home. If they end up purchasing the property you suggested, they'll likely refer you with greater enthusiasm, leading to more business opportunities!

Social Media

As part of your daily office routine, take a few moments each morning to like and comment on people's posts. This simple activity helps social media algorithms work in your favor. By interacting with others' content, you increase the chances of seeing their posts more often, and in turn, they'll see more of yours.

One of the powerful aspects of social media is its ability to offer a glimpse into people's lives through their posts. Whether it's photos of their dinner, reels from concerts, or videos of gender reveals, social media allows you to go behind the scenes. Keep an eye out for significant life events like pregnancy announcements, job transfers, or promotions. These milestones often present an opportunity for you to reach out and offer your services—whether it's helping someone find a new home, sell their current one, or both.

NOTE:

In Chapter 14: Social Media, I'll dive deeper into strategies for using social media to generate more business.

Important to Remember

☑ **Nighttime Routine**

The morning is shaped by the evening, making a nighttime routine crucial for setting yourself up for success the next day.

- Pick Out Your Clothes
  - This simple task conserves brain power for more important decisions the next day.
- Organize Your To-Do List
  - Write and prioritize everything you need to accomplish the following day, starting with the most challenging tasks.

- Read
  - The most successful people consistently dedicate time to reading each day.

✅ Morning Routine

A consistent morning routine can reduce stress, increase energy, and boost motivation, keeping you on track for success.

- Rehydrate
  - Drink a glass of water right after waking up to replenish fluids lost during sleep.
- Exercise
  - Morning exercise enhances focus, sharpens mental ability, and increases your energy throughout the day.
- Meditate
  - Meditation helps clear your mind, reduce stress, and mentally prepare for the day ahead.

✅ Office Routine

Your office routine is a list of essential business tasks that must be completed each day before focusing on other things.

- Prospect
  - Reach out to past clients, contacts in your database, new people you've met, or follow up on leads.
- Market Research
  - Stay up to date on market activity: check new listings, offers, and recent closings.
- Social Media
  - Engage with people's posts by liking and commenting to improve algorithm visibility and boost your online presence.

NOTES

Chapter 5
Expenses and Budgeting

In March 2019, I was sitting at a stoplight on my way home after a long day of work when my car speakers rang. Glancing down at my phone, resting on the charging platform of my center console, I saw it was my accountant calling. It felt odd—he rarely called this late. After a few more rings, I figured it was best to answer.

I tapped the green button and greeted him, expecting the usual few minutes of small talk. But something felt different this time. His tone was abrupt, and he quickly asked if I was sitting down. Caught off guard by his urgency, I hesitantly replied, telling him I was at a red light, driving home. Sensing the shift in my mood, he urged me to pull over. He said he'd wait.

As the awkward silence stretched, the red light felt like it was taking forever to change. I resisted the urge to ask what was wrong. Finally, the light turned green, and I hit the accelerator, heading for a nearby left turn lane. A few blocks later, I pulled into a White Castle parking lot, choosing a spot far from any other cars. Once I parked, I told my accountant I was ready and asked what was going on.

After a brief pause, he dropped the bombshell: after reviewing our family's tax information, we owed the federal and state governments over $50,000 combined. He kept talking, but I couldn't focus. The number was too overwhelming, echoing in my head. When he finally finished, I thanked him, numbly tapping the end button.

For a moment, I just sat there, trying to process the shock. Then the weight of it all hit me, and I broke down. I sobbed uncontrollably, gasping for breath as I tried to make sense of how this had happened. Tears streamed down my face as my mind spiraled, desperate to find an explanation. This went on for over 30 minutes, until I realized I needed to pull myself together—I still had to drive home.

I forced myself to take deep breaths, slowly regaining control. After a few minutes, I felt steady enough to drive. Wiping the tears from my face, I pulled down the mirror and tried to fix my appearance. The crying had left its mark, but I did my best to look normal before putting the car in drive.

I had to go home and explain to my wife that we owed much more than we had the means to pay.

Lesson Learned

During my time in corporate America, I became accustomed to having taxes automatically deducted from my paychecks. It became such a routine that I rarely even glanced at my pay stubs, assuming the deductions were accurate. So, when I received my first few commission checks in real estate, I was surprised to see that the only deductions were brokerage fees and the commission split owed to the brokerage.

In my fifth year in the industry, as my income began to grow, my mother, an accountant, advised me to start making quarterly estimated tax payments to both the state and federal governments. These payments were meant to account for the taxes that weren't being withheld from my commission checks. I followed her advice for several years, but in 2018, I grossly underestimated the amount I needed to set aside.

That year, I sold nearly $11 million in residential real estate, earning over $200,000—significantly more than in previous years. Unfortunately, my estimated tax payments were based on the lower income of the prior year, leaving them far below what I should have paid. This miscalculation resulted in a hefty tax bill that took my family over a year to pay off.

| Commissions

Real estate commissions are different from many other sales commissions because of the large dollar amounts involved in transactions, leading to substantial commission checks. For example, if a Realtor lists and sells a $200,000 home, they might earn 2.5% of the sales price, resulting in a gross commission (before splits or fees) of $5,000. Compare this to a car salesperson, who might sell a $20,000 car and earn about $300 (since car salespeople typically receive 20-40% of the dealership's gross profit on a vehicle).

Another key difference in real estate is the slower pace of transactions compared to other industries. In the earlier example, it could take a listing agent six months from their initial meeting with the sellers to the day they finally receive payment. On the other hand, a car salesperson could sell a car in a day and get paid within a few weeks.

> **NOTE:**
> Since Realtors aren't paid until a transaction closes, all the work leading up to that point is essentially unpaid. If a deal falls through, the Realtor may never get compensated for their efforts.

That being said, one of the advantages of being a Realtor is the variety of ways to earn a commission. Common avenues include:

- Representing a buyer or seller (or both) in a sales transaction
- Representing a tenant or landlord (or both) in a rental transaction

- Referring a buyer or seller to another Realtor for an agreed-upon referral fee or percentage (I'll cover referral fees in more detail in Chapter 11: Prospecting)

- Receiving a referral from another Realtor for a buyer or seller

Each of these methods has the potential to earn a Realtor thousands of dollars in commissions. However, it's important to remember that commission amounts can vary significantly from one transaction to the next, depending on a variety of factors.

Additionally, when you receive a commission is often unpredictable. The best way to manage these fluctuations is by consistently prospecting for new business. The fuller your pipeline, the more likely you are to receive regular income.

▌ 1099's

If you're an employee, your company is required to send you a W-2 by the end of January each year. A W-2 tax form provides essential information about the income you've earned, the taxes withheld, any benefits received, and other relevant details. You use this form to file your federal and state taxes.

As a Realtor, however, you're considered an independent contractor, not an employee. Instead of receiving a W-2, your brokerage will send you a Form 1099. A 1099 reports non-employment income to the IRS, such as your commission earnings.

The key difference between a W-2 and a 1099 is in the income reported. A W-2 shows your take-home pay after all deductions, such as taxes and benefits, are withheld. In contrast, a 1099 shows your gross income without any deductions, such as taxes, commissions, or fees.

For example, if your Gross Commission Income (GCI) is $50,000 and your brokerage takes $10,000 in fees or splits, your 1099 will show $40,000 as your net income.

▌ Taxes

Another major difference between being an independent contractor and an employee is how taxes are handled. In a traditional job, taxes are automatically withheld from each paycheck. As a Realtor, no taxes are deducted from your commission checks, which means you're responsible for paying your own taxes in the form of estimated quarterly payments to both federal and state governments. These payments are based on your expected income for the year and help reduce the amount you owe at tax time.

NOTE:

As a 1099 independent contractor, you typically won't receive a tax refund like a W-2 employee might. Instead, independent contractors often owe money at tax time. To avoid the mistakes I made, it's essential to work with an accountant who can guide you through setting up quarterly tax payments properly.

| Expenses

Being an independent contractor also changes how expenses are managed. For example, if you're an employee commuting to work, you pay for your gas out of pocket, just as you would for groceries. But as an independent contractor, you can deduct business-related expenses—like gas for work travel—to reduce your taxable income.

TIP:

Use the week between Christmas and New Year to review all of your accounts—both business and personal. This helps you assess where your money went over the past year and create a more efficient spending plan for the next year.

Write-Offs

One of the perks of being an independent contractor is the ability to "write off" or deduct business-related expenses. For example, marketing costs for a listing, business cards, and Realtor Association fees can all be deducted from your income to lower your taxable amount. If you earn $50,000 in commissions but have $10,000 in business expenses, you'll only be taxed on the remaining $40,000.

Health Insurance/Retirement Plans

Unlike many companies that offer benefits like health insurance and retirement plans to their employees, most brokerages don't provide these to Realtors. As a result, you're responsible for setting up and paying for your health insurance and retirement plans yourself. Fortunately, these costs can often be treated as business expenses and written off at tax time.

Budgeting

When I first started in real estate, I had no clear idea of what things would cost, let alone how to budget for my new venture. I was more focused on surviving than on making a budget. In hindsight, I should have set up a financial plan, even a small one, to allocate funds toward the essential costs of running my business. That way, I could have better prepared for the months when money was tight.

Budgeting can be challenging, especially if you're a new Realtor and don't yet know the full scope of your expenses. However, creating a budget helps keep you on track, preventing unnecessary spending. Start with what you know and adjust as needed.

Fixed Expenses

Begin by listing your fixed expenses—the ones that don't fluctuate month to month. This includes personal expenses like car payments, cell phone bills, and rent or mortgage payments, as well as business-related fixed costs like Realtor Association fees and brokerage fees. Totaling these will give you a clearer picture of the minimum annual income you'll need to cover your fixed costs.

Variable Expenses

Variable expenses, which can change from month to month, are harder to predict. Start by reviewing last year's variable expenses, then estimate what similar costs you'll face this year. For example, if you plan to sell two listings this year, calculate the costs of professional listing photos, flyers, and postcards for each one. This exercise will help you better estimate your variable expenses for the year.

> **TIP:**
> If you're a new Realtor, ask others in your office about their first-year expenses to get a better idea of what you can expect.

Once you've calculated both your fixed and variable expenses, you'll have a clearer understanding of how much income you'll need to generate to cover your costs. This will also show you how many sales you need to break even and turn a profit. For instance, if your total expenses for the year are $50,000 and your average commission is $5,000 per sale, you'll need to sell at least 10 homes to break even. Any additional sales beyond that will be profit.

> **NOTE:**
> Every dollar spent outside your business is one less dollar you can reinvest in your business.

Separate Bank Account

When Tesla was founded in 2003, one of the first steps was to set up a bank account specifically for the company's income and expenses. While you're not building the next Tesla, you are running your own business, so it's crucial to set up a separate bank account for your real estate business.

Having a dedicated business account makes it easier to track income and expenses, ensuring that you have a clear picture of how your business is performing. It also simplifies tax preparation, as your personal and business finances will be clearly separated.

> **NOTE:**
>
> Do your research when choosing a bank account. Some banks have minimum balance requirements or charge monthly fees, so find one that fits your business needs without unnecessary penalties.

Debit vs Credit Cards

In today's world, most business purchases—whether in person at a store or online—require a card. Whether you're buying equipment or paying for services, having a payment card is essential for running your business.

As a business owner, you generally have two options for the type of card you can use: a debit card tied to your business bank account or a credit card. Each option comes with its own set of advantages and disadvantages that can impact your business operations and financial management.

The Positives and Negatives of Debit Cards	
Positives	**Negatives**
✓ **Easy to obtain:** Most business checking accounts come with a debit card, so you likely won't need to apply separately.	✓ **No perks:** Debit cards generally don't offer rewards like points, cash back, or travel miles.
✓ **No credit check:** Using a debit card doesn't require a credit check, which can be beneficial if you're building or protecting your credit score.	✓ **No credit history:** Debit cards don't help you build a business credit history, which is important for securing loans or lines of credit in the future.
✓ **No monthly payments:** Since debit card purchases draw directly from your account, you don't need to worry about monthly payments or debt management.	
✓ **No fees:** There are usually no annual or transaction fees associated with debit card use.	

The Positives and Negatives of Credit Cards	
Positives	**Negatives**
Establishes credit history: Using a credit card helps build your business credit, which can be crucial for future financing needs.	**Monthly payments:** You'll need to make payments on your balance each month, which requires careful budgeting and cash flow management.
Offers perks: Many credit cards provide rewards like points, cash back, air travel miles, and discounts, which can help offset business expenses.	**Late fees:** Missing a payment can result in late fees, which can add up over time.
	Annual fees: Some credit cards charge annual fees, especially those offering premium rewards.
	Interest charges: If you don't pay off your balance in full, you'll be charged interest on the remaining amount, which can quickly increase your debt.

TIP:

Look for credit cards that offer rewards or points on the purchases you make. You can reinvest those points into your business to save on future expenses.

If you decide to use a credit card, take your time to shop around and find the one that best fits your business needs. Pay close attention to interest rates, annual fees, late fees, and other terms to ensure the card aligns with your financial strategy.

NOTE:

Retailers are charged a transaction fee every time a customer uses a debit or credit card. These costs are often passed down to consumers through higher prices. On average, debit card users pay $1,133 more annually than credit card users because debit cards don't offer perks like points, which can help offset these cost increases.

Creating a Corporation

NOTE:

Before deciding to establish a corporation, consult with an accountant and attorney to fully understand the responsibilities of running one and to determine which type of corporation best suits your business.

When I first started my real estate career, I was hesitant about creating a corporation. At the time, I wasn't making much money, and I assumed that the only reason to form a corporation was for tax benefits. However, after finally discussing it with both my accountant and attorney, I quickly realized there were more advantages than I initially thought.

Protection

In today's world, lawsuits can arise unexpectedly, and many attorneys are eager to help those looking to sue. Forming a corporation adds a layer of legal protection by ensuring that, in the event of a lawsuit, your corporation—not you personally—will be the entity being sued. This shields your personal assets, such as your home and possessions, from risk. Only assets directly associated with your corporation (like a company-owned car) are vulnerable.

Taxes

Another significant benefit of forming a corporation is the potential to lower your tax liability. With a corporation, you have the option to pay yourself as a W-2 employee, even if you're the sole member. This means taxes will be deducted from your salary when you pay yourself, usually on a quarterly basis, so by the time you file your taxes, a portion will have already been paid. When tax time comes, you'll only be taxed on the difference between your net income (after expenses) and your salary.

> **NOTE:**
> Paying yourself as an employee does not exempt you from taxes on that salary amount.

For example, if you earn $100,000 in commissions, pay yourself a $40,000 salary, and have $10,000 in expenses, your taxable income would be $50,000 ($100,000 commissions - $40,000 salary - $10,000 expenses). This can significantly reduce your tax burden.

> **TIP:**
> Consider using a payroll service like ADP to ensure the correct taxes are deducted and sent to the appropriate government agencies.

Things to Be Aware of When Forming a Corporation

- ✓ **Annual Report:** Each year, your state will require you to file an Annual Report, typically due on or before the anniversary date of your incorporation. This report often comes with a fee that varies by state.

- ✅ **Brokerage Payments:** You'll need to inform your brokerage to make payments in your corporation's name.

- ✅ **Business Bank Account:** Most banks require an EIN to open a business account in your corporation's name.

NOTE:

Requirements differ by state, so ensure you're fully aware of what your state mandates to keep your corporation in good standing.

Important to Remember

✅ **Commissions**

Multiple ways to earn a commission
- Represent a buyer or seller in a sales transaction
- Represent a tenant or landlord in a rental transaction
- Refer a client to another Realtor for a referral fee
- Receive referrals from other Realtors

✅ **1099s**

As an independent contractor, you'll receive a 1099 showing your net commissions for the year, which is used for tax filing.

✅ **Taxes**

Unlike W-2 employees, Realtors must make quarterly estimated tax payments to both federal and state governments.

✅ **Expenses**
- **Write-offs:** Business expenses such as marketing, association fees, and mileage can be deducted to lower your taxable income.
- **Health Insurance/Retirement Plans:** Most brokerages don't offer these, so you'll need to set them up on your own.

✅ **Budgeting**
- **Fixed Expenses:** Regular, consistent expenses like rent, car payments, or insurance.
- **Variable Expenses:** Irregular expenses that fluctuate, such as marketing or travel. Estimate these based on past experience and future goals.

✅ **Separate Bank Account**

Having a dedicated account for business income and expenses simplifies tax preparation and helps you track your finances.

✔ Debit vs. Credit Cards

Debit cards are tied to your bank account and don't offer perks, while credit cards often provide rewards like points or cash back but may come with fees.

✔ Creating a Corporation

- **Protection:** A corporation shields your personal assets in the event of a lawsuit.

- **Taxes:** Paying yourself as a W-2 employee helps reduce your tax burden at the end of the year.

- **Responsibilities:** Filing annual reports, notifying your brokerage of your corporation's name, and ensuring you have an EIN for a business bank account.

NOTES

Chapter 6
Should You Join a Team?

In early 2011 I grew more curious about how the real estate industry operates beyond just being a salesperson. I sought advice from veteran agents on how to expand my knowledge, and each one suggested that I get more involved in my local association. Around that time, the association had recently launched a new committee called the Young Professionals Network (YPN) of Realtors, and they were accepting applications for the following year's board. Although I had only been in the industry for a few years, I had already built a strong reputation and knew many of the Realtors on the current board, so I decided to apply.

After completing the application and interview process, I was selected to serve on the 2012 YPN board. The board consisted of 12 Realtors, all around my age. We met monthly at the Chicago Association of Realtors' main office on Michigan Ave to discuss various topics, mostly centered on planning events for the year and the charitable work we aimed to do. It didn't take long for me to realize that the board's other purpose was to build relationships with key members of the real estate community.

A few months into my tenure, I found myself with my fellow board members, packing toiletry bags for homeless people around Chicago. While doing so, I overheard one of the board members, Adam (not his real name), negotiating a sale over the phone. Another board member leaned over and commented, "He's always negotiating something." This was the first time I really paid attention to Adam, but his conversation piqued my curiosity.

Over the next few meetings, I made a point to get to know Adam better. I learned that we had a lot in common: we both grew up in the southern suburbs of Chicago, played hockey, and had ambitious plans for success. Even our future wives had gone to the same high school.

At that time, I was working at the same brokerage I had joined before leaving my cousin's team. I had just closed several transactions and launched my own branding. I felt great about the direction my business was heading and wasn't looking to change things. But that changed when Adam approached me with an offer to join the team he was building.

Adam had reached a point where he couldn't handle all the business coming his way and was looking for someone driven to join him. Over the next few months, we met several times. He explained how he was structuring his business and the vision he had for its future. His model relied heavily on investing in zip codes through sites like Zillow, Trulia, and Realtor.com, which provided leads whenever a buyer requested information about a property in an agent's chosen area.

In January 2013, we had our final meeting to discuss the structure of the team and my responsibilities. Adam outlined my duties beyond just selling: I would show the team's listings, help his buyers when he couldn't, and attend inspections for the team's properties. He also explained how I would be compensated for these tasks and how many leads I could expect each week.

Despite having a clear understanding of the role, I still had some reservations about joining a team—especially since my business was already gaining momentum. My biggest hesitation was that I wouldn't be able to pursue my goal of winning a top producer award. However, after careful consideration, I realized that while joining the team meant putting my goal on hold, the opportunity to fast-track my business growth was too good to pass up.

Ultimately, I accepted Adam's offer and joined his newly formed team.

Lesson Learned

Deciding whether to join Adam's team was one of the toughest decisions I've made in my career. Since my first day in the industry, winning a top producer award had been my primary focus. But at that point, it felt out of reach. After leaving my cousin's team, my business was growing, but not at the pace that would allow me to achieve my goal anytime soon. So, when the opportunity to join Adam's team arose, I saw it as a chance to accelerate my progress. What I didn't fully grasp at the time was how much sacrificing my personal goal would weigh on me.

During my first year on the team, my business grew rapidly, and I became so absorbed with the increased number of clients that I didn't have much time to think about anything else. Then, in March—15 months after joining—we were recognized as one of the top teams in the city. I was excited for the team, but when I saw Adam on stage accepting the award, a sense of emptiness hit me. As I watched him hold the award, I realized that no matter how much I contributed, as long as I was part of the team, I would never be the one on that stage.

That moment hit hard, but I pushed the feeling aside and stayed focused on growing my business. However, each year we won an award, and every time I watched Adam accept it, the sense of unfulfillment grew stronger. Eventually, I realized that I needed to go my own way, and two years after leaving the team, I finally achieved my goal of becoming a top producer.

While I don't regret joining Adam's team—I value the experience and the lessons learned—I wish I had taken more time to reflect on what truly mattered to me before making the decision. To this day, I still wonder how my career would have unfolded if I hadn't joined. Before joining any team, make sure you thoroughly understand what's important to you. That way, you can make your decision with confidence, without lingering thoughts of "what if?"

NOTE:

"Team" and "group" are interchangeable terms, with the lead agent typically deciding which to use. For simplicity, I'll refer to them as "teams" throughout this book.

▌ Basics of a Team

When I first joined my cousin's team, I had only a vague understanding of what a real estate team was. I'd heard them mentioned in my pre-licensing classes but never thought to research further. All I knew was that teams typically formed when an agent had more business than they could handle and needed help managing the overflow. It wasn't until a few months into my career that I realized how much more complex teams could be.

After spending time on multiple teams and observing others, I've found that while teams vary in size and structure, they tend to share a few common elements. Whether large or small, teams generally have similar foundational roles and organization, regardless of the brokerage they're based in.

Structure

A team's structure largely depends on how the leader decides to organize it and the team's size. Most teams follow a basic hierarchy, with the team leader at the top and the team members reporting to them. The size of the team typically dictates each member's roles and responsibilities. For instance, a smaller team might have an administrator who handles everything from marketing to paperwork to client concierge duties. On larger teams, different members may be assigned to each of these tasks individually.

Though there's no one-size-fits-all structure for teams, certain roles are commonly found across the board. These roles and their responsibilities may vary, depending on what the team leader assigns.

> **TIP:**
> Always ask for a detailed breakdown of the team structure before joining so you fully understand your role and responsibilities.

Common Team Roles

- ✅ Team Leader Personal Assistant
- ✅ Buyer Agent
- ✅ Listing Agent
- ✅ Marketing Director
- ✅ Transaction Coordinator
- ✅ Client Concierge

> **TIP:**
> I will explore each of these roles in greater detail in Chapter 15: Building a Team.

A simple example of a basic team structure

Team Leader

As an agent's business grows, they often reach a point where handling the influx of clients alone would mean sacrificing service quality. At this stage, agents face a crucial decision: either maintain their current level of business or continue to expand. Those who choose to keep growing often start a team, becoming the team leader in the process.

Much like a CEO of a company, the team leader oversees the team, with other members reporting to them. They determine the structure of the team and decide which members are needed to help grow the business. For instance, if the team leader has more buyer clients than they can handle, they might hire a buyer's agent to focus on those clients, allowing the leader to concentrate on listings. Or, if the team leader lacks time for marketing, they might hire a marketing director to handle promotional tasks. As the team grows, the leader's role typically shifts to recruiting, mentoring agents, setting team goals, and managing overall operations.

> **NOTE:**
> The first hire a team leader makes is usually out of necessity, to cover a responsibility they can no longer manage alone.

Additionally, the team leader is often the public face of the team. They are the central figure in marketing efforts and receive most of the accolades when the team is recognized. This includes being the focal point of team photos, accepting awards, and being featured in articles.

Having been part of two teams in my career, I've observed how different leadership styles can shape a team. From my experience and research, I've found that most teams tend to adopt the personality of their leader. For example, my cousin's team was more laid-back and casual, reflecting her personality, whereas Adam's team had a more structured and corporate feel, mirroring his. Not every leadership style suits every agent, so it's important to get a sense of the team leader's personality during interviews to see if you'd be a good fit.

It's Not Your Production Anymore

When I joined Adam's newly formed team, I was immediately thrown into the mix. He quickly began sending me buyer leads to work on. At first, it felt overwhelming, but over time I developed a system to follow up and keep everything organized (I'll explain this system in more detail in Chapter 12: Leads). These leads, combined with the fact that we were investing in sites that generated qualified buyers, allowed me to quickly scale my business. I closed more deals in the first 12 months on the team than I had in my entire previous career.

While everything was going smoothly, one issue began to surface as my sales volume increased. When making offers for my buyers, listing agents would often ask if I was a new agent, as they couldn't find recent sales under my name on the MLS. I had to explain repeatedly that I was part of a team and that all my production was recorded under the team leader's agent ID. Although this never affected my ability to get offers accepted, it was a constant reminder of the trade-off I had made.

One of the main sacrifices of joining a team is that all your sales are counted under the team's production, not your own. On the MLS, sales are typically attributed to the team leader's agent ID (primarily for awards and recognition purposes). This means that regardless of how much you sell, you won't receive individual recognition or be eligible for personal awards.

> **NOTE:**
> Some MLS systems now allow teams to have their own ID, with all team production being attributed to the team ID rather than the team leader's.

While giving up personal recognition may not sound appealing, there are benefits to consider. You can leverage the team's success in your marketing efforts. For example, when interviewing with a buyer or seller, you may be asked how many sales you've completed. As a new agent, this is a tough question to answer if you haven't closed any deals. However, as part of a successful team, you can confidently say, "I work with a team that did $20 million in sales last year. By hiring me, you're also hiring an entire team with a proven track record." This can be a significant advantage compared to sidestepping the question as an individual agent.

Marketing

After separating from my cousin's team and becoming an independent agent, the first thing I did was develop my personal brand. This was crucial because I could no longer rely on the team for marketing—I had to market myself. With no prior knowledge of branding, I worked with a loan officer who took me under his wing. Over the course of a month, he helped me design a logo, choose colors, and select a font (I'll discuss how to do this in more detail in Chapter 13: Branding).

Once my branding was complete, I began integrating it into all of my marketing efforts. The loan officer emphasized the importance of consistently putting my brand in front of people to create recognition. Following his advice, I started by posting about it on Facebook and LinkedIn, then using it regularly on these platforms. I also included my branding in monthly newsletter e-blasts to my database and on every mailer I sent out. Each month, I made it a priority to ensure my target audience saw my brand.

That changed when I joined Adam's team. As soon as I signed the paperwork, the personal brand I had plastered across all my marketing was replaced by the team's. My individual branding essentially ceased to exist.

One of the sacrifices you'll make when joining a team is giving up the ability to market your personal brand. Teams usually focus on promoting a unified brand to create awareness and generate more business for the entire group. This means that as a team member, your marketing materials will feature the team's branding, not just your own. For example, if you send postcards to your database, your personal details might appear, but the team's name, logo, and other required elements will likely be featured more prominently. You may also be asked to post about the team on your social media profiles to broaden the team's exposure.

NOTE:

Often, the team's name is based on the team leader's name. For example, if I started a team, I might call it the "Michael Opyd Team."

On the positive side, you will probably be included in the team's marketing efforts. This could mean being added to the team's website, appearing on listing materials, or being featured in videos posted on social media. While you may lose control of your personal brand, being part of a team's marketing could provide you with more exposure than you'd get on your own.

TIP:

When I joined my second team, I made the mistake of giving them access to my personal database for marketing. I thought I was being a team player, but after I left, I discovered they were still marketing to my contacts because I hadn't put safeguards in place beforehand. Make sure you don't make the same mistake I did.

| Income

When I began discussing the possibility of joining Adam's team, I wanted to clearly understand my responsibilities and how I would be compensated. After working with my cousin under an agreement where I only earned a percentage of the commission if the property sold, I realized I needed more financial security. I wanted to be compensated for my work even if the property didn't sell. Too often, I'd put in significant effort only to end up empty-handed if the deal fell through.

After explaining my concerns, Adam agreed to pay me every two weeks for the tasks I performed for the team, regardless of whether a sale was made. We created a list of responsibilities with corresponding compensation for each task, and I kept a log that Adam would review at the end of each pay period. This arrangement provided me with a sense of security, knowing that even if I didn't close a sale for an extended period, I would still have a steady income.

Of course, commissions remained the primary way I earned money on the team.

Commissions

My first transaction was for a rental. My cousin asked me to help someone she knew find an apartment in the city. Eager for any business, I accepted and began working with a woman close to my age who was looking for a one-bedroom, one-bath apartment with a monthly rent of $2,000. After showing her a few places, she decided to apply for one listed at $2,100 a month. We offered $2,000, and the landlord accepted. A few weeks later, my office received a check for $1,000—half the monthly rent, which was standard in my market. Shortly after, I picked up my first commission check for $675.

The check didn't include a breakdown, and I was confused about how my brokerage arrived at that number. I had expected more.

Commissions on Teams vs. Independent Agents

Commissions work differently when you're part of a team compared to being an independent agent. As an independent agent, commission splits are straightforward: you have a split with your brokerage, and that's the percentage you receive for each transaction (I'll explain this in more detail in the next chapter). But on a team, it's more complex. Your commission is based on the team leader's split with the brokerage and then your split with the team.

> **NOTE:**
> When you're on a team, you only have a commission agreement with the team, not with the brokerage.

In my case, my cousin had a 90% split with the brokerage, and I had a 75% split with the team. This meant that for every transaction, the office would first split the commission 90/10, with the brokerage keeping 10%. Then the remaining 90% was split 75/25 between my cousin and me.

For example, the $1,000 check was split so that my brokerage took $100. The remaining $900 was then split between my cousin and me, with her receiving $225 and me receiving $675.

Additional Notes on Commissions

To keep the example simple, I didn't include any brokerage fees, which are typically taken off the top. After fees are deducted, the remainder is split according to the team leader's agreement with the brokerage and your agreement with the team.

Varying Splits: Some teams have different commission splits depending on the situation. For example, you might have a base split of 75/25 for clients you bring in, but a 50/50 split for leads provided by the team.

Salaries and Commissions: Some teams offer a salary in addition to commission or may combine both structures.

Choosing to be part of a team means sacrificing a portion of your commission, but being on the right team can help you generate more business and support your growth. Ultimately, you'll need to decide if giving up a portion of your commission is worth the potential benefits for the future of your business.

À La Carte Items

The agreement I had with Adam, which included compensation for specific team tasks, quickly paid off. Since he was already stretched thin with the amount of business he handled, I had numerous opportunities to take on tasks he couldn't manage. In a typical week, I would conduct several showings for the team's listings, attend at least one inspection, and assist with Adam's buyers. This provided me with a steady income, which felt like earning a small salary. With this extra money, I was able to cover my bills and reinvest in my personal business. I began sending out monthly postcards to my database, writing handwritten notes throughout the year, and investing in a customer relationship management (CRM) tool, which allowed me to engage with my database more frequently. This, in turn, helped me generate more of my own business, resulting in more closed transactions outside of the team's leads.

When you're part of a team, you may be asked to perform tasks related to the team's business, which can include showing listings, picking up lockboxes, retrieving keys or items from clients, sitting through inspections, or taking down signs. During your interview with the team leader, ask for a list of responsibilities and whether you'll be expected to perform such À La Carte tasks. Also, inquire about how you'll be compensated for them. If there's no compensation, ensure there's another form of benefit that makes these tasks worth your time.

NOTE:

Another potential sacrifice is the loss of full control over your calendar. Some teams require members to share their calendars so the team's administrator can schedule events (both paid and unpaid) that you will need to attend, such as showing listings or attending property inspections.

Bonuses

On January 18th, 2013, Adam and I met for lunch at a café in Chicago's River North neighborhood. We had been discussing terms for a few weeks and were finally ready to review the employment agreement paperwork. After we ordered, Adam handed me the four-page agreement to look over. As I reviewed it, I noticed a new addition we hadn't discussed: a tiered bonus system that offered different payouts based on the team's total production. For example, I would earn a $500 bonus if the team sold $5 million in real estate, with the payout increasing as the team's sales grew. When I asked Adam about this, he explained that he added it as an incentive for the team's hard work. I appreciated this addition and felt confident we would hit the top tier in the first year (which we did).

Not all teams offer bonuses, and many team leaders prefer not to. For those that do, bonuses are typically tied to either the team's overall production or individual agent milestones. When discussing potential employment, ask whether the team offers bonuses and, if so, how they are structured. Make sure any bonuses are clearly outlined in your agreement before signing.

Understanding how you will be compensated can be confusing and frustrating if it isn't defined upfront. Before joining a team, ensure you fully understand how you'll earn income, and make sure the employment agreement clearly outlines all compensation methods. This will save you from future headaches.

TIP:

If your team offers À La Carte items, ensure your agreement specifies the dollar value for each task and when you will be paid for completing them.

Leads

On my first day working with Adam, we sat down at his kitchen table so he could walk me through how the leads worked. For about an hour, he explained how leads came in, how he would distribute them to me, how I was expected to follow up, and how we would track them. Adam had been working with these types of leads for a while and had seen a lot of success, so I listened carefully and took notes. The next day, Adam began sending me leads, and I started following up. Over time, I received hundreds of leads, many of which turned into closed deals for both myself and the team.

> **NOTE:**
>
> I'll go into more detail on how to follow up and convert leads in Chapter 12: Leads.

One of the main benefits of joining a team is the opportunity to receive leads regularly. A consistent flow of leads can help jump-start your career if you're new or get you back on track if you've been struggling.

> **NOTE:**
>
> Relying solely on team-generated leads shouldn't be your only strategy for generating business. Use the leads as a way to supplement your efforts, but focus on building your own business through your database and contacts.

Whether leads come from third-party sites like Zillow or Realtor.com, or from the team leader's overflow of business, being part of a team can help you close more deals now and in the future. Every closed deal creates the potential for repeat business and referrals down the line.

> **TIP:**
>
> Make sure your employment agreement clearly states who owns the client after a lead closes. Ideally, the agreement should allow you to retain the client as your own, regardless of whether you remain on the team.

Splits

When discussing the possibility of joining Adam's team, one of our main topics was how commission splits would work—specifically, the difference between closing a deal I generated versus closing a team-provided lead. I believed that if I did all the work to procure the client and close the deal, I should receive a higher percentage. Adam, on the other hand, felt that for the leads the team provided, my split should be lower.

We both presented our cases and understood each other's perspectives. In the end, we agreed on two splits: a "normal split" for deals I generated myself, which was higher, and a "team split" for leads the team provided, which was slightly lower.

Teams often offer different splits depending on the type of business you bring in, especially for team-generated leads. Leads usually come with upfront costs, and the team expects to recoup those expenses and earn a profit. When speaking with a team leader, ask them to explain how your commission split will work for your own clients versus team-provided clients. Make sure both splits are fair and clearly outlined in your agreement.

Team Employment Agreement

The night before my lunch meeting with Adam to review the employment agreement, I made a list of all the items I wanted included. I figured there could be distractions during the meeting, and I didn't want to miss anything important. Sitting at the dinner table in my condo, I reflected on our previous conversations and wrote down everything I could remember. The next day, I spent the morning reviewing my notes, ensuring that all the terms were spelled out as we had discussed. Feeling confident, I headed to meet Adam.

When I arrived at the café, Adam was already seated at a corner table. The room was mostly empty, providing the perfect setting for our discussion without much noise or distraction. After we ordered lunch, Adam pulled out the agreement from his work bag and handed it to me for review. I took my time reading it line by line, making sure everything was included. To my satisfaction, the agreement not only covered what I had noted but also included a few extra items I welcomed. I requested a few minor adjustments for clarity, and once Adam made those changes, I was ready to sign. After both of us signed the agreement, I officially became a member of his team.

A **team employment agreement** is a contract between an agent and a team (or brokerage, for independent agents). The document spells out the details of an agent's role, such as commission splits, any fees, and specific team requirements. It also outlines responsibilities like keeping your license active and completing continuing education. Each team has its own agreement, but certain elements should always be included.

Key Items Your Agreement Should Clearly Define

- ✔ **Commission split(s)** (for both personal and team-generated business)
- ✔ **À La Carte tasks** (list each task with a corresponding payment amount)
- ✔ **Database ownership** (ensure that you retain your database when you leave and that the team doesn't continue marketing to it)—This applies if you allow the team to market to your database or request them to do so.
- ✔ **Lead management** (how team-provided leads work and your responsibilities in following up, including any conversion targets)
- ✔ **Production credit** (whether sales are credited to the team leader's ID or your own)
- ✔ **Bonus payouts** (if applicable)

Small Teams vs. Large Teams

As the team leader, Adam focused on securing listings for the team. While he concentrated on signing up sellers, I took on the responsibility of working with many of his buyers, handling everything except negotiations. At the same time, as Adam secured more listings, I managed tasks that required being physically present at the property, such as showings, inspections, appraisals, and final walk-throughs. After a few months, the business needed additional support, so we decided to expand.

Adam quickly recruited another Realtor to join us, growing the team to three members. Shortly after, he hired a business administrator to handle scheduling, social media posting, paperwork, and serve as Adam's personal assistant. Over time, the team continued to expand, with more Realtors joining and additional administrative roles being filled. By the time I left, the team had grown to seven members.

Witnessing the team's evolution from a small group to a larger one, I observed the distinct differences that come with working in both small and large teams. Each has its pros and cons, and depending on what you're looking for, one may be a better fit than the other.

Small Team

When I first started working with Adam, the team had a different dynamic than after it grew. A smaller team has a much more intimate feel. We spent more time together, and our conversations were deeper and more meaningful. However, as the team expanded, it became harder for everyone to be together, and when we were, the conversations were more surface-level. If you prefer being part of something more inclusive and close-knit, a smaller team might be a better fit for you.

The Positives and Negatives of a Small Team	
Positives	**Negatives**
More personalized attention from the team leader	Responsibility for your own administrative work
Greater visibility in team marketing	More team-related duties
Access to more leads	Less brand recognition in the market

Large Team

Once the team grew to seven members, it adopted a different identity. The structure became more corporate, with Adam taking a more hands-off approach with the agents as he focused on expanding and marketing the team. This shift required team members to become more independent, often needing to find solutions on our own. If you prefer working in a structure that mirrors the corporate world, joining a larger team might be the better option for you.

The Positives and Negatives of a Large Team	
Positives	**Negatives**
Less administrative work, handled by other team members	Less personalized attention from the team leader
Access to more support and resources	Smaller commission splits
More agents to learn from	Less visibility in team marketing
Greater networking opportunities	More competition for leads

There are many pros and cons to joining a team. If you're considering becoming part of one, I highly recommend that you take the time to learn all the details about the team and carefully weigh your options before making a decision. Ultimately, you want to feel confident that the choice you made is the right one for you at that moment.

Important to Remember

 Basics of a Team

- **Structure**
  - Team Member Roles
    - Team Leader
    - Personal Assistant
    - Buyer Agent
    - Listing Agent
    - Marketing Director
    - Transaction Coordinator
    - Client Concierge
  - Team Leader: CEO of the team
  - All your sales production will be recorded under the team leader's ID and will no longer be credited to you directly

- **Marketing**
  - Teams typically focus on promoting the team brand to generate more business for all members.

- **Income**
  - Commissions
    - Your commission is based on the team leader's split with the brokerage and your split with the team.
      - For example, if the team leader has a 90% split with the brokerage and you have a 75% split with the team, the commission from any transaction will first be split 90/10 between the brokerage (which keeps 10%) and the team. Then, the remaining 90% will be split 75/25 between you and the team leader.
  - À La Carte Items
    - You might have opportunities to earn extra income by completing tasks related to the team's business.
  - Bonuses
    - Some teams offer bonuses based on the overall production of the team.

- Leads
  - Splits
    - Some teams provide agents with leads at a lower commission split than if the agent closed their own business.

✓ Team Employment Agreement

- The agreement should clearly define the following:
  - Commission splits (for both personal business and team-generated business).
  - À La Carte tasks (each task listed with a corresponding payment amount).
  - What happens to your database when you leave (ensure you retain ownership, and the team cannot continue marketing to it).
  - How leads provided by the team are managed and expectations for handling them.
  - Where production credit for closed sales goes (under the team leader's ID or your own).
  - Bonus payouts (if the team offers bonuses).

✓ Small Teams vs. Large Teams

- **Small Teams**
  - Tend to have a more intimate feel.
- **Large Teams**
  - Have a more corporate structure.

NOTES

Chapter 7
Joining a Brokerage

The sound of my alarm echoed off the walls of my bedroom at my parents' house as I reluctantly opened my eyes and dragged myself out of bed. I knew I had to get moving if I wanted to beat the inbound Chicago traffic and reach the office on time. After getting ready quickly, I filled my coffee cup with some Folgers Classic Roast from the pre-made pot in the kitchen, grabbed my work bag, and headed out for the 35-minute drive.

It had been a few weeks since I earned my real estate license and joined my first brokerage. Knowing it would be tough to work effectively from my parents' house or my girlfriend's apartment, I made it a point to go to the office as often as I could. From the outside, the office was welcoming—street-level with tall windows, some displaying the brokerage's name and logo, but most offering a clear view into the workspace.

On my first day, one of the agents told me that people passing by would sometimes stop in for help, and whoever greeted them would get the lead. Seeing this as a golden opportunity, I asked my Managing Broker if I could work from the conference room whenever it wasn't in use. She hesitantly agreed, so every day I set up shop there, hoping someone would walk through the door.

I also believed that being in the office would allow me to learn from the other agents and, especially, from my Managing Broker. As a new agent eager to absorb as much as possible, I occasionally knocked on her door when I hit a roadblock. At first, she didn't seem to mind my questions and would take the time to answer them. But after a few weeks, her responses grew shorter, her tone more frustrated, making it clear that I was becoming a nuisance.

In an attempt to ease her frustration, I began spreading my questions around—to my cousin, who I worked with at the time, and to other agents in the office. Since the brokerage didn't offer formal training or mentorship, most of what I learned early on came from seeking out advice wherever I could.

One day, while sitting in the conference room, I noticed a young man, probably in his mid-20s, walking slowly past the office windows, peering in as if he was unsure whether to come in. I watched as he hesitated outside the door before finally stepping inside. Seeing an opportunity, I quickly got up to greet him.

I introduced myself, and we began chatting. He explained that he was considering renting a place but didn't know where to start. He seemed nervous, often rambling and repeating himself. I did my best to ease his concerns and answer his questions, despite my limited knowledge. Just as he began to feel more comfortable, I heard my Managing Broker yell something from her office. Unsure of what she said, I ignored it and continued talking with the young man.

A moment later, the door to my Managing Broker's office swung open. I turned to see her standing halfway in the doorway with a disgusted look on her face. Glaring at the young man, she abruptly said, "Okay, that's enough—time to go, thank you," and unceremoniously kicked him out of the office.

Dumbfounded, I watched as the young man left, confusion all over his face. When he was out of sight, I turned back to my Managing Broker, trying to process what had just happened. Without hesitation, she coldly informed me that I had spent too much time with him and that he wasn't a serious client, so she "spared" me the effort. With that, she retreated into her office and shut the door.

As the weeks passed, my Managing Broker never mentioned the incident again. In fact, during my entire time at that office, she never offered me any further assistance.

Lesson Learned

When I began my real estate career, I didn't take the time to interview with different brokerages to understand how they support their agents. I immediately joined my cousin's team, which meant joining the brokerage she worked at by default. While that brokerage worked well for her—a seasoned agent who needed little support—it wasn't the best fit for me as a new agent who required significant guidance. Thankfully, after about a year, that office closed, forcing my cousin to move us to a new brokerage. At this new office, the Managing Broker was much more supportive, and I began meeting with him every two weeks.

This experience taught me that not all brokerages are created equal. I saw firsthand how different brokerages can be, which gave me valuable perspective. Joining a brokerage, especially your first, is one of the most important decisions you'll make for your business. You must thoroughly research and find one that offers ample support, provides practical education, and creates opportunities for success.

> **NOTE:**
> A brokerage is the company an agent works for. Brokerages can have multiple offices, typically sharing the same name across locations.

| Research

In early 2024, a close friend shared with me that his mother, who was living in Mexico at the time, had been diagnosed with cancer. A few weeks before, she began experiencing discomfort in her stomach. Initially, she thought it was nothing serious and ignored it, but the discomfort soon turned into unbearable pain. Finally, she made an appointment with her primary doctor, who, after performing a CT scan, revealed that she had a tumor the size of a peach growing on one of her kidneys. Believing surgery was not an option, the doctor advised starting chemotherapy immediately.

Unwilling to settle for one opinion, my friend threw himself into researching everything he could about his mother's condition. He spent hours on accredited websites and consulted doctors in Chicago who specialized in her type of cancer. After gathering extensive information, he concluded that while chemotherapy might be one option, it wasn't the only one. He decided to fly his mother to Chicago to seek additional medical opinions.

After visiting several doctors across different hospitals, the decision was made to remove the tumor through surgery instead of starting chemotherapy. On a Friday afternoon in March, she underwent surgery with the hope that the tumor could be safely removed.

A few hours later, it became clear they had made the right choice—the doctor successfully removed the tumor, and after a few months of recovery, my friend's mother resumed her normal life. Had my friend not done his research and sought additional opinions, his mother would have endured months of grueling chemotherapy with no guarantee of remission. Instead, she walked out of the hospital days later, surrounded by her family, full of strength and hope.

This personal experience parallels my journey in real estate. Throughout my career, I worked at three different brokerages—ranging from small to large—and was under the leadership of five different Managing Brokers, each with their own distinct style. Just as my friend's research led to the best possible outcome for his mother, I learned that careful research and comparison of brokerages is crucial to finding the right fit for your real estate business.

TIP:

When interviewing at brokerages, don't just rely on what the owner or Managing Broker tells you. Instead, seek out random agents at the office to get their unfiltered perspective. Most brokerages will refer you to agents who will give you the responses they want you to hear.

In the rest of this chapter, I'll walk you through the key areas to focus on during your interviews. Each plays a critical role in building your real estate business, so it's vital to understand them thoroughly before making your decision.

| Education

In 2017, Amazon launched the Amazon Technical Academy at its Seattle headquarters, offering employees new career opportunities. The academy provides courses developed by experienced Amazon engineers, taught by technical employees within the company. Graduates include former operations associates, program managers, executive assistants, support techs, and financial analysts. Impressively, more than 90% of these graduates have transitioned into Software Development Engineer roles, with an average compensation increase of 93%.

Amazon Technical Academy is just one of several educational initiatives the company offers. Programs like Career Choice, Machine Learning University, and apprenticeships provide professional growth opportunities across all levels of the company. Since its founding in 1994, Amazon has invested billions in employee education, recognizing its importance for both individual and corporate growth. This investment has helped Amazon become one of the largest companies in the world.

While many large companies, like Amazon, invest significantly in employee development, real estate brokerages often fall short. From my experience and research, most brokerages provide minimal education, typically geared toward experienced agents rather than helping new agents build their careers.

For example, in 2022, I met with a struggling agent over coffee. She had been in the industry for two years but was finding it hard to get her business off the ground. She told me that she had joined her current brokerage based on a colleague's recommendation, without interviewing at other ones. When I asked her about the educational support she received, she described a basic, hands-off approach. Her Managing Broker had directed her to watch pre-recorded training videos, but the content was too general and lacked practical, hands-on guidance. When she met with her Managing Broker for advice, she was told to start calling people and asking for business. It was clear that she, like many new agents, felt unsupported and unprepared for the challenges ahead.

In real estate, the responsibility for agent education lies with the brokerage. The National Association of Realtors (NAR) only mandates basic ethics training, and local associations charge fees for most courses. It's crucial for brokerages to offer more than the bare minimum, particularly for new agents. When interviewing with potential brokerages, ask about the specific education and support programs they offer.

NOTE:

Most brokerages tend to focus on educating experienced agents to help them increase sales, rather than on helping new agents establish their businesses.

Mentorship

In early 2015, I began conceptualizing what my own brokerage would look like. By then, I had enough experience in real estate to notice the gaps in how agents were treated at their firms, particularly in terms of mentorship and support. While I was still focused on growing my own real estate business, I spent late nights in my home office brainstorming ideas, scribbling thoughts on yellow notepads, and sketching logos on large paper pads. My office quickly began to resemble Russell Crowe's in A Beautiful Mind.

By the fall of 2015, I was ready to take my ideas further. The first thing on my list was education. Drawing from my experiences with a lack of support at various brokerages, I wanted to create a mentorship program that would be the core of my brokerage. It would combine everything I had learned, experienced, and built in my career, and present it in a clear, structured program to help new agents avoid the struggles I had faced.

In 2017, I officially opened my brokerage. Although I had made significant progress on the mentorship program, it wasn't fully complete until a few years later. By that time, I had gained more experience and partnered with a colleague, allowing us to finalize a comprehensive five-week one-on-one mentorship program. This program provided new agents with custom-built tools and real-time support, helping them start their real estate careers with confidence. Almost 50 agents went through the program in its first year, achieving average sales of $1 million to $2 million within 12 months of completion.

In addition to the structured mentorship program, we offered personal mentorship on demand. Agents could reach out to us for real-time support whenever they needed it, ensuring they had the answers they needed to guide their clients properly.

When interviewing at brokerages, be sure to ask about their mentorship programs. A mentor should be available to assist you not just in scheduled meetings, but whenever you have questions. They should also hold you accountable and help you stay on track toward your goals.

NOTE:

At many brokerages, the Managing Broker often serves as the assigned mentor.

A great mentor can significantly accelerate your learning and help you achieve your goals faster. Make sure you are assigned a mentor who you trust will help you get to where you want to be.

TIP:

If you're told you'll be assigned a mentor, ask to speak with them before joining the brokerage. It's important to get a sense of whether they are the right fit for you. If you don't feel confident in their ability to guide you, consider whether that brokerage is a good fit overall. Also, when speaking with a potential mentor, ask how many agents they currently mentor. This will help you gauge whether they have the time and capacity to provide the support you need.

Regular Trainings

As I mentioned in the introduction to this chapter, my first brokerage didn't offer formal training for its agents.

During my first few months, most of my learning came from seeking out answers from my cousin and other agents in the office. While I was getting my bearings, the brokerage itself was going through a transition. The owners weren't heavily involved in day-to-day operations, and when they realized it was more practical to close my office, they quickly decided to do so, transferring all the agents, including myself, to another office they owned. When I learned we were moving to the new office, I was excited. I had recently met a few agents from that office who shared that it had a dedicated training space and regularly offered classes. Since I wasn't receiving proper training at my current office, I felt like I was finally getting the opportunity to learn the basics I had been craving.

On my first day at the new office, I was shown where to sign up for upcoming classes, and I eagerly put my name down for all of them. The classes were held weekly at 10:00 AM on Tuesdays and Thursdays and were taught by the office's top-producing agents, covering a wide range of topics. They took place in a large room in the office's finished basement, which had U-shaped tables and a projector on a black cart that displayed slides onto a large pull-down white screen at the front of the room.

Every week, I made sure to arrive by 9:30 AM to get a seat near the front, where I could clearly see the screen. Although many of the topics were geared towards veteran agents, I did my best to ask questions when I felt lost and took as many notes as possible. I also made sure to request the instructors' presentations afterward so I could review them along with my notes. This weekly routine benefited me in countless ways. After a few weeks, I noticed my confidence growing as I became more familiar with the terminology. I finally felt like I was building a solid foundation of knowledge that would benefit me throughout my career, and I was also forming relationships with agents I could turn to with questions. While many brokerages offer regular training, not all provide programs specifically designed for new or newer agents.

When you sit down with the person interviewing you, ask them to provide examples of the training they offer. Look for topics relevant to new agents, such as:

- How to build and market to your database
- How to work with buyers
- How to work with sellers
- How to prospect for new business
- How to convert leads

TIP:

Request a recent training calendar to review what they've offered their agents over the past few months.

Support

At my first brokerage, I got used to doing almost everything myself, as neither office had much support staff. With only a few agents working in each office, the Managing Broker handled basic tasks like signing listing agreements, collecting paperwork, and paying agents. However, all other administrative tasks—such as inputting listings into the MLS, making changes to MLS listings, or creating marketing materials—were the agents' responsibility. I didn't mind doing these tasks, but when I moved to a new brokerage, I quickly realized how valuable having proper support could be.

The new brokerage was a local company with three offices, each offering a different level of support. Two of the offices were fully staffed with front desk personnel, an accounting department, a marketing department, technical advisors, and each had its own Managing Broker.

The biggest shift for me was being introduced to the brokerage's back-end system. The company had invested hundreds of thousands of dollars to build a well-designed, user-friendly portal. While it was intuitive, learning the entire system was overwhelming at first because of its size. Thankfully, any time I had questions, I could reach out to a technical advisor who patiently walked me through the process. After a few weeks, I was able to navigate the system with ease, which streamlined my business operations significantly. If I had questions about a commission check or needed help with an office procedure, there was always someone readily available to assist me. Having this level of support allowed me to offload many administrative tasks so I could focus on more important aspects of my business, like prospecting and building relationships.

When interviewing at a brokerage, ask the person you're meeting with to explain how they support their agents. Be sure to get specifics on who you would contact a question or issue and how their processes for assisting agents work. If the brokerage has solid support systems in place, they should be able to answer this question easily.

TIP:

If they mention having a back-end system, ask for a quick demo to see how it works.

| Commissions

In the fall of 2017, I had just one agent working at my brokerage. I had officially opened the doors a few months earlier and was spending a lot of time trying to recruit new agents. I knew my company was offering something different from what most agents were used to, but I figured that once I explained the advantages, it would make sense for them to come on board.

I decided to start by recruiting agents I knew well and had strong relationships with. First on my list was my good friend (let's call him Rick for confidentiality). Rick had been in the real estate industry longer than I had. He wasn't a top producer, but he was consistent, averaging around $5 million in production each year. For reference, in Chicago, agents typically need to hit $10 million or more annually to be recognized as top producers. I knew Rick would be a great fit for my new company, and since we had worked together at a previous brokerage, I also knew what that brokerage was offering him.

I took Rick out to lunch and walked him through everything my brokerage offered, comparing it to what he currently had, saving the commission conversation for last. Knowing Rick as well as I did, I already had an idea of what split he was currently on, so when the conversation turned to commissions, I offered him significantly more than what he was receiving. When I mentioned the number, I saw Rick's eyes light up, and I was sure I had closed the deal. We ended the lunch with Rick telling me he needed to think things over and would get back to me in a few days.

A few days later, Rick called to tell me, although he appreciated my offer, he had decided to stay with his current brokerage. We talked for a few more minutes as I tried to convince him to reconsider, but his mind was made up. I thanked him for his time and told him that if he ever changed his mind, the door was always open.

A few months later, I ran into Rick at a showing—he was showing one of my listings. After our clients left, we stayed back and chatted for a few minutes. He told me that after our meeting, he had asked the owner of his brokerage for a raise in his commission. Rick explained to the owner that he hadn't had a raise in a long time, had generated over $50 million in production over the past decade, and had never been a disciplinary issue, among other points. Despite this, the owner only offered him a 2% raise. At the time, 2% was less than the rate of inflation in Chicago, meaning Rick's raise didn't even cover the increased cost of living. He reluctantly accepted the offer, and although I continued to try to recruit him, he never joined my brokerage. To this day, he's still at the same company.

When it comes to commissions, the key thing to understand is that they are the primary source of income for brokerages. The higher the commission split a brokerage offers its agents, the less income they generate from those agents. From a business perspective, it makes sense for brokerages to avoid raising agent commissions because it cuts into their profits.

There are generally three types of commission plans that brokerages offer: a set commission plan, a capping plan, and a transaction fee plan. Each has its pros and cons. Before deciding which brokerage to join, make sure you fully understand the commission structure so there are no surprises once you get started.

Set Commission Plan

A set commission plan is one of the simplest structures for an agent to be on. Under this plan, the agent receives a fixed percentage of every commission earned, while the brokerage keeps the remainder, regardless of the agent's yearly production. For example, if an agent on a 70% split closes a deal that earns the brokerage $5,000, the agent would receive $3,500 ($5,000 x 70%), and the brokerage would retain $1,500 ($5,000 - $3,500).

Unlike other commission plans, the percentage doesn't automatically increase once the agent hits a certain production level. Any changes to the commission split typically occur when the agent feels they've earned a higher percentage and requests a change. At that point, it's up to the brokerage to decide whether to offer the agent a higher split and if so, by how much. Many brokerages favor set commission plans because they reward loyalty—an essential factor in running a successful brokerage, especially since agents can easily switch companies.

NOTE:

For new agents, it's common for brokerages to offer a starting split of 50/50 or 60/40. For veteran agents, the split may be higher depending on their average annual production.

The Positives and Negatives of Being on a Set Commission Plan	
Positives	**Negatives**
The split remains consistent and doesn't reset to a lower rate annually.	The split stays the same unless the brokerage agrees to increase it.
Easier to track and forecast earnings.	Agents often have to justify why they deserve a higher split.
Potential to negotiate a higher split over time.	Most brokerages cap the split at a certain percentage (e.g. 90% at $20 million in production) and don't raise it, even if the agent exceeds this in subsequent years.

NOTE:

Similar to set commission plans, some brokerages offer tiered plans. In these plans, an agent starts at a specific percentage split, and when they reach a certain level of production or commission, they automatically move up to a higher tier. For example, an agent on a 60/40 split must remain on that plan until they generate $3 million in sales within a calendar year. Once they reach that goal, they move up to a 70/30 split and continue at that level until they hit the next sales milestone.

Capping Plan

A capping plan is one of the most common commission structures used by brokerages, though it's less straightforward than a set commission plan. In a capping plan, agents start at a lower commission percentage, and only after generating a specified amount of commission income for the brokerage will their percentage increase for the rest of the year. At the beginning of each new year (or anniversary date), the plan resets to a lower percentage.

For example, if an agent is on a 60/40 split (60% to the agent, 40% to the brokerage) and is required to generate $10,000 in commission income for the brokerage, they would need to close enough transactions to earn $25,000 in total commissions ($25,000 × 40% = $10,000). Once this target is hit, their commission percentage automatically increases for the remainder of the year. At the start of the new year, the plan resets to the 60/40 split until they generate $10,000 in commission income again.

> **NOTE:**
>
> It's common for plan reset dates to be based on the agent's anniversary date with the brokerage rather than January 1st. For instance, if an agent started on February 1st, their plan wouldn't reset until February 1st of the following year.

The starting and maximum splits in capping plans are set by the brokerage. Typically, these plans start at 60/40 or 70/30 and max out at 90/10 or 95/5, depending on the agent's average annual production.

The Positives and Negatives of Being on a Cap Plan	
Positives	**Negatives**
☑ Newer agents can earn more once they hit the cap, as their split increases.	☑ The split resets annually, forcing agents to "start over" each year.
☑ If an agent caps early in the year, they can enjoy a higher income for the rest of the year.	☑ Some brokerages set a high commission cap, which can be tough for newer agents to achieve.
☑ The potential to reach a higher split can be a motivational factor.	☑ The reset can be discouraging, especially if an agent feels they've lost momentum from the previous year.

Transaction Fee Plans

A transaction fee plan has gained popularity recently. In this model, agents receive a high commission split but pay a fee for each transaction they close. Typically, there's a cap on these fees, after which the agent no longer has to pay them for the rest of the year.

For instance, if a brokerage charges a $395 fee per transaction with a cap of $9,000 in fees for the year, an agent would need to close 23 transactions ($9,000 ÷ $395) before the fee is waived for the remaining transactions that year.

The Positives and Negatives of a Transaction Fee Plan	
Positives	**Negatives**
✓ Agents can earn more with a higher split.	✓ The fee cap resets annually, forcing agents to start over each year.
✓ New agents may start with a higher split compared to traditional plans.	✓ Some brokerages add extra fees to transactions that agents must cover.
✓ Agents who cap early can enjoy higher earnings for the rest of the year.	✓ The cap is often set high, making it difficult for new agents to reach, which can limit their earning potential.

Understanding how a brokerage's commission plan works is crucial, but it's just as important to know about any additional fees and costs you'll be responsible for. Ensure that you thoroughly discuss these aspects during interviews with prospective brokerages to avoid surprises down the road.

Fees

When I joined my second brokerage, I was still working with my cousin. After realizing that our first brokerage was shutting down, we began exploring other options to find the best fit for us. As a veteran agent familiar with what most brokerages in the city had to offer, my cousin believed it would be best to join a local company that had been growing rapidly and provided services our previous brokerage lacked.

The new brokerage was entirely different from anything I had experienced in my career so far. The office we chose was housed in a three-story building, with each floor dedicated to a different service. The ground floor featured a reception desk staffed Monday through Friday from 9 AM to 5 PM, multiple conference rooms, a large open area for agents to work, and the Managing Broker's office. The second floor was home to the marketing department, where agents could request any marketing materials they needed, as well as the accounting office responsible for processing and paying commissions. The owner's office was also located there. The third floor boasted a room for weekly yoga classes and meditation sessions, complete with yoga mats and cushions.

Eager to take full advantage of everything the new office had to offer, I spent as much time there as possible, utilizing every available resource. I requested postcards from the marketing department to send to my database, took shifts at the office's lead computers (agents could sit for four-hour shifts at dedicated computers to collect leads from the brokerage's website), and consumed more free coffee than I probably should have. As I tapped into these new resources, my business started to gain momentum, and after a few months, I successfully closed a deal with one of my buyers.

After attending the closing, I headed straight to the office, rushing up the stairs to drop off my first commission check at the accounting office. I was excited to finally see the fruits of my hard work. The next morning, I arrived early and went directly to the accounting office, where my check awaited in a sealed white envelope with my name on it. The accountant, seeing my excitement, congratulated me with a high-five before handing over the envelope. After thanking him and eagerly returning the high-five, I hurried out to my car, wanting to open the envelope privately.

However, when I tore it open and saw the amount, my excitement quickly turned to confusion. While I knew I would only receive a percentage of the commission, I hadn't paid much attention to the fees the brokerage charged. Seeing them for the first time, I realized that while additional services can enhance an agent's business, they certainly come at a cost.

Understanding Brokerage Fees

Fees vary by brokerage but generally fall into two categories: **administrative** and **marketing**. Administrative fees are typically paid monthly or annually, while marketing fees are usually charged when the service is provided. When interviewing brokerages, always ask for a detailed breakdown of all fees agents are required to pay and how those fees will be collected.

Administrative Fees

At my new brokerage, the agents were paid using a standard 8.5 x 11-inch sheet of paper, divided into two sections. The top third of the page contained the actual check, displaying the net commission amount, with a perforated line allowing it to be easily detached for deposit. The bottom two-thirds of the page detailed a full breakdown of all fees and deductions from the original commission amount received by the office, resulting in the net commission. It also showed my year-to-date commission total.

As I reviewed my first check, I quickly realized how brokerages make money beyond commissions. There was a $250 transaction fee, a $250 processing fee, a $7.10 printing fee for the pages I had printed since joining, and a $1,000 errors and omissions (E&O) insurance fee, which gets deducted annually from every agent's first check of the year. After all the deductions, the amount on my check was $248.33, meaning I had earned just 13% of the gross $1,875 commission I had dropped off.

There are many different administrative fees a brokerage might charge its agents. Below is a list of the most common ones to look out for when interviewing with brokerages:

Common Administrative Fees

- **Errors and Omissions Insurance (E&O Insurance)**
  This insurance protects the brokerage in case an agent makes a mistake during a transaction that leads to legal action. Most brokerages charge an annual E&O fee, typically due either at the beginning of the year or on the agent's anniversary date.

- **Desk or Office Fees**
  These fees apply to agents who rent a designated desk or office space within the brokerage. They are usually paid monthly.

- **Transaction Fees**
  Some brokerages charge a fee on every transaction, which is deducted from each commission check the brokerage receives.

- **Processing Fees**
  Brokerages may charge this fee to cover the cost of an administrative employee who processes the brokerage's paperwork. Like transaction fees, these are deducted from commission checks.

- **Printing Fees**
  Some brokerages charge agents per page for printing at the office, with fees varying based on whether the pages are printed in color or black and white. Some brokerages may offer a set number of free pages each month, with fees applying only if an agent exceeds that limit.

NOTE:

Most brokerages deduct administrative fees from the gross commission amount before splitting the remainder between the agent and the brokerage. For example, if an agent has a $250 transaction fee and the brokerage receives a $5,000 commission check for a recent closing, the brokerage will first deduct $250 from the $5,000. The remaining $4,750 is then split between the agent and the brokerage according to their agreed commission split.

Marketing Fees

After moving to my new brokerage, I continued working with my cousin on her team for about a year. As part of the team, all our marketing efforts were dedicated to promoting the team as a whole. In our agreement, my cousin, as the team leader, covered all the marketing expenses. With a full marketing department at our disposal, we frequently utilized their services to create a variety of marketing materials.

Around a year after joining my cousin at the new brokerage, I felt ready to strike out on my own and build my business independently. Once we amicably parted ways, one of my first tasks was creating new marketing materials to promote myself. I set up a meeting with the brokerage's marketing department and asked them to design a postcard I could send to my database, announcing my new venture. The marketing team presented a few variations, and after selecting one, I asked them to print 100 postcards. A few days later, I mailed them out, completely unaware that I would eventually need to pay for the service.

Fast forward three months, and I successfully placed a rental client in a $2,000-per-month apartment. As the tenant's agent, I was entitled to half of the first month's rent ($1,000) as commission. However, rental commissions are often mailed directly to the brokerage, meaning I had to wait for the listing agent's office to send my check. Two weeks after the lease was signed, I received an email from the accounting department letting me know my commission check was ready.

Excited, I picked up the envelope and, as before, retreated to my car to open it in private. To my dismay, the check amount was once again significantly lower than I had expected. Puzzled, I reviewed the breakdown at the bottom of the statement. That's when I realized the postcards I had ordered came with a cost, which the brokerage had fronted. Rather than asking for payment upfront, my brokerage deducted the marketing expenses from future commission checks. Coming from my cousin's team, where marketing costs were covered, I had foolishly never thought to ask about these fees.

Important Considerations for Marketing Fees

When interviewing with brokerages, it's crucial to ask about their marketing options—specifically, what services are free, which ones come at a cost, and how those costs are handled. Marketing fees can vary widely depending on what the brokerage offers. Some charge upfront, while others, like my brokerage, subtract the costs from future commission checks. Below are a few common marketing fees you might encounter:

Common Marketing Fees

☑ **Listing Brochures**
Printed materials distributed to potential buyers for listings. Brokerages may offer various pricing options based on the quality, quantity, and length of the brochures. Pricing can also depend on whether the brokerage charges for design services.

☑ **Headshots/Video Bios**
Professional headshots or video bios for agents to use in their marketing. Some brokerages offer these services for free, while others charge a fee.

☑ **Listing Sign Installation**
Some brokerages offer a service to install "For Sale" signs and riders indicating status changes, such as price reductions or pending offers.

☑ **À La Carte Services**
These include a variety of printed marketing materials, such as postcards, property information flyers, or door hangers.

Final Thoughts

Fees are an inherent part of working with a brokerage, and each one has its own fee structure. Before making a decision, fully understand what fees you'll be responsible for and how they will be billed. This will not only help you determine which brokerage is the best fit but also assist you in creating an effective budget for your business.

| Tools

My cousin had been a Realtor long before I joined her, and by the time I came on board, she had already built a system tailored to her business style and the brokerage she worked with. When I first joined her team, I naturally assumed the best approach was to replicate her systems. I spent the initial weeks learning how her business operated and recreating everything to match her setup. I also relied heavily on the team for tasks that most independent agents would handle themselves. Everything was new to me, and it never crossed my mind that her way of doing things might not suit my style.

Our differences in approach became more apparent when we moved to a new brokerage and I started experimenting with the tools they offered. The first few months after separating from my cousin's team were chaotic. I quickly realized how dependent I had become on the team's tools and systems. Once I was on my own, I had to restructure my business to fit my style and fill the gaps that the team had been covering.

To get back on track, I set up meetings with my brokerage's administrative staff to learn the ins and outs of the tools they provided. My brokerage was tech-savvy, relying heavily on a custom-built website paired with a Customer Relationship Manager (CRM) platform. These tools were designed to generate leads and nurture relationships with clients. After several months of learning and adjusting, I felt comfortable with the tools and had rebuilt my systems.

Most brokerages offer agents a set of tools, either for free or at a cost. From my experience, certain tools are particularly beneficial, especially for new agents. When interviewing at a brokerage, ask them what tools they provide and whether there are associated fees.

Basic Tools to Look For

- ✅ **CRM (Customer Relationship Manager):**Organizes contacts and helps improve client relationships.

- ✅ **Electronic Signature Software:** Enables clients to sign documents quickly and easily from any device.

- ✅ **Agent Website:** Helps consumers find agents online and serves as a marketing tool.

> ### NOTE:
> Some brokerages offer tools for a limited time for free, similar to a trial period, after which you may need to pay to continue using them.

| Leads

My second brokerage was founded by two entrepreneurs who wanted a business they could operate year-round, unaffected by Chicago's unpredictable weather. Their first venture, a bike rental company along Lake Shore Drive, was limited by the harsh winters, so in 1998, they pivoted and started a real estate brokerage.

The company was established just as the internet began to flourish. Recognizing the potential of this new technology, the owners invested heavily in creating a website where consumers could search for properties by simply signing up. By capturing this information, they were able to provide their agents with leads. The platform proved to be a valuable asset for the company, and I was eager to take advantage of it when I joined.

To access the leads platform, the brokerage provided two dedicated computers on the second floor, near the marketing department. Each computer was enclosed by four-foot-high walls made of blue foam, perfect for hanging scripts with push pins. Agents were allowed to sit for four-hour shifts from Monday through Saturday, gaining access to any consumer information collected during their shift from website sign-ups.

I took as many shifts as I could, and over time, I worked with about two dozen leads, resulting in four successful closings. However, each time I closed a lead, I was reminded of the importance of not relying solely on these leads. Instead, they served as a supplement to my business, not the core of it.

When a brokerage provides leads, they typically offer them at a lower commission split to cover the cost of generating the leads. For example, a brokerage might require a 40/60 split (40% to the agent and 60% to the brokerage) for any lead they provide, instead of the agent's usual split. When I parted ways with my cousin, I was given two commission structures: one higher split for my personal business and a lower one for leads generated by the brokerage. Although I understood the reasoning behind this, it was still hard to accept the larger deductions, especially since the amount of work I put into each transaction was the same, if not more, than for the clients I brought in myself. That said, I knew that bringing home some money was better than bringing home none at all.

> **NOTE:**
>
> Leads from outside your personal contacts should be used to enhance your business, not form its foundation. The core of your business should come from people you know and market to regularly (I'll go into more detail about building and generating business from a database in the next chapter).

A brokerage can offer you an abundance of leads, but if you don't know how to convert them, it won't make a difference. Before committing to a brokerage that provides leads, ask if they also offer training on converting those leads.

> **NOTE:**
> In Chapter 12: Leads, I'll explain how I improved my conversion rate from under 1% to nearly 25%, and how you can too.

| Marketing and Branding

In 1989, computer scientist Tim Berners-Lee proposed an idea for "linked information systems" while working at CERN (The European Organization for Nuclear Research) in Switzerland. At the time, institutions like MIT and Stanford University had developed complex internal systems for sharing information, and Berners-Lee aimed to connect CERN's system to these networks. He outlined his vision that year and continued developing it over the following years. In 1991, he wrote and published the first web page, a simple outline of the WorldWideWeb project.

CERN initially shared access with other institutions before opening it to the public. Two years later, Berners-Lee released the source code into the public domain, making it free and accessible to anyone. Shortly after, web browsers began to appear, and the World Wide Web quickly became the most popular information-sharing system of its kind.

Neither Berners-Lee nor his colleagues could have anticipated the profound impact the Web would have across all industries, particularly real estate. Before the internet, a Realtor's job was vastly different. To get documents signed, agents had to print out pages and meet with clients in person. Calendars weren't digital but handwritten in notebooks. To market themselves, Realtors spent substantial amounts of money on ads in newspapers, bus benches, billboards, and flyers.

Agents also relied heavily on their brokerages to generate business. Brokerages spent significant sums to attract clients, as the only way for buyers to search for properties was by visiting a brokerage office and flipping through a three-ring binder filled with printed listing sheets. Today, buyers can accomplish the same task in seconds by simply opening an app on their phones.

While the internet transformed how consumers search for properties, it also revolutionized how Realtors market themselves. In the pre-internet era, agents benefited from promoting their brokerage's name, which was familiar to consumers due to the brokerage's marketing efforts. Today's Realtors have an array of digital tools at their disposal, allowing them to market themselves more efficiently. As a result, agents are now creating personal brands through their own efforts. Free digital marketing has replaced the days of spending large sums on traditional advertising and enables agents to reach a broader audience more quickly. Posting on social media, building custom websites, making videos on a smartphone, and sending e-blasts to thousands with a single click have freed agents from depending on their brokerage for marketing.

However, many brokerages still prefer to promote their name over that of individual agents. When interviewing with a brokerage, ask how they allow agents to market themselves. Ideally, you'll want a brokerage that supports your personal brand rather than restricting it. The best brokerages understand the power of branding and let their agents be the focal point of marketing efforts, rather than the brokerage itself.

> **NOTE:**
>
> Every market is different, and the brokerage's name holds varying levels of importance in each. If you're in a market where the brokerage's name carries more weight than the agent's, recognize this and leverage that name while also promoting your own brand.

Given how challenging it is to build a real estate business, selecting the right brokerage can be the difference between success and failure. Be sure to interview with multiple offices and ask as many questions as necessary to gather the information you need. After doing your research, choose the brokerage that best fits your needs.

> **TIP:**
>
> Don't settle! Many agents regret joining the first brokerage they interview with, only to later discover better options through colleagues.

| Leaving a Brokerage

In the second week of January 2013, I scheduled a morning meeting with the owner of my brokerage, where I had worked for several years. I was nervous going into the meeting because I was about to tell him I was leaving for another brokerage. Having never done this before, I wasn't sure what to expect.

On the day of the meeting, I walked up to the second floor and saw the owner's office door open. He was sitting behind his desk, focused on his laptop. I stood in the doorway for a few seconds, but he didn't look up, so I knocked on the door to get his attention. He invited me in and asked me to close the door. I sat down in one of the chairs in front of his desk and started the conversation with small talk, asking how he was doing. The owner and I had only exchanged quick greetings in the past, so the situation felt awkward. I decided to get straight to the point—I told him I was leaving the brokerage and moving to another one that I felt was a better fit for my business.

Without hesitation, he responded, "OK, I understand," without asking why I made the decision or if there was anything they could do to keep me. His quick, impersonal reaction made me feel insignificant, but I didn't let it deter me. I told him I had eight company-provided leads I'd been working on for a while and would like to take them with me. He agreed, offering me a 50% split on those leads, which was actually 10% better than if I had closed them with the brokerage. I thanked him for his time and left the meeting. The next day, I joined my new team.

Going into the meeting, I had a few important things I wanted to address. Although the meeting itself was brief, the company admin I spoke with afterward helped ensure I kept what was rightfully mine.

Leaving a brokerage can be a tricky situation, and I've heard horror stories from other agents about their experiences. Some have faced shouting matches and been told they would fail if they left. However, in most cases, leaving is amicable. When you decide to leave, there are several key things to address and prepare for to ensure a smooth transition.

Items to Address

Company-Provided Leads
Ask to keep any company-provided leads you're currently working on. If they push back, try negotiating a referral fee agreement.

Active Listings
Request to take your active listings with you. Some brokerages may require the listings to remain under the old brokerage.

> **NOTE:**
> If you can take them, you'll need to sign a new listing agreement with your new brokerage and likely cancel and relist the properties in the MLS after your transfer.

Pending Transactions
Clarify how properties with pending sales will be handled. Typically, they will close under the old brokerage, and you will be paid based on your previous split.

To Do Before You Leave

Download Your Database
If your contacts are stored in a company-provided CRM, make sure to download them before you leave. Those are your contacts, and you are entitled to them.

Update Your Materials
Write a checklist of everything that needs to be updated with your new brokerage details, including marketing materials, email signature, social media profiles, and business cards.

Notify Your Clients
Send an email to your database explaining the change, why you made the move, and how it will benefit them.

TIP:

Take the time to make the transition smooth by keeping communication open and professional with both your clients and the brokerage.

Important to Remember

✅ **Research**

- Before joining a brokerage, schedule interviews with multiple firms and do your homework to compare their offerings. Find one that supports your goals and growth.

✅ **Education**

- The brokerage is responsible for providing agent education, but much of the training is often geared toward veteran agents.
- **Mentorship**
  - When interviewing, ask about the mentorship program. Find out if you'll be assigned a mentor who is available to guide you when needed.
- **Regular Training**
  - When interviewing, ask about the mentorship program. Find out if you'll be assigned a mentor who is available to guide you when needed.
- **Support**
  - Inquire how the brokerage supports its agents. Ask for specifics on who to contact with questions or concerns, and clarify their process for assisting agents.

✅ **Commissions**

- **Set Commission Plan**
  - In a set plan, agents receive a fixed percentage of every commission dollar earned, with the remainder going to the brokerage.
- **Capping Plan**
  - Agents stay at a lower percentage until they generate a set amount of commission income for the brokerage. Once the target is met, the commission rate increases for the rest of the year before resetting to the base percentage.
- **Transaction Fee Plans**
  - Agents receive a high commission but are charged a transaction fee for every deal closed. The plan often includes a cap on fees, meaning once the cap is reached, no further fees are charged until the next year.

✅ Fees

- **Administrative Fees**
  - Brokerages charge fees for various administrative tasks. Common fees include:
    - Errors and Omissions Insurance (E&O)
    - Desk or office fees
    - Processing fees
    - Printing costs

- **Marketing Fees**
  - Fees for marketing services provided by the brokerage. Typical charges include:
    - Listing brochures
    - Headshots or video bios
    - Listing sign installation
    - À la carte services (postcards, flyers, door hangers)

✅ Tools

- **Key tools to look for in a brokerage:**
  - CRM (Customer Relationship Manager)
  - Electronic signature software
  - Agent website

✅ Leads

- Some brokerages offer leads to agents at a reduced commission split that favors the brokerage. Clarify these terms before signing.

✅ Marketing and Branding

- Many brokerages prioritize their name over the agent's. When interviewing, ask how much flexibility you'll have to market yourself and your personal brand.

✅ Leaving a Brokerage

- When leaving a brokerage, make sure to address key points and prepare in advance:
  - **Items to Address**
    - **Company-Provided Leads**
      - Request to keep the leads you're currently working on.
    - **Active Listings**
      - Ask to take your active listings with you.
    - **Pending Transactions**
      - Clarify how sales in progress will be handled.

□ **To Do Before You Leave**

○ **Your Database**
- If your database is in a company-provided CRM, download it.

○ **Items to Update**
- Make a list of everything that needs updating—marketing materials, email signatures, social media profiles, and business cards.

NOTES

PART
02
Build »

Chapter 8
Database

"I'm freezing," I thought as I sat in my car, parked outside my parents' house, waiting for it to warm up on a cold fall day in 2009. I sipped from my dark blue plastic coffee mug filled with homemade coffee, hoping to warm up. Glancing past the cup, I noticed the clock reading 8:07 AM. Realizing I might be late for my first day of training, I quickly reversed out of the driveway, shifted into drive, and headed toward the north side of Chicago.

By 8:54, I pulled into the parking lot of a converted church and found a spot near the back. Grabbing my work bag and coffee, I hurried inside, eager to escape the cold. Stepping through the large wooden doors, I was greeted by a spacious room that still retained the character of the church it once was. Eccentric woodwork and stained glass adorned the hundred-year-old building. I approached the registration table, where a kind woman checked me in and directed me to an available seat at one of the tables.

The room buzzed with conversation, filled with Realtors of all ages chatting like old friends. The overlapping conversations echoed off the high ceilings, making it hard to concentrate. Spotting an open seat near the front, I made my way over and sat down, facing away from the stage.

In front of me was a large three-ring binder, which, judging by others' binders at the table, appeared organized for each day of the weeklong training. Before I could open it, one of my tablemates introduced themselves, and I made the rounds introducing myself to the others, wrapping up just before the training began.

The session kicked off with the trainer explaining the week's agenda before diving straight into the first section of the binder: databases. He emphasized that a well-maintained database is the core of every successful Realtor's business. To succeed, we had to nurture it continuously.

The morning flew by in a three-hour sprint. The trainer moved quickly through the material, pausing only to answer questions. The intensity surprised me, making it hard to keep up with all the new information. The training was interactive, requiring us to write down as many names and contacts as we could, practice scripts with our tablemates, and brainstorm marketing ideas.

When noon arrived, the trainer gave us a 30-minute lunch break. While the others left, I stayed seated, snacking on a few granola bars I'd swiped from my parents' pantry. My head buzzed from the onslaught of information, and my messy notes were barely legible. I used the break to decompress and mentally sort through everything.

True to his word, the trainer called everyone back exactly 30 minutes later, resuming the fast-paced session. The rest of the day mirrored the morning's intensity, with more script practice, a scheduled 15-minute break at 2:30, and a block of time for us to call five of the contacts we had written down earlier.

As the day wound down, the trainer spent the final 30 minutes reinforcing the value of our databases. He shared stories of agents he had trained, agents who made over a million dollars a year by focusing solely on their databases. They built thriving real estate businesses by marketing to their contacts a few times each month. By the end of his talk, I felt like I'd struck gold, convinced that my real estate career was going to be much easier than I'd originally thought.

After the weeklong training concluded, I was filled with a sense of confidence—and a bit of cockiness. I bragged to people that I was going to sell millions of dollars in real estate over the next year and make a ton of money. Following the trainer's advice, I immediately began marketing to my database of around 100 people several times a month. But reality soon hit. Building a real estate business from scratch was much harder than I had anticipated, and my early confidence quickly turned into self-doubt.

Despite my slow start, I didn't stop marketing to my database. Every year, I made sure to contact my database at least 28 to 30 times through various means, mostly emails and postcards. Slowly but surely, my persistence paid off. Business started trickling in from the people I'd been marketing to. As I added past clients to my database, referrals began to follow.

Year after year, the results compounded. By the time I decided to stop selling, I was working solely with referrals from my database and past clients, making a comfortable living from the relationships I had carefully nurtured over time.

Lesson Learned

Looking back at the beginning of my real estate career, I realize how naive I was to think I could build a successful business quickly. I got swept up by the excitement of the training session and failed to ground myself in reality—life quickly did that for me. Although I didn't implement much of what I learned during that week-long course, one lesson stuck with me: the importance of focusing on my database. From the moment I completed that training until the last day I sold real estate, I never stopped marketing to my database.

Much of my success came from my commitment to consistently reaching out to my contacts multiple times a month. I've also noticed this same practice among the top Realtors I've spoken with across the country. They all have large databases and remain in constant communication with them, year after year. In fact, when they create their yearly budgets, the majority of their spending goes towards marketing to their contacts in one way or another.

Throughout the rest of this chapter, I'll guide you through the process of building a database from scratch and how to market to it effectively—even if you have no budget. Of all the chapters in this book, this one is the most critical. If you take away only one lesson, I hope it's the importance of consistently building and marketing to your database. This practice will determine whether you become a thriving Realtor or one who constantly struggles to survive.

Building a Database

If I asked you to name a soda company, what's the first one that comes to mind? How about the second? Can you name a third? When I give this test to agents, most will respond with Coke or Pepsi first, followed by the other, and half can't even name a third. This exercise illustrates the importance of being the first Realtor people think of when real estate comes up. Statistically, people can name only three Realtors, so if you're not the "Coke" or "Pepsi" in their minds, you're missing out on business—whether they're in the market or referring someone.

Marketing to your database is about creating brand recognition among your contacts. Your goal is to ensure that anything related to real estate immediately triggers a thought of you. For example, if one of your contacts overhears someone at a party talking about selling their home, your name and face should instantly pop into their head.

The most effective way to do this is by gathering as many names and contacts as possible and implementing a marketing plan that reaches them consistently throughout your career. Building a database isn't difficult, nor is it ever complete. Initially, it takes some time to set up, but after that, it's simply a matter of adding new contacts as often as possible.

Organization

Before diving into the process of building a database, you first need a place to store all your contacts, one that allows you to organize, edit, and update information easily. When I first started, I didn't have the money for a CRM, and my brokerage didn't offer one, so I created my own using an Excel spreadsheet. I used that system until I joined my second brokerage, which provided a custom CRM with features like automated emails and reminders, helping me stay connected with my contacts.

If you're just starting out, don't rush to spend money on a CRM if your brokerage doesn't provide one for free. Use something simple and free, like Google Sheets, and focus your budget on marketing to your database—whether that's sending postcards, buying small gifts, or hosting client appreciation events.

TIP:

If you do use a CRM, make sure it's easy to extract your contacts, especially if it's a brokerage-provided system. Your database belongs to you and should move with you if you ever switch brokerages.

If you build your own database in Excel or Google Sheets, ensure you include key fields like name, phone number, email, address, birthday, and notes. Regardless of what system you use, make sure it's easy to navigate and organize.

Your Phone

In the 1960s, the United States and the Soviet Union were locked in a Cold War, where actions spoke louder than words. Both nations raced to prove their dominance in space, each vying to be the first to land a person on the Moon and demonstrate their leadership on the global stage. For much of the race, the Soviet Union led, with the two countries trading space achievements until 1969, when NASA successfully sent astronauts Neil Armstrong, Buzz Aldrin, and Michael Collins on a historic mission to the Moon.

The Space Race marked a significant milestone in human achievement, propelling technological advancements forward. The computers used during the Apollo 11 mission were cutting-edge for their time, but they pale in comparison to the technology we carry in our pockets today. The computing power in modern smartphones far exceeds that of all the computers combined during the Apollo 11 moon landing in 1969.

Since Steve Jobs introduced the original iPhone in 2007, forever changing the smartphone landscape, we've grown so dependent on these devices that we often overlook their incredible basic functions. One of these is the ability to store thousands of contacts. Your phone is the modern equivalent of a 30-year-old Yellow Pages book, but instead of flipping through hundreds of pages, you can search for a person's name in seconds with just a tap. Your phone is the ultimate starting point for building a database. Not only do you already have the contact information of hundreds, if not thousands, of people, but you likely know many of them personally. This familiarity increases the likelihood that they'll be open to receiving helpful information from you (I'll cover how to approach this later in the chapter).

To start building your database, export all of the contacts from your phone and add them to your chosen contact management system. Below are instructions for exporting contacts from both iPhone and Android devices.

Exporting Contacts from Your Phone

For iPhone:

- Go to your contacts app and select all contacts.

- Tap "Share" and send them to your email as a .vcf file.

- Open the file on your computer and import it to your chosen system (Google Sheets, Excel, or CRM).

For Android:

✔ Open your contacts app, select "Manage contacts," and tap "Export."

✔ Choose your preferred export location (Google Drive, for example).

✔ Download the exported .vcf file and import it to your system.

By starting with your phone, you'll have a solid foundation for your database, filled with contacts who are likely already familiar with you.

Social Media and Database Building

Social media began in 1997 with the short-lived profile uploading service Six Degrees, followed by Friendster in 2001. These early platforms attracted millions of users, requiring them to sign up with an email address—a process that wasn't new, as sites like LiveJournal and Blogger had already implemented it. However, as people became more accustomed to using the internet for various needs, signing up for sites with an email address became more common, helping social media gain traction.

In 2005, at the dawn of social media, only 5% of Americans used these platforms. Today, nearly 70% of Americans, along with over 2.6 billion people globally, are active on social networking sites.

Social media has become an integral part of our daily lives. While there are many ways to leverage it for your business (which I'll discuss further in Chapter 14: Social Media), you can also use social platforms to build your database. Sites like Facebook and LinkedIn allow you to export your friends and connections, offering another opportunity to expand your contact list. Just as the contacts in your phone likely know you personally, so do many of your social media connections, making them more receptive to your marketing efforts.

How to Export Contacts from Facebook and LinkedIn

Facebook:

✔ On your computer, open Facebook.

✔ Go to "Settings."

✔ Under "Your Information," click "Download Your Information."

✔ Select "Download or Transfer Information."

✔ Choose "Friends" under "Specific Types of Information."

✔ Set the date range to "All Time."

✔ Click "Create Files."

LinkedIn:

- Click the "Me" icon at the top of your LinkedIn homepage.

- Select "Settings & Privacy" from the dropdown menu.

- Click "Data Privacy" in the left pane.

- Under "How LinkedIn uses your data," click "Get a copy of your data."

- Select "Connections."

- Click "Request Archive."

- Enter your password and click "Done."

- You'll receive an email with a link to download your list of connections.

NOTE:

Unfortunately, Instagram does not provide a way to export your contacts.

Think Outside the Box

Exporting contacts from your phone and social media is a great start for building a large database, but if you're aiming to grow even more, think beyond the obvious. Consider adding people like your hair stylist, dog walker, fellow church members, social club acquaintances, neighbors, your dentist, doctor, your children's school teachers, and anyone else who comes to mind. Don't worry if you don't have a close personal relationship with some of these people—this exercise is about adding names to market to. The larger your database, the more opportunities you create to generate business.

Fill in the Blanks

When we learn something as simple as someone's name, we form neural connections in our brains. These synapses create new circuits between nerve cells, essentially remapping the brain. According to Johns Hopkins University, those synapses strengthen or weaken based on how often we're exposed to an event.[1]

In other words, the more frequently you can get in front of someone, the better the chances they'll remember you. That's why, as you build your database, it's crucial to gather as much information from people as possible. The more contact details you have—like phone numbers, emails, and home addresses—the more ways you can reach them. For instance, if you only have a phone number, you're limited to calling or texting. But with an email or home address, you can also send emails or mail them directly.

Once your contacts are in one place, the next step is filling in any missing information. You can easily do this by reaching out to each person. Use the information you already have as an opportunity to reconnect. For example, if you only have a phone number, call or text to ask for their email and home address. If you only have an email, send a message asking for their phone number and address.

NOTE:

Break your list into manageable chunks and tackle it over a few days instead of trying to do it all at once.

When I first built my database, I had around 100 contacts, and roughly 75% of them were missing either a phone number or email. To fill in the gaps, I used the simple script below, which I would send via text or email:

Script

Hey [Name], I hope all is well! I'm reaching out to see if you wouldn't mind sharing your email and address. I've started a new career in real estate and would love to send you helpful info from time to time. I promise not to spam you! :)
[Your Name]

Don't worry if someone chooses not to share their information. Not everyone will feel comfortable doing so. However, in my experience—and from the agents I've mentored—most people are receptive, especially if they know you.

Another important thing to remember: your database should never be complete. Continuously focus on adding new contacts to create more business opportunities. Every person you add is another potential client, and you never know where it might lead.

▌ Marketing

If you Google "Biggest mistakes Realtors make at the beginning of their career," you'll find countless articles with answers ranging from poor communication with clients to ineffective time management. While these are common missteps for new agents, one crucial oversight I rarely see mentioned is the failure to consistently market to their database.

One of my biggest regrets early in my career was not focusing enough on marketing to my contacts. My original touch plan—my strategy for contacting my database—consisted of 28-30 touches per year. This included a monthly newsletter e-blast, a monthly postcard, and a quarterly market update email to each contact, along with a few personal touches like handwritten holiday cards and birthday texts. In hindsight, if I wanted to accelerate my business, my plan should have included at least 50 touches per year.

As a newer agent, you face the challenge of replacing the names of Realtors already familiar to your contacts with your own. To achieve this, you need to put yourself in front of your database as often as possible to build brand awareness. The fastest way to do this is by having a well-thought-out plan for regular, consistent contact.

Touch Plan

Benjamin Franklin, the famous inventor from the 1700s, once said, "If you fail to plan, you are planning to fail!" Although these words were spoken over 200 years ago, they still ring true today. I've seen this firsthand during my time owning a brokerage. Many veteran agents came to me for help, having experienced past success but now feeling stuck and unsure of how to revive their business.

When I sat down with these agents, I asked them how they were staying in contact with their database. Most of the time, their responses were scattered, describing a few things they had done in the past, but rarely did I hear about a well-thought-out plan. They often shared stories about losing clients to other agents, simply because those clients had forgotten about them. The problem was clear: they had stopped regularly "touching" their contacts, abandoning the core practice that separates successful agents from those who struggle. After our conversations, many agents started reaching out to their databases again. Those who did saw positive results, while those who didn't, unfortunately, remained stuck.

To see positive results yourself, you need to create a structured plan for how you will market to your database. Start by considering how you prefer to communicate. Do you enjoy making phone calls, or would you rather only call when necessary? Would you prefer texting over calling? Maybe you enjoy sending emails or would like to craft a monthly newsletter. If your budget allows, you could even send postcards or other mailers. There's no "right" way to market to your database—the key is to choose methods you enjoy, so the process doesn't feel like a burden. If it does, you're more likely to lose interest and stop altogether.

Your touch plan should include at least two touches per month, although I highly recommend more, especially if you're a new agent building your business or a veteran looking to reignite a stalled one. Once you decide on your approach, write out your plan and keep it somewhere easily accessible. For example, I used a simple Google Sheet every year to track my plan. Whenever I completed a touch, I'd mark the cell green to show it was done, or red if I missed it. This helped me stay on track and review how many touches I had made by year's end.

> **TIP:**
> Set calendar reminders on your phone to prompt you to complete your touches regularly.

Video Messages

Video has rapidly become one of the most preferred ways for people to consume information. In fact, 79% of consumers would rather watch a video about a product than read about it. This trend makes video messaging a powerful marketing tool, especially when integrated into your touch plan as a Realtor. With smartphones readily available, sending a video via text or email ensures a high likelihood of it being seen, and the impact is more lasting—information conveyed through video is 68% more likely to be recalled than information through text alone.[2]

Surprisingly, despite video's effectiveness, only a handful of Realtors I've spoken with use video messages regularly, and even fewer send them via text. Most prefer to email their video messages or rely on third-party services. However, if you're on a budget, video text messaging is a highly accessible way to stay top of mind with your contacts. A simple 20–30 second video expressing that you were thinking of them, or offering a friendly hello, can do wonders in keeping your name fresh in their minds.

> **TIP:**
> Personalize each video to the recipient—it could be a simple greeting, a thank you, or even a quick update. Personalized messages are more impactful and could spark a meaningful conversation that leads to new opportunities.

Personal Drop-Bys

Every year around Thanksgiving, a top-producing Realtor I know rents a van and fills it with about 25 pies from a local bakery. Before loading the pies, he adds a handwritten note to each, addressed personally to the recipient. He then embarks on a preplanned route, delivering the pies to his contacts' homes. The whole event takes about three to four hours, but the effort pays off—he typically receives at least one referral a year from each person on his list.

> **NOTE:**
> If your budget doesn't allow for pies, you can replicate this gesture with something inexpensive, like a $.50 packet of seeds.

Drop-bys aren't for everyone in your database. Reserve this personal gesture for select contacts—those who regularly send you business or are repeat clients. You can also spread out your drop-bys throughout the year, not just during the holidays. The key is consistency. You want your contacts to expect it so much that if you skip a year, they'd reach out to ask why.

Top 25 List

Your top 25 list consists of your most valuable contacts—the ones who regularly send business your way or frequently use your services. These are your "raving fans," people who advocate for you to everyone they know.

If you've been in the industry for a few years, you likely already know who these people are. If you're a newer Realtor, take a close look at your list and identify which contacts might become your biggest advocates.

> **NOTE:**
> It's common to add or replace contacts on this list over time.

Once you've identified your top 25, make sure to show them how much you appreciate their support each year. Beyond drop-bys, you can host client appreciation events or, if your budget allows, plan an all-expenses-paid trip for your top clients.

For newer agents with smaller budgets, don't let that stop you from finding creative ways to express appreciation. A simple handwritten card, as mentioned earlier, can go a long way. It's not about how much you spend; it's about being consistent and making your clients feel valued. Whatever you decide, treat these top contacts well!

The Six-Figure Newsletter

By my third year in real estate, I was still struggling to get my business off the ground. The housing market was recovering from the 2009 crash, and I began to wonder if real estate was the right path for me. I had been consistently marketing to my database but wasn't seeing the results I expected. Instead of making any drastic changes, I decided to analyze what I was currently doing.

Through this process, I discovered that my newsletter was the one marketing tool generating consistent engagement. The platform I used, Mailchimp.com, provided detailed statistics, and I noticed a steady increase in my newsletter's open rate. In my first year, my open rate was around 10%, but by the second year, it had climbed to 17%. That 7% jump gave me the confidence that I was doing something right.

However, I wanted to take it further. My research showed that the average open rate for real estate newsletters was 21.7%.[3] I knew I was on track to surpass that industry average in my third year, but I wasn't satisfied with just average. I set an ambitious goal: I wanted to hit a 50% open rate, believing that if half my database opened my newsletter, my business would soon take off.

I spent the next week researching how to make my newsletter more effective. By the end, I identified several strategies to increase engagement and boost my open rates.

> **NOTE:**
> Building an effective newsletter that achieves high open rates takes time—so be patient!

Subject Lines Matter

Currently, over 4 billion people worldwide use email daily, and more than 347 billion emails are sent and received every day. On average, each person receives 121 emails per day.

Email plays a crucial role in both communication and business transactions. It's the second most preferred way to communicate, just behind texting, with almost 50% of people saying they would rather email than use other methods. With such a high volume of emails flooding inboxes, standing out can be a challenge unless you have a strategy. The key to getting your emails noticed and opened starts with crafting an effective subject line.

To grab attention, your subject line needs to break away from the typical patterns we see in email inboxes. Here are a few strategies to make your subject lines stand out:

- Add one or two emojis 😊 (but no more than two).

- Capitalize entire words, for example, REAL ESTATE.

- Use brackets around words, like this: [REAL ESTATE].

> **TIP:**
> Always include the phrase "Real Estate" in your subject line. Even if your contact doesn't open the email, they'll still associate your name (in the "from" section) with real estate, which helps build brand awareness.

Timing is Everything

In the early days of sending newsletters, I didn't have a set schedule. My send times varied, from 9:00 AM to 6:00 PM, with some outliers like 8:20 PM and even 11:30 PM. As I reviewed the data, I realized my best open rates occurred when I sent newsletters at 10:00 AM CST. After consistently sending them at this time, my open rate steadily climbed.

According to HubSpot, the best time to send marketing emails is between 8:00 AM - 11:00 AM CST, followed by 11:01 AM - 2:00 PM CST. The worst times are between 12:00 AM and 2:00 AM CST.[4] My findings aligned perfectly with HubSpot's research.

> **TIP:**
>
> Test different send times to determine when your audience is most likely to engage. Also, keep your send time and day consistent—this builds anticipation. For example, I sent my newsletter at 10:00 AM on the first of each month. Also, set calendar reminders to send your newsletter at the designated time each month.

Provide Value

When I reviewed my early newsletters, I realized I was missing a key element: I wasn't providing enough valuable information. My emails typically started with a personal update, followed by a real estate-related article, and concluded with a summary of something I had recently done in real estate, such as closing a rental or attending a training. At the time, this layout made sense to me, but after researching newsletters more thoroughly, I realized it was severely lacking in value.

The most effective newsletters are those that consistently offer value to their readers. If a newsletter is solely focused on selling, people quickly lose interest and either ignore it or unsubscribe. Once I understood this, I revamped my entire approach, adopting what I now call the "give, give, give, give, take" layout. This means providing four valuable items (the "gives") before ending with something I'd done recently in real estate (the "take").

> **TIP:**
>
> To streamline the process, create a newsletter template in your program of choice so you can easily reuse it each month instead of starting from scratch.

I began by updating the top section to include a branded header. Next, I changed the message section to offer relevant real estate updates or market information, along with any personal notes I wanted to share. I then included three articles with eye-catching images—either from the article itself or one I found on Google—and linked to the full content. Finally, I added a recent sale, new listing, or real estate activity to show I was an active Realtor, including a link to view the property on a third-party site like Zillow or Realtor. com (people love looking at real estate!).

> **TIP:**
>
> Add a short video of yourself discussing the market at the beginning instead of writing it out. Video is often more engaging for readers.

After making these changes, I noticed an immediate improvement in engagement. More people opened the emails, clicked the article links, and even checked out the real estate listings at the end.

> **NOTE:**
>
> Don't forget to include your social media links at the bottom, along with any necessary compliance information.

Test It

One important lesson my research taught me was the value of previewing your newsletter before sending it out. When you send a newsletter, you're not just delivering content— you're also broadcasting your brand. Any errors, whether in spelling, punctuation, or formatting, can reflect poorly on your professionalism. To build brand awareness, it's crucial to avoid anything that might tarnish your reputation.

Before sending your newsletter to your entire database, send it to yourself first. Most platforms offer the option to view a live version of the email as if you were one of your contacts. Use this feature to review your newsletter carefully for errors, broken links, or improper formatting.

> **NOTE:**
>
> Around 80% of people open emails on their smartphones, so ensure your newsletter is properly formatted for mobile devices.

Statistics

Technology has evolved rapidly since I began my career, and many platforms have added data features that give you deeper insights into your newsletters' performance. When I first started using MailChimp, I only had access to a few basic stats. Now, platforms like MailChimp provide detailed analytics for every aspect of your newsletter, allowing you to see what's working and what's not.

By reviewing these stats regularly, you can make real-time adjustments to improve your strategy. Use the data to your advantage and optimize your newsletters based on what your audience engages with most.

> **TIP:**
>
> Reach out to any contact who frequently clicks on your newsletter. If someone is interacting with it a lot, they may be considering entering the market.

Resend It

During a meeting with one of my agents, I learned a simple trick I wish I had known earlier in my career. She mentioned that she resends her newsletter the day after its initial send, which led to a significant increase in her open rate—around 20%. Intrigued, I researched this technique and found that MailChimp allows you to resend an email to those who didn't open it the first time. If a recipient did open it, they won't receive the resend.

This revelation changed my approach. By resending the email, I was able to get my name in front of more people. Even if they didn't open it again, they still saw my name and real estate, reinforcing brand awareness. Additionally, this method increased my open rate by giving people another chance to view the newsletter.

I started using this trick, setting a calendar reminder on the second day of each month to resend my newsletter. My first attempt boosted my open rate from 45% to 65%, adding 80 more opens from my 400-person database! I continued using this strategy throughout my career and maintained a 65% open rate. I highly recommend incorporating this tactic to improve your own open rates quickly.

> **NOTE:**
>
> Don't worry if someone unsubscribes from your newsletter. Not everyone will want to receive it. Focus on the people who stay engaged.

In 2019, I shifted my focus from selling real estate to growing my company. Even though I cut back on personal marketing, I never stopped sending my newsletter. Despite the reduced marketing effort, business continued to flow in, and I consistently averaged $5 million in production and six-figure income—thanks to a newsletter that took just 30-45 minutes a month to create.

If you're not already using a newsletter in your marketing strategy, I strongly recommend it. From my research and conversations with agents, most don't use this simple tool—but those who do often see fantastic results.

Important to Remember

✅ **Building a Database**

- Statistically, people can name up to three Realtors. If you're not top of mind, you're unlikely to get their business.
- **Organization**
  - Store your contacts in an organized system, such as a Google Sheet or CRM.

- **Your Phone**
  - Start building your database by exporting contacts from your phone and adding them to your system.
- **Social Media**
  - Export contacts from Facebook and LinkedIn to add to your database.
- **Think Outside the Box**
  - Add anyone you can think of beyond your phone and social media, such as your hairstylist, dentist, or neighbors.
- **Fill in the Blanks**
  - Reach out to contacts for missing information (name, email, phone, home address).

Marketing

- Consistently put yourself in front of your contacts to build brand recognition.
- **Touch Plan**
  - Develop a plan to contact your database multiple times a month using various methods (calls, texts, emails, mailers, etc.).
  - **Suggestion:** Aim to contact your database 50 times a year.
- **Handwritten Cards**
  - Include handwritten cards in your plan. Personal touches leave a lasting impression.
- **Video Messages**
  - 79% of consumers prefer video over reading about a product. Send 20-30 second personalized video messages to your contacts.
- **Personal Drop-Bys**
  - Drop off a small gift for contacts who refer business or are repeat clients.

Top 25 List

- Identify your top 25 contacts who regularly refer you or use your services, and show appreciation with specific gestures (e.g., handwritten notes).

The Six-Figure Newsletter

- Sending a monthly newsletter is a powerful marketing tool.
- **Subject Lines Matter**
  - Use capitalized words, emojis, and brackets to make your subject lines stand out.

- **Timing is Everything**
  - The best time to send marketing emails is between 8:00 AM - 11:00 AM CST or 11:01 AM - 2:00 PM CST. Avoid sending emails between 12:00 AM and 2:00 AM CST.
- **Provide Value**
  - Use a "give, give, give, give, take" format. Provide four pieces of valuable content and end with something real estate-related, like a recent sale or listing.
- **Test It**
  - Always send the newsletter to yourself first to check for errors or formatting issues before sending it to your contacts.
- **Statistics**
  - Regularly review the statistics provided by your email platform to see what's working and adjust accordingly.
- **Resend It**
  - Resend your newsletter the next day to contacts who didn't open it the first time.

NOTES

Chapter 9
Buyers

In 2012, a friend of mine referred me to a colleague who was considering buying a place. To protect his identity, I'll call him John. A few days later, I received a text from John asking if I'd be interested in helping him. Thrilled at the opportunity to work with another buyer, I suggested we meet as soon as possible to discuss the buying process and better understand his needs.

Three days later, I sat in a small conference room at my brokerage, reviewing my notes while waiting for John to arrive. As I went over my presentation materials one last time, I noticed a man enter the office. He was about 5'10", with short dark brown hair spiked in the front, dressed in a well-worn blue suit, a white dress shirt without a tie, and scuffed brown dress shoes.

John scanned the office until he spotted me in the room to his left. He smiled and walked over, opening the door as I stood up to greet him. After a brief round of small talk, we took our seats, and I jumped into my presentation. When I finished, I asked John to tell me more about what kind of property he was looking for. He explained he wanted a one-bedroom, one-bath condominium near Lake Michigan, with a budget of around $200,000. His preferences didn't extend much beyond that.

Not wanting to take up more of his time, I thanked him for meeting with me and told him to keep an eye out for emails from the MLS with potential properties. I also introduced him to a mortgage professional to help him get pre-approved before we started viewing homes. For two weeks, I sent John an endless stream of properties while he went through the pre-approval process. Once he was ready to start looking, we set a day and time to meet. I reviewed the list of properties he had marked as favorites, but they were so varied that it was hard to detect any consistent pattern. Still, I picked out some options I thought he might like, feeling confident that we'd find something quickly.

Our first outing took about two hours as we toured a variety of condominiums along the lake. Unfortunately, none caught John's interest. We agreed to go out again the following week, and I was sure I had a better sense of his preferences. However, once again, he didn't find anything he liked. This continued for over three months. Every weekend, I spent hours showing him nearly every one-bedroom, one-bath unit along the lake, but nothing stood out to him.

Finally, after showing John more than 60 properties, he found one that he was seriously interested in. Curious, I asked him why this particular place stood out compared to the others. He explained that he loved the open kitchen, the lake view, the updated finishes, the walk-in closet, and—what surprised me—the proximity to the harbor. Confused, I asked why the harbor mattered. John explained that his parents owned a boat they sometimes kept there, and he wanted to be able to walk to it easily whenever they visited.

Lesson Learned

One of the biggest mistakes new agents make is not asking enough questions during the initial buyer consultation to fully understand the buyer's needs and preferences. Many agents, eager to have a client and appear busy, rush to start showing properties without gathering enough information. This leads to more time spent showing a large number of properties, trying to figure out the buyer's preferences, and results in wasted time for both you and the client.

In John's case, if I had asked more follow-up questions during our first meeting, he likely would have mentioned his parents' boat and his desire to live near the harbor. That information would have allowed me to focus on properties close to the harbor, saving us both time and energy.

When you meet a buyer for the first time, it's crucial to spend enough time learning what is important to them and why. While most buyers will have a general idea of their needs, such as the number of bedrooms and baths, price range, and property type, they are often less focused on specific location preferences or must-have features. Your role is to play detective, asking the right questions to narrow down their true preferences before setting up property searches. I'll explain how to do this later in the chapter, but before you can start showing homes, you first have to sell yourself—this happens during the buyer's presentation.

❙ Buyer Presentation

A common misconception among Realtors is thinking that their main job is to sell properties. In reality, selling properties is only 10% of the job—90% is selling yourself. You are trying to convince the person or people in front of you to choose your services over those of other Realtors in the market. The buyer's presentation is where this happens, so it should go without saying that you need to have a great presentation and a strong grasp of what you're talking about.

Besides the content of your presentation, there are a few other key factors that can help you put yourself in the best position to sell your services.

NOTE:

To avoid buyers ghosting you, send a calendar invite with all the meeting details. A calendar invite increases the chances of buyers attending the meeting since it shows up on their schedule, and most people are more likely to commit once they confirm it.

Location

Choosing where to meet a potential client is often an overlooked decision, but there's significant psychology involved in selecting the right venue. Typically, you have two options: meeting at your office or in a public space. Both options have their merits, and you'll hear arguments in favor of each. However, based on my research and experience, I believe that meeting in a public place is the better choice for a first encounter. Let me explain why.

When meeting someone for the first time, we naturally tend to put our "guard up." This reaction is part of our brain's built-in defense mechanism, dating back to the Stone Age. Back then, our ancestors had to constantly protect themselves to survive. While we no longer face threats like Sabertooth Tigers, our brains retain these ancient defense mechanisms.

To make a good impression and sell ourselves effectively, we need to lower the buyer's defenses. One of the quickest ways to achieve this is by choosing a location where the potential client feels safe—such as a public place. Meeting in a public setting reduces anxiety because the likelihood of danger is minimal. In contrast, meeting a stranger in an unfamiliar office may make the client more guarded.

A buyer in a public place is more likely to relax and open up, while a buyer in an office might remain defensive for longer. This is the main reason I prefer meeting in public spaces—it helps build trust faster without having to work through their heightened defenses.

Presentation Goals

The primary goal of your presentation is to become the agent your clients choose to buy their home. However, there are several other important objectives you should aim to accomplish during the meeting to ensure future success for both you and your buyers.

One key goal is to set clear expectations. This is crucial because it establishes the tone for your working relationship and provides a reference point throughout the buying process. For instance, one common reason transactions fall apart is due to misunderstandings during the home inspection. Many buyers mistakenly see the inspection as a chance to negotiate a lower price by identifying cosmetic issues. However, the true purpose of a home inspection is to protect buyers from purchasing a property with major defects or safety hazards, not to secure credits for minor repairs. By addressing this early on, you set the right expectations, helping buyers focus on significant issues during the inspection, rather than superficial ones.

Another objective of your presentation should be to educate buyers about current market conditions. Before meeting with a Realtor, buyers often form opinions based on information from friends, online searches, and third-party sites like Redfin. Unfortunately, these sources can lead to inaccurate perceptions of the market. Taking time to explain the real state of the market ensures buyers are better prepared when they're ready to start shopping.

Additionally, it's important to guide buyers through the home-buying process. Many of your initial clients, especially as a newer agent, will likely be first-time buyers who may feel overwhelmed by the process. Walking them through each step—from start to finish—helps them feel more confident and prepared for what lies ahead.

Lastly, help buyers understand that finishes and aesthetics are not as critical as they might think. Shows like Million Dollar Listing, Selling Sunset, and countless HGTV programs have fostered unrealistic expectations about the appearance of homes. Many buyers now expect high-end finishes, regardless of their budget. While there's nothing wrong with wanting luxury features, it's often more practical to focus on the needs rather than the wants. For example, is an open layout more important because they entertain often, or are they prioritizing a kitchen with quartz countertops and white cabinets? By emphasizing the importance of the unchangeable aspects of the home and explaining that cosmetic updates can be done later—on their terms and budget—buyers can make smarter, long-term decisions and maximize their return on investment when it's time to resell.

Understanding these goals is essential for helping buyers make quicker and more informed decisions.

Presentation Layout

Just as there's psychology behind choosing the ideal location to meet a buyer, the same applies to structuring your presentation. Your presentation should flow in a way that takes the buyer on a journey, starting with building rapport and ending with a comprehensive understanding of the home-buying process.

The opening of your presentation is crucial because it's where you establish trust. To do this effectively, begin by sharing your experience in the industry and any credentials you possess. Once the buyer feels comfortable with you, the door is open to set expectations and guide them through the buying process.

NOTE:

As a new agent, you may not have much experience or many credentials yet. In this case, highlight relevant aspects of your background, such as previous sales roles, and showcase any skills that would benefit your buyers, like a strong work ethic or attention to detail.

Once you've gained their trust, the next step is to educate them on the current market conditions. As mentioned earlier, buyers often come to the table with preconceived notions about the market, which may be inaccurate. It's your job as a professional to provide clarity, ensuring they have realistic expectations as they enter the market.

Next, guide them through a detailed overview of the buying process, starting with the search. For instance, explain how you'll set them up on an automated MLS search, the amount of notice you need to schedule showings, and what to look out for during viewings, both in person and online (e.g., poor-quality photos). Also, outline the paperwork process. Then, walk them through the steps that follow once they've found a property they're interested in. For example, you'll conduct a Comparative Market Analysis (CMA) to assess the property's market value, explain the home inspection process, and clarify their responsibilities for loan approval. Finally, discuss what will happen on closing day.

The final section of your presentation should focus on helping buyers distinguish between their needs and wants. The essential elements of a property—such as location, layout, and natural light—are needs because they cannot be changed. Meanwhile, wants are typically cosmetic, like paint colors, cabinets, or flooring. By emphasizing the importance of focusing on needs, you'll help buyers narrow down their options to properties that truly fit their practical requirements. This approach not only streamlines their decision-making process but also leads to quicker, more informed choices.

Limit Text

To sell yourself effectively to the buyer, you need to demonstrate that you know what you're talking about. The best way to do this is by limiting the text on each slide. Stick to a few key bullet points and, at most, a couple of images. A slide overloaded with text doesn't convey expertise. It's similar to watching a TED Talk—no one wants the presenter to read from a script. Instead, you expect them to share their knowledge confidently because they are an expert. Buyers are no different. Use bullet points as a guide to highlight key topics, but focus on making eye contact and walking buyers through the details in a conversational way.

NOTE:

I strongly recommend practicing your presentation until you can deliver it with minimal glances at your notes. Rehearse in front of a mirror or with someone who can provide feedback. The more familiar you are with the material, the more likely it is that buyers will trust you and want to work with you.

Paper vs. Tablet

When it comes to presenting to clients, you have two main options: using paper or a tablet. The first option, printing your presentation, is preferred by some agents because it allows for note-taking during the meeting and provides buyers with a tangible takeaway. However, paper can seem outdated, especially to younger buyers who may expect their Realtor to be as tech-savvy as they are. This perception could potentially be a turn-off.

The second option is to use a tablet or laptop. Most agents have transitioned to this approach because it offers greater flexibility and allows for a more visually engaging presentation.

With attention spans averaging around eight seconds, it's crucial to use tools that keep buyers engaged. The more captivated they are, the better your chances of making a sale.

> **NOTE:**
>
> It's important to explain how Realtor commissions work. Take time to walk buyers through the process, including how both you and the listing agent are compensated. The more transparent you are, the more trust you'll build with your clients.

Needs vs. Wants

Earlier in this chapter, I mentioned my experience with a buyer named Steve and how I made the mistake of not asking enough follow-up questions during the initial consultation. This is a common mistake I see agents make early in their careers. They gather basic information about what buyers want, then quickly set up a property search without digging deeper into why those things matter to the buyer. The more information you extract upfront, the more focused your buyer's search will be, and the less likely you'll end up showing them over 60 properties, as I did.

When you begin asking buyers what they're looking for, start by focusing on their needs—items that are non-negotiable. These include factors like the number of bedrooms, bathrooms, or proximity to public transportation for commuting. Also, take the time to find out why these are non-negotiable. Understanding the reason behind their needs helps keep your clients on track if they start straying from their criteria. For example, if you know they need a three-bedroom, two-bathroom home because they have children, you can remind them of this when they ask about a two-bedroom property they found on Redfin that "looks nice." This prevents them from pursuing a property they're not seriously considering and saves you from wasting time.

Once you've identified their needs and the reasons behind them, you can move on to discussing their wants—the features they would prefer but aren't essential. For instance, they might want a finished basement but are fine with an unfinished one they can renovate later.

> **NOTE:**
>
> Buyers often focus more on their wants than their needs. It's your job to refocus them whenever you notice they're drifting.

Another common mistake I see agents make is not narrowing down the neighborhoods their clients are seriously considering. Many agents set up searches in too many areas at the start and then try to narrow them down as they show properties. This approach leads to wasted time and too many showings. Instead, find out upfront which neighborhoods your buyers are truly interested in and why. For example, do they need to be in a certain area for a school district or because it's close to family?

Most buyers will have two or three main neighborhoods in mind, plus a few they've heard about or Googled but don't know much about. For these secondary options, I recommend advising clients to explore them first. If, after doing their due diligence, they can see themselves living there, then you can set up a property search. If your clients insist on considering five or six areas, offer to take them on an exploratory showing. Drive them to one property in each area—one you choose based on what you think they'll like—and discuss each neighborhood while driving. After the showings, review the areas together and decide which ones can be eliminated.

| Buyer's Presentation Follow-Up

One of the most important aspects of working with potential buyers is knowing what to do after the meeting ends. The newer generation of buyers—Millennials, Gen Z, and beyond—tend to interview multiple agents before deciding who will represent them. Often, you won't know for days, weeks, or even months whether they'll choose to work with you. That's why following up after your initial meeting is crucial to keep your name fresh in their minds.

Your first follow-up should happen right after the meeting. Buyer consultations, especially for first-time homebuyers, can be overwhelming. Sending a follow-up email with more details about what you discussed gives them a chance to absorb the information at their own pace. Having a pre-prepared email template for this is ideal.

After the initial follow-up, establish a plan to regularly check in with the buyers until they make their decision. I recommend contacting potential buyers weekly. Every Monday, reach out via call, text, or email. It's helpful to add value with each touchpoint, whether by sharing a relevant article, providing information about a new development, or offering insights that show you're thinking about their best interests.

TIP:

Set a calendar reminder to ensure you don't forget to follow up with any potential buyers. A system like this ensures no one falls through the cracks.

| What Next?

Once a buyer has chosen you as their agent, it's time to complete the essential tasks that come with onboarding a new client. These include setting up property searches, adding the buyer to your client spreadsheet or tracking system, and introducing them to your preferred mortgage professional. To ensure consistency, create a New Buyer Checklist that you can easily access. This checklist will help you follow the same process for every buyer and avoid skipping any steps.

> **TIP:**
> It's important to provide the same level of service to every buyer. When a client refers you to someone else, they'll likely talk about everything you did for them. This means the new buyer will come in with certain expectations. If you don't meet those expectations, the new buyer may be less likely to refer you—or if they do, it won't be with the same enthusiasm as the original client.

Setting Up Property Searches

To prevent overwhelming your buyer when setting up property searches (especially on the Multiple Listing Service), focus the search criteria based on the information they provided during the buyer's consultation. For instance, if your client is interested in a specific neighborhood, limit the search to that area rather than the entire town. This approach ensures that your client only receives listings from neighborhoods they're interested in, making it easier for them to narrow down properties they want to view.

Additionally, name the searches in a way that's easy to understand and keep organized. I recommend using the neighborhood name so that when your clients view the listings, they immediately know they are only seeing properties from their desired location.

> **NOTE:**
> If your client isn't finding what they're looking for, even with focused searches, it's okay to adjust the criteria. You can expand the search boundaries, remove restrictions on the number of bedrooms or bathrooms, or relax overly specific requirements. Sometimes, you'll need to tweak the search parameters to provide your client with more options to consider.

Look Daily for Properties to Send

Many agents rely on automated property searches and wait for buyers to select the homes they want to view. To stand out from the competition, take time each day to personally search for properties to send your clients. Set a goal of sending at least one property a week, even if it's not a perfect match, to show that you're proactive and committed to finding the right home for them. If they end up buying a property you found, their perception of you—and how they recommend you to others—will improve significantly.

> **NOTE:**
>
> Searching for properties daily can be time-consuming, especially with multiple clients. To simplify this, create a client profile for yourself on your MLS and set up daily property searches based on your clients' criteria. This way, you receive listings as if you were a buyer, allowing you to quickly review and send the best options to your clients.

▌ Showings

For buyers, shopping for properties is the most exciting part of the home-buying process. It's their chance to step into potential new homes and see in person what they've only viewed online. However, as an agent, you need to ensure you're more than just a glorified chauffeur during showings.

Don't Overwhelm

The first showing is usually when buyers are most excited and eager to see as many properties as possible. The problem with this approach is that after seeing too many homes, they tend to blend together, making it hard for buyers to remember key details. I recommend limiting showings to around five or six properties per outing. This keeps the experience manageable and helps buyers more easily decide which homes they're truly interested in.

> **NOTE:**
>
> After each showing or at the end of the day, gather feedback from your clients. Ask them which homes are definite "no's" and why, and which ones they are seriously considering. Understanding their reasoning will help both you and the buyers narrow down the options.

To stay organized, I suggest using a document like the example below. This is a replica of a Google Document I created in Google Drive. Each time I take a buyer out, I open a new document, paste the schedule, and organize the showings in the most efficient order. After making the requests, I share the document with my buyers and update it as responses come in from listing agents. This helps clients know the schedule, where we're starting, and which properties we'll be visiting (or not visiting).

> **NOTE:**
>
> Plan your showings around your schedule. For example, if you're showing homes in the morning and have afternoon appointments in the south, arrange the first showings to finish as far south as possible to make your next appointments easier to reach.

Sample Showing Schedule

Client Name and Date

Color Code System

> **GREEN = CONFIRMED**
>
> **RED = CANNOT SHOW (Under Contract, Cancelled, Temp Off Market, etc.)**
>
> **BLACK = STILL WAITING ON RESPONSE**

TIME	PROPERTY ADDRESS	SHOWING INFO
10:00 AM	123 Main St	Agent Will Meet Us
10:30 AM	456 Market St	Accepted An Offer
11:00 AM	789 State St	Emailed Agent

Anyone Can Open A Door

Showing properties is an art that often takes years for agents to master, but it doesn't have to if you understand your role. Any agent can unlock a door and let buyers wander aimlessly, but great agents actively guide their clients through the property. Whether you choose to lead or follow your clients, your main role is to point out potential concerns that could cost them money in the future. For instance, if you notice water stains in the basement, inform them that it could indicate a possible foundation leak that should be inspected further.

As you walk through each room, engage your clients by discussing furniture placement ideas, highlighting key features like quartz countertops or high-end appliances, and suggesting cosmetic changes that could make the home better suited to their style.

Your goal with each property should be to help your clients see the complete picture. By the time they walk out, they should have enough information to make an informed decision about the home.

| Comparative Market Analysis (CMA)

A Comparative Market Analysis (CMA) helps determine the market value of a property by comparing it to similar properties that have recently sold. When conducting a CMA or "running comps," it's best to approach it like an appraiser, as they will ultimately determine the property's value during the appraisal process for financing.

> **NOTE:**
>
> Appraisals are only required for buyers who finance their purchase and are scheduled by the buyer's mortgage lender. If your client is paying in cash, an appraisal typically isn't needed unless they opt to pay for one themselves.

Appraisers use the Sales Comparison Approach, which calculates a property's value based on the sale prices of comparable properties in the same neighborhood. To do this, at least three comparable properties sold within the last year in an open, competitive market are required. When performing your CMA, aim to find three solid comparables to help provide a clear value range for the property.

> **TIP:**
>
> When sharing your pricing opinion, offer a range instead of an exact number. This leaves more flexibility for negotiations and avoids anchoring your clients to a specific price that could make it harder for them to agree to different terms.

Every market is different, so consult with someone knowledgeable in your area—whether it's a mentor, managing broker, or team leader—to ensure you conduct your CMA correctly.

▌ Negotiations

Real-life negotiations aren't as dramatic as what you see on TV. Most of what's shown is designed to entertain, with real negotiations having already occurred behind the scenes. In reality, negotiations often happen through calls, emails, or even texts, and rarely in person. These discussions also tend to be much simpler, typically revolving around price, though all terms should be taken seriously to secure the best deal for your buyer. To navigate negotiations effectively, here are a few key steps:

Understand What's Important to Your Buyers

Before submitting an offer, have a detailed conversation with your buyers to understand which terms matter most to them beyond price. Many buyers, especially first-timers, tend to fixate on the price, but other factors can be just as crucial. For example, do they need to close by a certain date because their lease is expiring? Or do they need a closing cost credit to help with costs beyond the down payment? Understanding these priorities will allow you to focus on negotiating the terms that matter most and make concessions where necessary to meet their needs.

Discover the Seller's Motivation

Before making an offer, it's helpful to find out why the seller is selling. Sellers rarely list their home without a reason, and understanding their motivation can give you a strategic edge. For instance, are they selling because they need more space due to a growing family? Or are they relocating for work? Knowing this can be valuable when negotiating an offer and tailoring the terms to make your buyers' offer more attractive.

Just as buyers have priorities, sellers do too. Speak with the listing agent to see if they're willing to share any insights about what's important to the sellers, aside from price. This knowledge can help you negotiate for what your buyers need while making the offer more appealing to the sellers. Keep in mind, though, that not all listing agents will share this information, as some may feel it weakens their negotiating position. Still, it never hurts to ask.

Work with the Listing Agent

When we think of negotiation, we often imagine dramatic scenes from movies or TV—whether it's a corporate standoff in a boardroom or a tense encounter between a hero and villain, each trying to gain the upper hand. While these depictions are entertaining, they are far removed from the reality of negotiating residential real estate transactions.

In real estate, it's best to view the other Realtor as an ally, not an adversary. Negotiations should not be personal. It's about finding terms that both your clients and the seller's clients feel good about. From my experience, the best negotiations happen when both agents work together to create a win-win transaction.

Here are some recommendations for working effectively with the listing agent:

- **Be Responsive**
  Answer calls, emails, and messages from the listing agent promptly. This demonstrates your professionalism and commitment.

- **Share Information**
  Provide necessary documents, disclosures, and answers to the listing agent's questions quickly. This keeps the negotiation process moving smoothly.

- **Collaborate on Solutions**
  If issues arise during negotiations, work with the listing agent to find solutions that satisfy both parties. Cooperation often leads to better outcomes.

Approaching negotiations with collaboration sets a positive tone for the rest of the transaction. Remember, having an offer accepted is just the first step toward closing the deal. As you'll see later, there are many additional steps where you and the listing agent will need to continue working together to reach the closing table.

TIP:

When submitting an offer to a listing agent, take the time to craft a professional offer email. Include all necessary documents, provide clear details about the offer, and present everything in a polished manner. This makes a great impression and shows that you know what you're doing, which can go a long way toward getting your offer accepted.

> **NOTE:**
>
> Negotiations can be overwhelming, especially in your early years in the industry. Don't hesitate to reach out to a mentor, Managing Broker, Team Leader, or a seasoned agent you trust. They can guide you through unfamiliar scenarios and help you navigate challenges.

Once an Offer is Accepted

Unlike many industries, when a buyer and seller agree on the terms of a sale, the transaction is far from over. Most closings take 30 days or more, and getting the offer accepted is just the first of many steps before your clients can officially call the home theirs.

> **TIP:**
>
> Include all relevant parties' information (buyer, lender, attorney, etc.) on the contract upfront to avoid needing to provide it later. Same goes for listings as well (seller, attorney, building manager, etc.).

Escrow/Earnest Money

After the offer is accepted and all paperwork is signed, the next step is for the buyers to deliver the escrow or earnest money to the entity holding it (such as the listing company, title company, or another third party). This money acts as a deposit from the buyers, showing the sellers they are serious about purchasing the home. If the transaction goes through, the earnest money is applied toward the down payment. In most cases, the money is refundable if the transaction is canceled within the appropriate time frame. The amount varies, so consult with a mentor, Managing Broker, Team Leader, or veteran agent for guidance on what is appropriate.

Property Inspection

The property inspection is one of the most common points where a deal can fall apart.

> **TIP:**
>
> Before the home inspection, send your clients a pre-inspection email explaining the role of the inspector, what they'll be looking for, and reminding them to focus on latent defects and safety hazards rather than cosmetic issues. This helps set expectations and ensures they know what to prioritize during the inspection.

While Realtors do their best to spot potential issues when showing a home, we can't catch everything in a short visit. A licensed home inspector, however, performs a thorough examination of the property, identifying any defects, safety hazards, or maintenance items.

TIP:

Always attend the home inspection. This is a valuable learning opportunity for you as an agent and gives you the chance to address any concerns your clients have directly with the inspector. These conversations can help put your clients at ease about the inspection results.

The inspector compiles their findings into a detailed report, usually complete with pictures, descriptions, and maintenance tips.

Once the report is received, schedule a time to discuss any concerns with your buyers. It's essential to remind them to focus on significant issues, such as latent defects or safety hazards, as these are the only items that can typically be negotiated with the seller. Cosmetic issues, on the other hand, are considered normal wear and tear and can't be used as leverage in negotiations.

NOTE:

Examples of latent defects include a malfunctioning dishwasher, while safety hazards could include an overloaded electrical panel. Cosmetic issues, like floor scratches or dents in a fridge door, are normal in a used home.

Loan Process

The most common way buyers purchase a property is by securing a loan from a lending institution. Buyers work closely with a mortgage professional who will guide them through the entire loan process. This typically includes verifying the buyer's income and expenses, reviewing their credit history, and ordering an appraisal.

NOTE:

The appraisal is conducted by a third-party appraisal company hired by the mortgage lender. After the appraisal is ordered, the appraiser contacts the listing agent to schedule a property visit. The appraiser will then conduct a market analysis and produce a report based on their findings. Their role is to confirm that the agreed-upon purchase price aligns with the market value of the home.

Once the mortgage professional determines the buyer is qualified to purchase the home and the appraisal supports the purchase price, the lender will issue a "clear to close," meaning the loan is approved and the closing can be scheduled.

> **TIP:**
>
> Aside from inspections, poor communication is one of the leading reasons transactions fall apart. To avoid this, conduct weekly check-ins with your mortgage professional and attorney (if your clients are using one). Pick a specific day each week to request updates via email, including your buyers on the message. This ensures everyone stays informed and prevents missed deadlines or confusion from derailing the transaction.

| Final Walk-Through

Once the closing is scheduled, the next step is to arrange the final walk-through. This is an important step, as it gives the buyers one last chance to inspect the home before signing the paperwork. I recommend scheduling the final walk-through as close to the closing as possible to reduce the chance of any issues arising before the sale is finalized. For instance, if the walk-through happens two days before closing, everything may appear fine, but if heavy rainfall causes the basement to flood the next day, the buyers would be unaware of the issue. Once they sign the paperwork, they would be responsible for handling the flood damage as the new owners.

The final walk-through also allows the buyers to verify that any repairs or replacements the seller agreed to after the inspection have been completed. For example, if the seller agreed to replace a non-working dishwasher, the buyers can confirm this before proceeding to the closing.

| Closing

Closings can take place in various locations, but they typically occur at title companies and are scheduled during normal business hours (Monday through Friday, 9 a.m. to 5 p.m.). Closings are not scheduled on weekends.

> **NOTE:**
>
> The title company's role is to research and insure the title of the home. The title insurance policy that buyers purchase protects them from any potential liabilities, making it a crucial part of the closing process.

At closing, buyers will need to bring their driver's license (or state-issued ID or passport) and a certified check for the funds required (if the amount is over $50,000, it typically needs to be wired from the buyer's bank to the title company). Buyers will be required to sign a significant amount of paperwork, most of which relates to the loan, as well as the title and closing statement. Once all paperwork is signed, the title company's representative (often called a "closer") sends the documents to the lending institution. After reviewing and approving the documents, the mortgage lender will release the necessary funds to the title company. At this point, the closing is complete, and your buyers officially own the property!

> **TIP:**
>
> I recommend attending as many closings as possible and bringing a small gift for your buyers. Being present shows your clients that you've supported them throughout the entire process, and it's also a great opportunity to ask for referrals from anyone they know who might benefit from your services.

▎After Closing

A common mistake some agents make is treating their clients as just another transaction, disappearing after the sale closes. Over my career, I've worked with many clients who chose me because their previous agent didn't stay in touch after the closing. That agent failed to remain top-of-mind, so when those clients were ready to buy or sell again, they didn't consider using the same agent.

To ensure your buyers remember you after the closing, incorporate them into a follow-up marketing plan. Add them to your monthly newsletter, mailing list, and connect with them on social media. Set calendar reminders to follow up on the anniversary of their closing. A combination of these strategies increases the likelihood that your clients will return to you for future transactions and refer others to your services.

> **TIP:**
>
> Build a solid team of trusted professionals, including a mortgage broker, attorney, inspector, contractor, plumber, electrician, structural engineer, accountant, and financial planner. A strong network will enhance your ability to serve your clients.

Important to Remember

✔ **Buyer's Presentation**

- **Purpose:** Sell yourself and convince buyers to use your services.
- **Location:** Choose between your office or a public place.
- **Goals**
  - Set expectations about the buying process and the market.
  - Help them differentiate between needs vs. wants.
- **Layout**
  - Start by building trust and explaining market conditions.
  - Walk them through the buying process and key property factors.

- **Limit Text:** Use minimal text, focusing on key bullet points and pictures as discussion starters.
- **Paper vs. Tablet:** Tablets offer a modern touch, but choose based on your audience.

Needs vs Wants

- Identify buyers' must-haves (needs) vs. nice-to-haves (wants).
- Narrow down their preferences as much as possible.

Buyer's Presentation Follow-up

- Send a detailed email recap of the presentation, including important details not in your slides.

What's Next?

- Set up property searches and introduce your mortgage professional.

Setting Up Property Searches

- Focus searches based on buyers' consultation information.

Look Daily for Properties to Send

- Be proactive; aim to send properties to buyers regularly.

Showings

- **Don't Overwhelm:** Show 5-6 properties per outing.
- **Guide the Walk-Through:**
  - Point out potential costly defects.
  - Discuss furniture placement and noteworthy finishes.

Comparative Market Analysis (CMA)

- Use the Sales Comparison Approach like appraisers do.
- Focus on closed sales and provide a value range for negotiation flexibility.

Negotiations

- **Real-Life Negotiations:** Simpler than portrayed on TV.
- **Understand Buyer's Priorities:** Discuss terms that are most important besides price.
- **Find Seller's Motivation:** Ask the listing agent why the seller is selling and what matters most.
- **Work with the Listing Agent:**
  - Treat them as an ally, not an adversary.
  - Be responsive, share information, and collaborate on solutions.

✅ Once an Offer is Accepted

- **Escrow/Earnest Money:** A good faith deposit from the buyer, applied to the down payment at closing.
- **Property Inspection:** A licensed inspector reviews the property for defects and safety hazards.
- **Loan Process:** Buyers work closely with a mortgage professional to secure financing.
- **Final Walk-Through:** The last opportunity for buyers to inspect the home, typically just before closing.
- **Closing:** Occurs at a title company, where a representative facilitates the process.
- **After Closing:** Add buyers to your follow-up database and marketing plan.

NOTES

Chapter 10
Listings

It was a beautiful February morning in 2014. The sun warmed my face as I approached the large gray-stone building ahead of me. With each step, my nerves grew, knowing I was about to interview for my first potential listing. I had spent time practicing my listing presentation and reviewing comparable properties, so I felt confident about pricing the property. Excitement bubbled inside me as I prepared to share my thoughts with the seller.

My hand trembled as I reached for the buzzer next to the building's front door and pressed the button for the second floor. The sharp, ear-piercing sound rang from the buzzer box. After a few seconds of silence, a return buzzer went off, unlocking the large wooden door in front of me. I climbed the two flights of stairs, where the seller—whom I'll call Nicholas to maintain confidentiality—stood at the threshold, ready to greet me. Nicholas was a tall, slender man in his early fifties, with short brown hair streaked with gray. His hair had an unkempt, casual look, matching his attire of jeans, a sweatshirt, and well-worn Nike low-tops. After we shook hands, Nicholas invited me to view his second-floor, two-bedroom, two-bath condominium.

Once inside, I asked Nicholas to give me a tour of the property. As we moved from room to room, I took notes on my iPad, while also making an effort to quickly build rapport with him. After about ten minutes, we finished the tour and sat at his dining room table to talk. We engaged in a bit of small talk before I placed my iPad in front of him and began my listing presentation. Once I finished, I answered his questions and then asked a few of my own, including why he was selling the property.

Finally, it was time to discuss the price. Before the meeting, a mentor had advised me to ask the seller what they thought the property was worth before revealing my own assessment (I'll explain why this is important later in the chapter). Eager to share his thoughts, Nicholas told me he had done some market research and believed the home was worth around $300,000. Hearing this, I tried my best not to react, as it was significantly higher than what I had in mind. Keeping a poker face, I suggested we review the Comparative Market Analysis (CMA) I had prepared before diving further into the price discussion.

I proceeded to walk him through the properties currently on the market, those with pending offers, and the recently sold properties. At the end of the presentation, I explained that I believed the property was worth closer to $250,000 and suggested listing it at $260,000 to allow some room for negotiation. I could tell Nicholas wasn't happy with my suggestion. After a few awkward seconds of silence, I said, "Well, we could always test the market, so if $300,000 is what you'd prefer, I'm okay with that." Nicholas, now pleased with my flexibility, responded, "Great, let's move forward. What's next?"

Six months later, we had only a handful of showings. The feedback from the agents was consistent: it was a great unit but overpriced. During that time,

I tried everything to attract buyers. I hosted weekly open houses, posted regularly on social media, and sent out multiple e-blasts, but nothing seemed to work. Despite all my efforts, I couldn't bring in a buyer, and Nicholas ultimately canceled our agreement.

A few weeks after informing me of his decision, he re-listed the property with another agent at the $260,000 price I had originally suggested and ended up selling it for $250,000 two months later.

Lesson Learned

A common mistake many agents make is taking on overpriced listings. Often, this happens because agents are eager to secure the listing, so they agree to whatever price the seller wants. Unfortunately, more often than not, the property doesn't sell, leaving the agent with wasted time and money—not to mention the risk of appearing ineffective in the seller's eyes.

Whenever you go into a listing appointment, it's important not only to impress the sellers with your presentation but also to agree on a price that gives you a real chance to sell the home. As the expert, you must offer suggestions that help make the home more marketable. This balance is essential—not just to secure the listing but to ensure it closes successfully. After all, no matter how many listings you have, if none of them sell, you don't get paid.

❙ Comparative Market Analysis (CMA)

I previously explained what a CMA is, but there are some key differences between a CMA for a buyer and a CMA for a listing that I want to address. The main difference lies in the types of property statuses included in the analysis. A CMA for buyers focuses solely on properties that have recently closed. However, for listings, you need to consider not only recently closed properties but also active listings (your competition) and contingent listings (which could become future comparables). Including all of these factors helps you suggest a competitive list price, both for when the property goes live and for future market changes.

TIP:

When determining the value of a property in your CMA, I recommend offering a price range rather than a single market value. A range provides flexibility for future price adjustments and during negotiations. Sellers tend to fixate on a single price, which can create challenges if price reductions are necessary later or if a lower offer comes in.

Additionally, you likely haven't seen the property in person at this point, and after doing so, you may need to reevaluate the suggested price. A range makes this easier.

> **TIP:**
>
> Before walking the seller through the CMA, ask them what they believe the home is worth. After explaining the CMA, you can then share your thoughts on the property's value. Letting the seller go first helps you explain the comparable properties in a way that guides them toward understanding if their price expectations are too high, too low, or accurate.

Each market is different, so make sure to consult with someone knowledgeable about yours (such as a mentor, Managing Broker, or Team Leader) to learn how to properly conduct a CMA.

Know the Details

In addition to understanding the property's value, it's crucial to know as much as possible about the property and its surrounding area before meeting with the sellers. Start by using the Multiple Listing Service (MLS) to research the property. Old listings can provide valuable insights. Afterward, use Google and Google Maps to familiarize yourself with the key attractions and amenities that potential buyers will be interested in. For example:

- What school district is it in?
- Where is the nearest grocery store?
- Where is the nearest gym?
- How close is it to public transportation?
- How close is it to an expressway?
- Where is the nearest park?

Demonstrating that you're knowledgeable about both the property and its surroundings can significantly increase your chances of being selected as the listing agent. Additionally, this information will be helpful when creating the listing itself.

Property Walk-Through

Unlike working with buyers, where your first meeting might be at a public place or office, your initial meeting with a seller will almost always be at the property they're looking to sell. To give an accurate price evaluation, you need to see the property in person. It's similar to buying a used car—you can only learn so much from photos; seeing it in person is essential to determine if the asking price is fair. When walking through a property, agents typically use one of two methods.

The first method is to walk the property without the seller. Agents who prefer this approach usually hand the seller a printed marketing packet, similar to a listing presentation, and ask them to review it while the agent takes notes on the property as if they were a buyer.

Once the walk-through is complete, the agent sits down with the seller to discuss their findings.

The second method involves the seller walking the agent through the property. Agents who use this approach take notes as the seller talks, then sit down afterward to present their evaluation.

Both methods have pros and cons, and I've tried both. Personally, I prefer the second option. I've found that walking the property with the seller helps build trust, and a trusting seller is more likely to choose me over other agents. Sellers also enjoy talking about their property, and I use this time to gather information that can be useful later in the process. For example, I once had a seller who was hesitant about accepting an offer we had negotiated. Before calling him, I reviewed my notes from the listing appointment and saw that he mentioned being tired of the creaking sounds his hardwood floors made, but he couldn't afford to replace them. During our conversation, I brought up the creaky floors, and he started laughing. That reminder eased his concerns, and he ultimately accepted the offer.

> **TIP:**
>
> Before deciding on a method, try each one at least once to see which works best for you and your business. Afterward, reflect on how each method made you feel and which aligns more with your style.

▎Listing Presentation

In the previous chapter, I discussed the importance of delivering a strong presentation to sell yourself. Your listing presentation needs to be just as compelling as your buyer's presentation. Any seller you meet with is likely interviewing other Realtors, so the quality of your presentation and the depth of your knowledge will play a significant role in securing the listing.

Aside from the content of the presentation itself—which I will outline shortly—there are a few key steps to consider if you want to put yourself in the best position to sell your services.

> **TIP:**
>
> To ensure sellers don't forget about your meeting, send them a calendar invite with all the details included. This increases the likelihood that the sellers will be home and prepared for your meeting since it will appear on their calendar. As many people are strict about their schedules, the invite helps them remember and commit by confirming their attendance.

Presentation Goals

While the main goal is to secure the listing, there are several other key objectives you'll want to achieve to ensure success in selling the property.

The first goal is to set clear expectations. Often, when a seller decides to list their home, they come with preconceived notions about the process and what they can expect. It's crucial to address these expectations by providing a realistic outlook on current market conditions, the property's true market value, and an accurate timeline for the sale.

Another important goal is to build trust and rapport with the seller. Establishing a strong relationship not only boosts the seller's confidence in your abilities but also makes the entire process smoother and more enjoyable for both parties.

You should also aim to showcase your expertise and knowledge of the market. This includes offering a thorough market analysis, discussing recent sales in the area, and explaining the marketing strategies you'll use to attract potential buyers.

Finally, it's essential to demonstrate that your commitment and dedication to selling their property are stronger than any other agent's in the market.

Presentation Layout

Just like with your buyer's presentation, it's important to structure your listing presentation in a way that leads to the best results. It should take the sellers on a journey—starting with building trust and rapport, and ending with them feeling confident in your ability to sell their home for the highest possible price within a timeline that works for them.

The beginning of your presentation is your chance to make the sellers feel comfortable with you. Share details about who you are and your experience in the real estate industry.

> ### NOTE:
> If you're a new agent without much experience or credentials, focus on highlighting any relevant skills or past experiences that could benefit the sellers, just as you would with buyers.

Giving them insight into your background and credentials helps set the stage for managing expectations and guiding them through the selling process.

> ### TIP:
> Use the same introduction slides for your listing presentation as you do for your buyer's presentation. This will help you memorize them more quickly and keep your approach consistent.

Once you've earned their trust, the next step is to explain the current market conditions. Sellers, like buyers, often come into the meeting with their own perceptions of the market, and it's your responsibility as a professional to adjust their expectations where necessary. This way, when their property goes on the market, they'll have a clear understanding of what to expect.

Next, regardless of whether the sellers have sold a property before or not, take time to walk them through the process that will unfold until an offer is accepted. This includes gathering all necessary information about the property, signing listing paperwork, arranging for photos, marketing the property, and showing it. Discussing these steps will help sellers know what to expect if they choose you to list their home.

It's important to explain the costs involved in selling a home so that sellers fully understand their financial obligations. Walk them through your fees as well as other expected costs on closing day, such as Realtor fees, attorney fees, title fees, and any tax prorations. Being upfront about these expenses helps the sellers make informed decisions.

NOTE:

Make sure to clarify how Realtor commissions work. Take the time to explain how both you and the buyer's agent are paid, so there is no confusion. The more transparent you are, the better.

Several factors help sell a property, including proper pricing, a good location, effective marketing, and accessibility for showings. Explain to the sellers what contributes to a successful sale and where their property excels or falls short. Setting clear expectations upfront is essential. For example, if the home is nicely updated but only available for showings one day a week, explain that this restriction will limit the buyer pool. This limitation could extend the time on the market, resulting in lower offers from buyers hoping for a "deal."

A significant part of your presentation will focus on what you do to sell homes. Sellers will want to know how your approach differs from other Realtors they're interviewing. Use the next portion of your presentation to outline your method. Share your marketing plan, including HD photos, 3D walkthroughs, floorplans, videos, social media ads, and more. Explain how you schedule showings, how you gather and use feedback from agents who show the home, and what additional steps you take while the home is on the market and after an offer is accepted.

TIP:

While the property is active, send your sellers a weekly update detailing the previous week's activities, any feedback you've received, and any suggestions to help the property sell faster (e.g., a price adjustment). Once an offer is accepted, send both the attorney (if one is involved) and your clients weekly updates to keep everyone informed about the transaction's progress.

The final part of your listing presentation should cover any additional details the seller needs to know when working with you. For example, how long is your listing agreement (3, 6, 12 months?), are there any upfront fees (such as marketing fees), and what happens if the seller wants to cancel the listing early? Be as transparent as possible to avoid any confusion later on.

Limit Text

Just like with a buyer's presentation, to effectively sell yourself to the sellers, you must be able to confidently verbalize your expertise. The best way to do this is by limiting the text on each slide. Stick to a few key bullet points and incorporate relevant images. Reading from a slide filled with text doesn't convey mastery of the subject. Instead, use the bullet points to guide your discussion, while focusing on engaging with the sellers as you walk them through the information.

> ### NOTE:
> I highly recommend practicing your presentation until you only need to glance down occasionally. Practice in front of a mirror or with someone who can offer feedback. The more familiar you are with the presentation, the more confident and convincing you'll be, increasing the likelihood that the sellers will choose to work with you.

Paper vs. Tablet

When it comes to presenting, as with working with buyers, you have a couple of options for how to deliver your listing presentation. The first option is to print the entire presentation. Some agents prefer this method because it allows them to jot down notes directly on the pages and provides something tangible to give to the sellers as a takeaway. However, the downside is that paper can come across as outdated, particularly to younger sellers who may expect their Realtor to be more technologically savvy. This could potentially be a turn-off if the seller values a more modern approach.

The second option is to present on a tablet (or laptop). Most agents have transitioned to this method because it offers greater flexibility and the ability to create a visually engaging presentation that holds the seller's attention. Keep in mind that most people have an attention span of about eight seconds, so it's crucial to use tools that maintain engagement. The longer you can hold the seller's attention, the better your chances of closing the deal.

| Brutal Honesty

One of the biggest disservices you can do to both the seller and yourself is not being truthful about what needs to be done to sell their home. Often, sellers are unable to see their property's shortcomings. As a Realtor, it's your responsibility to point out everything that could impact the sale. For example, if the home has a lot of clutter, you need to tell the seller they'll need to remove as much as possible to showcase the property's true size. Similarly, if the walls are painted a dark color, suggest repainting with a brighter, neutral color to make the space feel more inviting.

Other key areas to focus on include:

- Removing all personal photos
- Reducing oversized furniture
- Clearing unnecessary items from kitchen countertops
- Ensuring the property is professionally cleaned and remains clean throughout the selling process
- Fixing anything broken and replacing burnt-out lightbulbs

TIP:

When having these conversations, emphasize the importance of completing these tasks before any marketing begins. The photos and marketing materials you create will play a crucial role in attracting attention to the home and maximizing its sale price.

| Seller Questions

An essential element of the listing appointment is understanding the seller's motivation for selling, along with gathering any details about the home that will help you market it effectively. Knowing their motivation allows you to stay aligned with their goals and refer back to it if they lose focus during the process. Additionally, learning about any unique features that make the home stand out from the competition can give you an edge when speaking with potential buyers and agents.

To get this information, come prepared with a specific list of questions to ask throughout the meeting. Make sure to take notes on their responses so you can refer to them later when needed.

| Listing Presentation Follow-Up

Before moving on to what happens once a seller agrees to work with you, it's important to touch on the follow-up after your listing consultation. Sellers typically interview multiple agents before deciding who will represent them. Sometimes, you won't know for days, weeks, or even months whether the seller will choose you. This is why following up after your initial meeting is crucial to keeping your name at the top of their mind.

The first follow-up should come right after your meeting. Listing consultations can be overwhelming for sellers, so having an email template ready to send, which recaps the details of your conversation and includes the CMA as an attachment, can be very helpful for them to reference later.

After the initial follow-up, develop a plan to check in with the sellers regularly until they make a decision. I preferred to follow up with potential clients weekly, typically on Mondays, through a call, text, or email. Each time, I tried to provide value—whether it was sending a relevant article, sharing new market information, or offering something else that showed I had their best interests in mind.

TIP:

Set a calendar reminder or use another tool to ensure you don't forget to follow up with potential sellers. Having a reminder helps prevent anyone from slipping through the cracks.

New Listing Checklist

Getting chosen as the seller's agent is just the first step in a series of tasks that need to be completed before the listing can go on the market. From signing the listing paperwork to completing all the marketing materials, you want to ensure that every box is checked so you can focus on selling once the listing goes live. The best way to do this is to create a checklist of everything that needs to be done, in the order it should be completed. This ensures no steps are missed and helps maintain consistency across all your listings.

TIP:

To stay consistent and avoid missing steps, I recommend creating your new listing checklist in a digital tool like Google Notes. That way, for each new listing, you can simply copy and paste the checklist into a new note. This also allows you to manage multiple listings at once without confusion.

Gather ALL Property Information

One mistake I made early in my career was rushing to list properties before I was fully prepared. Eager to get the listing on the market, I often skipped gathering essential information upfront. This resulted in having to frequently contact the seller and do last-minute research when buyers or agents asked questions I couldn't answer. Once I started gathering all the information at the beginning, I eliminated many of these questions by including the details in the MLS listing or a marketing brochure.

I recommend creating a comprehensive list of questions to ask your sellers about the property to gather as many details as possible. Base the questions on what you would expect a potential buyer to ask.

Here are a few suggestions to get you started:

- How old are the furnace and AC units?
- How old is the roof?
- How old is the water heater?
- Have there been any flooding issues?
- Are there any foundation issues?

TIP:

Be sure to ask about any showing restrictions, if any items are excluded from the sale (e.g., a chandelier or wine fridge), and if the seller needs a specific time frame once an offer is accepted (e.g., 60 days).

Providing this information to buyers upfront allows them to focus solely on the property during viewings, rather than being distracted by asking numerous questions during the tour.

| Listing Description

A listing description plays a crucial role in selling a property. After buyers view the photos and online marketing materials, they often turn to the description to decide if they want to see the property in person. If the description doesn't effectively represent the home, it can turn buyers off, leading them to focus on other properties. This can result in a longer time on the market and may cause the seller to question their choice of agent.

Think of the listing description as an opportunity to highlight features that aren't immediately visible in photos or other marketing materials. For example, describe the kitchen countertops, the type of hardwood flooring, or the brand of the kitchen appliances. Use keywords to emphasize the finer details that make the home special and grab the buyer's attention.

Here are a few examples:

- Granite or quartz countertops
- Stainless steel (name brand) appliances
- Wide-plank oak hardwood flooring
- Heated ceramic tile flooring
- (Name brand) soaker tub

NOTE:

Keywords also help attract more attention on third-party real estate sites, as they are often used in searches. Make it a point to include as many relevant keywords as possible in your description.

Tailor your description to fit the specific property. For instance, if you're listing a fixer-upper, focus on its potential by saying something like, "easily replace an old kitchen countertop with beautiful new white quartz." For a high-end listing, emphasize the luxury features by highlighting name-brand finishes throughout. There's no one-size-fits-all approach to listing descriptions—each home is unique, so ensure your description accurately reflects the property.

TIP:

If you get stuck, consider reviewing similar recently sold listings on the MLS for inspiration from what those agents wrote.

| Marketing

On January 9, 2007, in a keynote address at the Macworld Conference & Expo held in Moscone West in San Francisco, California Apple CEO Steve Jobs introduced the iPhone, and how consumers consume information was changed forever. Fast forward to today and cell phones (and tablets) have become the place where we get a majority of our information from. According to the National Association of Realtors (N.A.R.), in 2020 76% of homebuyers used a mobile or tablet search device in their home search and 97% of homebuyers used the internet.[1] This means to market a home today, Realtors need to focus on operating in the digital space to get the most amount of eyes on their listing, and it all starts with the photos.

Photos

In the mid-2000s, Zillow and Trulia were launched to give consumers a way to search for properties independently, without needing a Realtor to set up an MLS search. Initially, these platforms were accessible only on computers or laptops, but with the introduction of the iPhone and mobile applications, they quickly became available on mobile devices. Since then, both the platforms and the way consumers use them have evolved. As we've become accustomed to scrolling and swiping quickly, capturing a consumer's attention has become more challenging. Consumers are also far less forgiving when they encounter something unappealing. This is where professional, high-quality photos make all the difference.

When potential buyers browse platforms like Zillow or Redfin, they see the first photo of a property and immediately form a judgment about whether they are interested—similar to the way users swipe on apps like Tinder or Bumble. If the first photo catches their attention, they'll proceed to view the rest. Therefore, it's essential that every photo of your listing looks its absolute best. I recommend using a professional photographer and opting for HD photos rather than taking the photos yourself. This ensures that the property looks as attractive as possible to buyers viewing it online.

> **TIP:**
> Before scheduling the photoshoot, work with the seller to ensure the home is photo-ready. This includes professional cleaning, removing personal photos, eliminating unnecessary or oversized furniture (to make the space feel larger), painting walls in neutral colors if needed, and decluttering the home.

360 Virtual Tour

Before the COVID-19 pandemic in 2020, 360 virtual tours, also known as 3D tours or Matterports (named after the company that pioneered the software), were just beginning to gain traction. While city agents frequently used them, they hadn't fully caught on in many suburban markets. The pandemic changed that. Due to health risks, buyers began relying more heavily on online marketing to preview homes before deciding whether to see them in person. Although the height of the pandemic is behind us, buyers' habits have stayed the same. Today, buyers still review all online marketing materials before choosing to visit a home in person. This shift makes virtual marketing, or the lack of it, increasingly critical in selling a property now and in the future.

In addition to the reasons mentioned above, here are a few other benefits of incorporating 360 virtual tours into your marketing strategy:

- These tours can be added to most MLS platforms and automatically flow through to third-party sites like Zillow and Redfin, making them accessible to a wide audience.
- They serve as excellent marketing tools for your social media, email campaigns, and even direct mail. You can also include a QR code linked to the tour in any print materials you produce.
- Offering a 3D tour can help you win listings, as not every agent provides this service. It's an effective way to set yourself apart from the competition.

These tours are becoming popular nationwide and will likely continue to grow in demand. Many companies offer these services now, and the costs have become more affordable over time, making them accessible even to newer agents.

Social Media

When using social media to market your listings, it's important to post regularly to maximize visibility.

> **NOTE:**
> I'll dive deeper into using social media for marketing your listings in Chapter 14: Social Media.

Here are a few suggestions to get started with your posts:

- ✅ Pre-market the listing as "coming soon" before it goes live on the MLS.
- ✅ Announce when the listing is officially on the market.
- ✅ Post whenever you're hosting an open house.
- ✅ Share updates when there's a price adjustment.
- ✅ Announce when an offer has been accepted.
- ✅ Celebrate the closing once the deal is complete.

> **TIP:**
>
> Don't hesitate to repost your content. Most people won't see your initial post due to the fast pace of social media platforms. Reposting increases the chances of reaching a larger audience. Also, make it a priority to follow as many Realtors in your market as possible on the platforms you're using. This increases the visibility of your listing, as many Realtors may not be aware of it from just the MLS posting.

Open Houses

Open houses have been a part of the real estate industry since the early 1900s, originally serving as a primary way to market listings. Over the years, their role has shifted. Today, they are more of a lead generation tool for Realtors to connect with potential buyers who don't yet have an agent.

That being said, open houses can still be a useful marketing opportunity. Most MLS platforms allow Realtors to input open house information into a listing, which then syndicates to hundreds of websites connected to the MLS. This makes the open house visible to consumers across various platforms. Additionally, you can promote open houses on social media, providing an opportunity to market both the listing and yourself.

> **NOTE:**
>
> Less than 2% of homes sell directly because of an open house, so be sure to set the right expectations with your sellers before hosting one.

E-Blasts

An email campaign is an effective way to generate more attention for your listings.

> **TIP:**
>
> Most email marketing platforms allow you to create multiple templates for recurring use. I recommend building templates for new listings, price adjustments, and open houses to save time and maintain consistency.

When you secure a listing, send an e-blast to Realtors who may have interested buyers, both before the property hits the market and afterward.

> **TIP:**
>
> Focus on Realtors who have recently sold homes in the area or who do a lot of business nearby. You can typically find their contact information on the MLS.

Continue to send follow-up emails for price adjustments, open houses, or other updates.

> **NOTE:**
>
> I'll go into more detail about email marketing campaigns in the next chapter.

Postcards

Postcards are another long-standing marketing tool. While they aren't as popular as they once were, they can still be an effective way to market your listing. The best strategy is to send postcards to the surrounding homes in the neighborhood of the listed property.

> **TIP:**
>
> The United States Postal Service offers a program called **Every Door Direct Mail** that allows you to send postcards to any carrier route for a minimal cost. Visit www. usps.com/business/every-door-direct-mail.htm for more information. Canva.com is an excellent tool for designing postcards, with options to create templates for future use. If you have a specific list of recipients, expresscopy.com can send postcards directly to them.

Depending on your budget, you can send multiple postcards to announce the listing, promote price adjustments, advertise open houses, and share when the home is sold.

> **NOTE:**
>
> To grow your business, focus on acquiring as many listings as possible. Listings provide an opportunity for Realtors to market themselves. The more marketing you do, the more exposure you get, and more exposure leads to more business. Sending postcards to neighbors, especially after a sale, is a great way to promote your services.

▌ Live on the Market

As you can tell from everything covered above, a lot of work goes into getting a property ready to go on the market. However, once the listing is live, the work doesn't stop there. Having a listing is one thing, but selling it is another. The rest of this chapter will guide you through that process.

Marketing

While pre-marketing a property before it goes live is often a good idea, the real marketing effort begins once the property is officially listed. As soon as the listing is posted on the MLS, it will start appearing on third-party sites almost instantly. This is when you should execute the marketing plan you've outlined for the property. Anything you promised the sellers—whether it's sending an e-blast to local agents or mailing postcards to neighbors—needs to be set in motion.

> **NOTE:**
>
> Every property is unique, so it's crucial to have a clear marketing plan for each listing before the presentation. This allows you to explain it thoroughly to the sellers.

Sellers will expect you to deliver on everything you promised during the listing presentation. Failing to do so could leave a negative impression, which could not only impact your future dealings with that client but also affect your chances of receiving referrals.

Marketing doesn't end once the property is listed. You must continue to promote it until it sells. This means regularly posting about it on social media, sending additional e-blasts, calling or texting local agents, hosting open houses, and more.

> **TIP:**
>
> Write out your full marketing plan with specific dates for each action. This will help you stay on track and ensure you fulfill all the promises made to the sellers.

Weekly Check-Ins

Depending on the market, it might take some time to sell your listing. During this period, your sellers will want to know what's happening. A great way to keep them updated is through weekly check-ins. Provide a recap of how many showings occurred (even if there were none), any feedback you received from those showings, how your marketing efforts are progressing, and any suggestions you have for getting the property sold (such as a price adjustment). These updates not only keep the seller informed but also remind them of the hard work you're putting in, which is important as many sellers may start questioning their choice of agent as time passes.

> **TIP:**
>
> I've found that it's best to conduct weekly check-ins via email. This creates a documented record that can be referenced later. It also prevents any details from being forgotten, as might happen with phone calls.

Showing Feedback

Gaining insight into what buyers think after viewing a property is invaluable. This feedback can help you understand why a buyer may or may not be interested in making an offer. You can use this information to adjust your listing in real-time, while also keeping the property on the minds of Realtors whose clients are interested.

To obtain this feedback, you'll often need to request it directly from the Realtor who showed the property. You can do this via email, call, text, or by using a program like ShowingTime.

> **TIP:**
>
> Follow up frequently with Realtors who provide positive feedback (at least once a week). This keeps the property fresh in their minds and allows them to check in with their buyers to gauge ongoing interest.

Once you receive the feedback, it's essential to track it. Consider using a Google Sheet, Google Doc, or another digital tool to organize feedback for each listing.

> **NOTE:**
>
> I strongly recommend personally showing your listings. Many agents rely on lockboxes and allow the buyer's Realtor to handle the showing, but that Realtor won't know the property as well as you do. By being present, you can highlight details that might otherwise be overlooked and get immediate feedback from the buyer and their Realtor, which you can share with your seller.

| Negotiations

Negotiating on behalf of a seller is similar to representing a buyer, with the key difference being that sellers are often more emotionally attached to the property. This personal connection can add a layer of complexity that you'll need to navigate. The best way to handle this is by understanding what's important to your sellers and reminding them why they're selling.

What's Important for Your Sellers

When you present an offer to a seller, they often focus solely on the price. While price is important, there are many other terms that need to be considered as well. For example, is the closing date acceptable? Did the buyers request certain pieces of furniture to be included in the sale?

> **TIP:**
>
> Be sure to read through the entire offer carefully and understand all the terms before presenting it to your sellers.

Walk through each aspect of the offer with your sellers and determine which terms are most important to them and which ones they're flexible on. Knowing what matters most to your sellers will help you prioritize those items in negotiations and allow you to make concessions where necessary to secure the deal.

> **TIP:**
>
> Before discussing an offer with your sellers, review your notes from the listing presentation to remind yourself of any important details they mentioned.

Find the Buyer's Motivation

Buyers don't typically make offers without a clear motivation. Understanding why the buyer is interested in your listing can provide valuable insight and help you negotiate more effectively. The easiest way to find out the buyer's motivation is to speak with the buyer's agent. Ask them what drew the buyer to your listing over others they've seen.

> **TIP:**
>
> When talking to the buyer's agent, ask what terms—besides price—are most important to the buyers. This information can help you secure more favorable terms for your sellers.

Work with the Buyer's Agent

As mentioned in the previous chapter, it's important to view the listing agent as an ally, not an adversary. The same approach applies when you're on the listing side and working with a buyer's agent. Keep in mind that it's not about you or the other agent—it's about your clients and reaching terms that both parties feel good about. Below are the recommendations from the previous chapter that also apply when working with a buyer's agent:

☑ **Be Responsive**
   Promptly respond to calls, emails, and messages from the buyer's agent. This demonstrates your commitment and professionalism.

☑ **Share Information**
   Provide all necessary documents, disclosures, and promptly answer questions from the buyer's agent. This facilitates a smoother negotiation process.

☑ **Collaborate on Solutions**
   If any issues or obstacles arise during negotiations, work together with the buyer's agent to find solutions that satisfy both parties.

> **NOTE:**
>
> Negotiations can be overwhelming, and you're likely to encounter scenarios you're unfamiliar with during your first few years in the industry. I highly recommend seeking advice from your mentor, managing broker, team leader, or a veteran agent you trust. They can help guide you through any challenges that come up.

Once an Offer is Accepted

Once an offer is accepted on the seller's side, the process is similar to that on the buyer's side, but with key differences in how certain milestones are handled.

> **TIP:**
>
> As mentioned in the previous chapter, outside of the inspection, one of the main reasons transactions fall apart is due to poor communication. To prevent this, conduct weekly check-ins with the attorney (if your clients are using one), the title company (if applicable in your state), and the buyer's agent to get updates on the status of the buyer's loan. Choose a consistent day each week to send an email requesting updates. I prefer to include the sellers on these emails to the attorney, ensuring everyone is in the loop and providing a record of communication for future reference. This helps prevent missed deadlines or confusion about the process.

Escrow/Earnest Money

Just like when working with a buyer, after an offer is accepted and all parties have signed the necessary paperwork, the next step is for the buyer to deliver the escrow or earnest money to the entity holding it (whether it's the listing company, a title company, or another third party). This money acts as a deposit, made in good faith to demonstrate that the buyers are serious about purchasing the home. If the transaction proceeds to closing, this money is typically applied toward the buyer's down payment.

The funds are generally refundable if the buyer or seller cancels the sale within the appropriate window of time. The amount of earnest money required varies depending on several factors. Make sure to consult with your mentor, managing broker, team leader, or a veteran agent for guidance on what amount is appropriate and why.

Property Inspection

Although a home inspection is primarily for the buyers, it's beneficial for you, as the listing agent, to attend as well. Not only does this give you an opportunity to learn more about how the property functions, but it also allows you to answer any questions the inspector might have. This can help eliminate concerns and make the report cleaner. For instance, if the primary bedroom has a jet tub and the inspector doesn't know how to operate it, they might report it as non-functional, causing the buyers to request a replacement or financial compensation. However, if you're present, you can contact the sellers to clarify how the tub works, which can alleviate any concerns. The more comfortable the buyers feel about the property, the better the chances of the transaction closing smoothly.

TIP:

To avoid potential issues arising during the home inspection that could jeopardize the sale, consider suggesting a pre-listing inspection for the sellers. This allows them to address any problems before the property goes on the market.

Appraisal

One of the key differences when representing the seller is the involvement in the appraisal process. While buyer's agents typically don't get involved, the listing agent does. When a buyer is financing the purchase, their mortgage lender will order an appraisal. Once the order is placed, the appraiser assigned to the file will contact the listing agent to schedule a day and time to view the property.

NOTE:

The main purpose of an appraisal is to confirm that the agreed-upon purchase price aligns with the market value of the area. Lenders rely on appraisers to ensure they are not financing more than the property is worth, which could lead to financial losses for the lender.

Appraisers often want to see the entire property, both inside and out. They may take measurements and make notes on anything that helps them provide the most accurate evaluation possible.

TIP:

I highly recommend attending the appraisal and bringing at least three comparable properties, along with notes on each. Sharing this information with the appraiser can help them better understand the property's value.

| Final Walk-Through

One common reason a sale can fall apart at the last minute is when the property is not left in the condition the sellers agreed to. This can include not removing all of their belongings, failing to leave the property clean, or not completing the repairs or replacements they promised during the inspection. To ensure the home is ready for the final walk-through, it's a good idea to follow up with the sellers a few days before to confirm they are taking the necessary steps.

Closing

On the listing side, it's common for sellers not to attend the closing. Typically, sellers pre-sign all the closing documents ahead of time, so it's not always necessary for the listing agent to be present. However, if your sellers do plan to attend, I strongly recommend attending as well. Being there shows your clients that you're with them throughout the entire process. Additionally, the closing is an excellent opportunity to ask for referrals—clients may know others who could benefit from your services.

After Closing

As mentioned in the previous chapter, maintaining the relationship with your clients after closing is crucial. Once the paperwork is signed, you go from regular communication to minimal contact, which can cause clients to forget about you—potentially costing you future business.

To keep yourself top of mind with your sellers after closing, add them to your follow-up marketing plan. This could include adding them to your monthly newsletter, your mailing list, following them on social media, and setting a calendar reminder to check in on the anniversary of their closing. A combination of these strategies increases the likelihood they will use your services again and send you referrals.

TIP:

Surround yourself with a reliable team of professionals you can trust, including a mortgage broker, attorney, inspector, contractor, plumber, electrician, structural engineer, accountant, and financial planner. This ensures you can provide clients with trusted referrals throughout the process.

Important to Remember

✔ **Comparative Market Analysis (CMA)**
- Take into account what is currently on the market, what is pending, and what has recently closed.
- Use a market range for the property's value, rather than an exact price, to leave room for negotiation.

✓ Know the Details

- Do your research before the listing presentation:
  - Which school district is it in?
  - Where is the nearest grocery store?
  - Where is the nearest gym?
  - How close is it to public transportation?
  - How close is it to the expressway?
  - Where is the nearest park?

✓ Property Walk-Through

- Two methods:
  - Walk the property without the sellers, viewing it as a buyer would.
  - Have the sellers walk you through the property.

✓ Listing Presentation

- Most sellers interview multiple agents, so your presentation must stand out.
  - Presentation Goals:
  - Set clear expectations about the process and the market.
  - Establish trust and rapport.
  - Showcase your expertise.

- **Presentation Layout:**
  - Build trust and sell yourself.
  - Explain current market conditions.
  - Walk through the costs of selling.
  - Discuss factors that help a property sell.
  - Explain your strategy for getting properties sold.
  - Address additional important details (e.g., length of listing agreements, any upfront fees).

- **Limit Text:**
  - Use only a handful of bullet points and a few images as prompts. Your presentation should be mostly spoken from memory.

- **Paper vs. Tablet:**
  - Printed materials may feel outdated, while a tablet is more modern.
  - Choose based on your audience.

Brutal Honesty

- Point out anything that could affect the sale, such as:
  - Removing personal photos.
  - Reducing oversized furniture.
  - Clearing unnecessary items from kitchen countertops.
  - Ensuring the property is professionally cleaned and stays clean throughout the selling process.
  - Fixing broken items and replacing burnt-out lightbulbs.

Seller Questions

- Prepare a specific list of questions to ask throughout the meeting.Removing personal photos.

Listing Presentation Follow-up

- Send a detailed email recap of your presentation, including any additional important details not covered in your slides.

New Listing Checklist

- Create a checklist of tasks to complete when securing a new listing, ensuring no steps are missed.

Gather ALL Property Information

- Prepare questions to ask your sellers about the property:
  - How old are the furnace and AC units?
  - How old is the roof?
  - How old is the water heater?
  - Have there been any flooding issues?
  - Are there any foundation issues?

Listing Description

- Use the listing description to tell buyers about features that aren't visible in online marketing.
- Highlight finer details that make the home special using keywords to catch a buyer's attention.

Marketing

- According to the National Association of Realtors (N.A.R.), 76% of homebuyers used a mobile or tablet in their home search in 2020, and 97% used the internet.
- **Photos:**
  - The first thing people see; they need to stand out and draw attention.

- **360 Virtual Tour:**
  - Gives potential buyers a virtual walk-through of the property before deciding to see it in person.
- **Social Media:**
  - Post about your listing at different stages:
  - Pre-market it as "coming soon" before going live on the MLS.
  - Announce when it is officially on the market.
  - Promote open houses.
  - Post about price adjustments.
  - Update when an offer is accepted.
  - Celebrate when it closes.
- **Open Houses:**
  - Still a relevant way to market both the listing and yourself.
  - Promote open houses on social media.
- **E-blasts:**
  - Send an e-blast to Realtors who might have buyers for the home before and after listing it.
- **Postcards:**
  - Send postcards to homes in the surrounding area of the listing.

Live on the Market

- Market the property consistently, as promised to the sellers, until it sells.
- **Weekly Check-ins:**
  - Provide sellers with weekly updates.
  - Share feedback, suggest improvements (e.g., price reductions), or refresh the listing if needed.
- **Showing Feedback:**
  - Request feedback from buyer's agents to get their professional opinion and gauge interest.

Negotiations

- **What's Important for Your Sellers:**
  - Besides the price, what other terms in the offer matter to them?
- **Find Buyer's Motivation:**
  - Talk to the buyer's agent to learn why the buyers chose your listing over others.
- **Work with the Buyer's Agent:**
  - Treat the other agent as an ally, not an adversary.
  - Be responsive, share information, and collaborate on solutions.

✅ Once an Offer is Accepted

- **Escrow/Earnest Money:**
  - Delivered once an offer is accepted.
  - Acts as a good faith deposit to show the buyers' commitment to purchasing.
  - Applied to the buyer's down payment if the transaction proceeds.
- **Property Inspection:**
  - The most common point where deals fall apart.
  - A licensed inspector will examine the property for defects and safety hazards.
- **Appraisal:**
  - Required for buyers using financing.
  - The appraiser will contact the listing agent to set a time to view the property.
  - The appraisal ensures that the purchase price aligns with the market value.

✅ Final Walk-Through

- The buyer's last chance to see the home before signing the paperwork, typically right before closing.

✅ Closing

- Typically held at a Title company, where a representative facilitates the process.

✅ After Closing

- Add sellers to your follow-up database for continued marketing and future referrals.

NOTES

Chapter 11
Prospecting

"If I were to hand you a ready, willing, and able buyer who's prepared to spend $60,000, would you take it and work with them?" A heavy silence filled the room. The young man across from me, dressed in a perfectly tailored blue and black checkered suit, white collared shirt, and black tie with a matching pocket square folded into the shape of a rose, looked at me in confusion.

It was my third year running the real estate company, and my new partner and I had been working tirelessly to recruit agents. So far, we had nine agents, including ourselves, but we knew that to survive and grow, we needed many more. Through a combined effort— reaching out to agents, posting ads on LinkedIn, sharing on social media, and relying on word of mouth—we were averaging about one new agent meeting per week.

When the young man walked into my office, his professional attire immediately signaled that he was serious about making real estate his career. After a firm handshake, I gave him a tour of the office. As we made small talk, I could feel his energy and enthusiasm, which left me with a positive impression. He seemed like he could be a great fit for our company. Once we settled into the conference room, sitting across from each other, he told me a little about himself. I explained how we encouraged our agents to build their business and brand without the restrictions of traditional brokerages. As I spoke, I watched his body language and expressions, and my excitement grew. Even though he was new to real estate, it felt like he had the drive and determination to succeed—and wasn't afraid of hard work.

After finishing my pitch, I began explaining what he could expect as a new agent entering the industry and how difficult it is to build a real estate business. I always made sure new agents understood what they were getting into so they could commit comfortably to this lifestyle. I emphasized the importance of gaining as much experience as quickly as possible, which meant working with as many clients as he could.

This led me to ask a question we posed to every new agent we interviewed, to gauge how serious they were about the career—whether they truly wanted to put in the work or just liked the idea of being a Realtor. I asked, "If I were to hand you a ready, willing, and able buyer with a $60,000 budget, would you take it and work with them?"

After a few seconds of silence, his smile faded, replaced by a look of disgust. When he finally processed the question, he responded, "No, I only want to work with million-dollar clients."

Upon hearing that, I ended the interview immediately, telling him we weren't the right fit for each other, and escorted him out.

A year later, my partner looked up the young man's production on the MLS to see how much business he had done. When I asked, "How much did he do?" my partner replied, "None."

Lesson Learned

When I first started my career, I was eager to work with any clients I could. I understood that to survive those crucial first years, I had to take on whatever opportunities came my way—not just to earn money, but to gain as much experience as possible. Most of my early transactions involved helping people find rentals at low price points ($1,000–$2,000) in areas of the city where I didn't always feel comfortable. It wasn't until my third year that I finally closed my first sale—a condo on the south side of the city for $62,500. However, those initial rentals and sales laid the foundation for the success I would later enjoy in my career.

When entering this industry, it's essential to accept as many clients as possible to learn quickly. But there's an art to working with any client who comes your way. To do this successfully, you must understand the range of personalities you'll encounter and how to navigate each one effectively.

| Personalities

In early 2016, I was introduced to a new real estate search site called Truepad (which closed down in 2018). The platform asked Realtors to provide their opinions on properties they toured with buyers to help homebuyers find the best-valued homes. From the moment I used Truepad, I loved it and made it a habit to review every property I toured. The platform also had a ranking system for agents based on how accurately they could predict a property's final sales price. With my frequent use, I quickly became one of the highest-ranked Realtors and was regularly asked for feedback by the site's developers.

As the company grew, they introduced a feature offering buyer leads to agents, and due to my ranking, I was invited to join the pilot program. After successfully closing a few leads, a representative I often spoke with asked if I'd be interested in representing the company's owner, who was looking to buy a condominium in the city. I agreed, and the representative introduced me to Tom (name changed for confidentiality) via email. Within minutes, Tom replied with a short message detailing what he was looking for, when he was available to view properties, and asking me to select listings that fit his criteria as closely as possible.

A week later, I picked up Tom and his wife for our first tour. It was immediately clear that Tom's email was a preview of his no-nonsense approach. During the property viewings, Tom kept everything brief—if he didn't like a place, he'd say so and walk out without hesitation. His wife, on the other hand, was much more patient and considerate. She would linger a bit longer, acknowledging my efforts and the listing agent's time in showing us the property.

After our first day of showings, it was clear that Tom was a Type A personality, while his wife was a Type B. Recognizing that both were involved in the decision-making process, I adjusted my approach to accommodate their contrasting styles. With Tom, I remained direct and efficient. With his wife, I was patient and detailed. Being able to navigate both personalities seamlessly allowed me to help them find a property they both loved.

Understanding a client's personality type and knowing how to work with them is an essential skill that's rarely discussed but plays a crucial role in a Realtor's success. In your career, you'll encounter hundreds of people, each with their own unique traits. Your ability to adapt and respond to each individual's needs will build trust and make clients want to work with you.

Type A — The Go-Getter

Type A individuals are high achievers—competitive, ambitious, and highly organized. They are acutely aware of time and use it efficiently. Type A personalities are proactive and goal-oriented, constantly pushing boundaries and stepping outside their comfort zone. These individuals can often be workaholics, driven by deadlines and an eagerness to help others.

However, Type A individuals tend to experience higher levels of stress and anxiety. They may feel less satisfied in other areas of life, such as health or relationships, and are often status-conscious. Their impatience stems from their high value of time.

Another characteristic is aggression, which can manifest both positively and negatively. Type A individuals may use this drive to achieve their goals, striving to be the best. On the downside, they may sometimes overlook the needs of others. They can be hasty, impulsive, and hyper-alert, often getting frustrated or angry quickly.

Type B — Relaxed and Social

The Type B personality is almost the opposite of Type A. They are relaxed, consistent, and steady, finding enjoyment in the process rather than focusing solely on outcomes. Type B individuals have a calming influence on others and are more peaceful and grounded. It takes a lot to make them angry or frustrated. Less competitive, they value the experience more than winning or losing.

Type B individuals are often more tolerant of others, making them excellent in social situations. They tend to have a rich social life and many friends, finding it easy to relax and have fun with others. Type B personalities are perceptive and sensitive to others' emotions, while remaining emotionally stable themselves. Their patience and empathy make them well-suited for roles such as therapists, writers, or actors.

On the flip side, Type B individuals can procrastinate, often leaving tasks until the last minute. They sometimes need the pressure of a deadline to spur them into action. Their less acute awareness of time can also result in being late for meetings or appointments, and they may struggle to make quick decisions.

Type C — The Rule-Abiding Perfectionist

The Type C personality shares some traits with Type A but with noticeable differences. One key trait is perfectionism. Type C individuals tend to focus on details, often reviewing their work multiple times to ensure accuracy. They place a high value on doing an excellent job. However, unlike Type A, Type C individuals are less aware of time, meaning their quest for perfection can sometimes make tasks take much longer than necessary.

Type C personalities are consistent, reliable, and tend to follow the rules closely. They are ideal in safety-critical roles due to their thoroughness and attention to detail. More introverted than their Type A counterparts, they prefer meaningful conversations with one or two people and shy away from surface-level banter in larger groups. They also avoid conflict, as they value stability and the status quo.

Routine is important to Type C individuals, and they prefer focusing on one task at a time. Any disruption to their routine can cause stress or frustration. They prioritize stability and security, making decisions based on logic rather than emotion. Type C personalities are often deep thinkers.

However, their attention to detail and desire for perfection can sometimes lead to missed deadlines or extended time spent on tasks. They can feel overwhelmed if too much is happening at once and may need time alone to process information. Decision-making can take longer, as they prefer to gather all the facts and details before reaching a conclusion.

Type D — Distressed and Sensitive to Others

The "D" in Type D stands for distressed, and these individuals tend to lean toward negativity. However, Type D personalities also have many positive qualities.

They are warm and peaceful on the outside, with a deep sensitivity to the emotions of others. Type D individuals have a realistic view of life and are generally resilient. They seek security and enjoy helping others, often offering valuable advice. They rarely give up and can be a source of wisdom for those around them.

On the downside, Type D personalities often feel isolated, lonely, and weighed down by negative emotions. Despite experiencing more negativity than other personality types, they tend to suppress their emotions out of fear of rejection, choosing not to share their feelings with others.

Type D individuals frequently worry and may occasionally feel pessimistic or gloomy about life.

| Be Likable

Dwayne Johnson began his wrestling career in 1996 after being cut from the Calgary Stampeders in the Canadian Football League. He made his WWF (World Wrestling Federation) debut the same year, wrestling under the name Rocky Maivia. Over the next year, while winning the Intercontinental Championship, audiences grew increasingly hostile, rejecting his character with chants of "die, Rocky, die" and "Rocky sucks" during his matches.

After returning from a serious knee injury in August 1997, Johnson abandoned the Rocky Maivia name, instead referring to himself in the third person as The Rock. From that point on, The Rock's popularity skyrocketed, and he transitioned from wrestling to acting, becoming one of the highest-paid actors in Hollywood. Leveraging his social media platforms to showcase his infectious personality, he has since become known as one of the most charismatic and likable people on the planet.

People are naturally drawn to those they find likable because likability builds trust and rapport. Being likable can help you win over clients and create raving fans who speak highly of you. Even if you aren't naturally charismatic, there are plenty of ways to become more likable.

Smile

Likability is often synonymous with friendliness, and nothing conveys friendliness like a smile. Your facial expressions speak volumes about your personality and demeanor, so be mindful of them. Smile when appropriate—it will instantly make you seem warmer and more approachable.

> **TIP:**
>
> When meeting someone, smile immediately before saying or doing anything else to make a positive first impression.

Listen

We often get caught up in our own thoughts and don't always pay attention to others' concerns and preferences. In conversation, instead of interrupting or rushing to share your point of view, focus on what the other person is saying. Use it as an opportunity to connect with them.

> **TIP:**
>
> Ask plenty of questions and let the other person share. People tend to enjoy conversations with those who show genuine interest in them.

Find Common Ground

People are naturally attracted to those with similar interests. When meeting someone new, try to find common ground, such as hobbies, sports, movies, books, music, or fashion — anything that can create a connection.

> **TIP:**
>
> Before meeting a client for the first time, look them up on social media to discover common interests you can mention during your meeting.

Mirroring

One of the quickest ways to build rapport is by mirroring the other person's behavior. Mirroring involves subtly mimicking their body language and speech patterns. For example, if your client crosses their legs, do the same. If they speak quickly, pick up your pace to match theirs. This creates a subconscious connection, fostering trust.

> **TIP:**
>
> Pay attention to the specific words the person uses and mirror them. If they say "home" instead of "house," do the same.

Be Authentic

Don't try to be someone you're not. Likable people come from a place of security and confidence in who they are. If others sense that you're being inauthentic, they'll struggle to connect and trust you.

Likability is important. Many of the opportunities in your career will come through other people, and people tend to give opportunities to those they like. Focus on being likable, and people will want to work with you.

> **TIP:**
>
> Use the other person's name frequently in conversation. This personal touch will ensure they remember how you made them feel.

| Ideal Client

In Chapter 3, I discussed how the brain focuses on what we direct it to. For instance, when I pulled up to that six-way stop in my new car and noticed three other cars just like mine, it was because my brain was focused on my car, as I was sitting in it. The same principle applies when identifying the type of clients you want to work with. Once you know exactly who your ideal client is, your brain will start to recognize them more easily in public and help you understand how to attract them.

For example, when I was selling real estate, I knew I wanted to work with people who were close to my age and in a similar stage of life. Understanding the specifics of my ideal client allowed me to tailor my marketing efforts to appeal to them. As a Millennial, I knew that my generation had been in the workforce for a few years and was starting to buy their first homes. Additionally, Millennials were heavy users of Facebook. With this in mind, I posted articles targeted at first-time homebuyers, shared tips about the buying process, and told stories about my clients' experiences. I also tailored my monthly newsletter to include content they would find informative, with a stronger emphasis on buying rather than selling.

Knowing who my ideal client was also helped me identify potential clients more quickly when meeting new people. When I met someone who seemed like a good fit, I would naturally bring up real estate, asking about their current situation and whether they were considering buying in the near future. While I had similar conversations with others, I knew I had a better chance of converting these ideal prospects into clients because my focus and mindset guided me toward that outcome.

NOTE:

While working with your ideal client is preferred, don't neglect other client opportunities that come your way.

Understanding the type of person you want to work with will make it easier to recognize these people in your daily life. However, maintaining a constant stream of clients requires consistent effort.

| A.B.P. (Always Be Prospecting)

During my second year on my second real estate team, I spent almost every day working from Starbucks. Our office was in an area with paid parking, and after racking up over a thousand dollars in parking fees the previous year, I decided it would be smarter to work somewhere with free parking. I had some success picking up rental clients at Starbucks when I first started my career, so I figured the coffee shop would once again provide opportunities to meet people.

My routine was to arrive at Starbucks around 8:00 AM, get settled at a table, and then head to the barista to order my coffee. Most mornings, there wasn't much of a line, so I'd get my coffee quickly (this was before mobile ordering existed). But one March morning, the place was unusually crowded. I had to take a seat by the window, and after setting up, I joined a line of six people, becoming the seventh.

In front of me was a man about my age, with neatly combed light brown hair, wearing a dark gray suit that looked like he had bought it off the rack the day before—clearly not tailored, as it was a bit oversized. He paired the suit with a white dress shirt and a solid red tie. As I observed him, I noticed he pulled out his phone and unlocked it. When he did, I saw he had the Zillow app on his screen. So, I struck up a conversation, asking, "What do you think of the Zillow app?"

We chatted about Zillow as we moved through the line. Eventually, I mentioned I was a Realtor and handed him my business card, telling him to reach out if he was ever in the market (though in hindsight, I should've asked for his information or connected on LinkedIn).

Two weeks later, I received a text from an unfamiliar number, and thinking it was spam, I ignored it. The next time I opened my messaging app, I saw the text again. Before deleting it, I decided to read it—and it turned out to be from the young man I'd met at Starbucks. He mentioned he was considering buying a place and asked if I'd be interested in meeting to discuss the process.

A few days later, we met again at the same Starbucks. After agreeing to work together, we spent the next month viewing properties before he decided on a one-bedroom, one-bath condominium in the building next to the Starbucks where we met. A month later, we closed on the sale. Since then, I've helped him buy and sell five different properties, and he's referred me to several others. Altogether, I've closed over $3 million in real estate sales— all from a simple conversation in line at a Starbucks.

Prospecting isn't just something you do during a designated time each morning; it's something you do all the time, every day. Whether you're in line at the grocery store or watching your kid's soccer game, there's always an opportunity to prospect for new business. Anytime you're in a conversation with someone, no matter where you are, make it a priority to mention you're in real estate.

TIP:

To steer a conversation towards real estate, ask the other person what they do for a living. More often than not, they'll feel obligated to ask you the same, giving you the perfect opportunity to let them know you're a Realtor.

The more opportunities you create for yourself, the more business you'll generate!

| Your Database

In Chapter 8, I went into detail about how to prospect your database and why it's so important. If you don't remember what you read, I highly recommend going back to reread it before proceeding further.

When prospecting your database, there are two key objectives: 1) getting your name and brand embedded in the minds of your contacts so they remember you, and 2) generating business. The first takes time and happens organically, but the second can happen much sooner. The best way to start generating business right away is simply to ask for it.

When marketing to your database, don't hesitate to ask your contacts to reach out if they need your services or to refer you to others who do. Even if they don't need your help at the moment or don't know anyone who does, you're planting the seed for future opportunities. This helps build your pipeline. Calling, texting, or emailing them individually can make this especially effective.

TIP:

In all of my marketing efforts, I always include the line: "If you or anyone you know needs my help, please do not hesitate to reach out!"

Remember, people don't like being sold to, so when asking for business or referrals, avoid being pushy. Otherwise, you risk turning them off.

Social Media

When social media emerged in the early 2000s, it revolutionized the way Realtors could market themselves and connect with a broader audience—for free. This was a stark contrast to how Realtors had to promote their services before. Now, Realtors can not only promote themselves to their contacts but also gain insights into the lives of those people.

One of the main appeals of social media is the ability to stay updated on what's happening in others' lives. People frequently post updates, allowing us to witness their lives unfold—especially when it comes to major life events.

Milestones such as having babies, job promotions, or relocations are often shared on social media. In the past, learning about these events might have taken much longer, whether through word of mouth, mail, or direct communication. Now, we can witness these moments in real time simply by tapping an app and scrolling through our feeds.

For Realtors, these life events present incredible opportunities, as they are often key drivers for buying or selling real estate. Seeing these posts in real time allows you to reach out and offer your services at the perfect moment. Twenty years ago, by the time a Realtor learned about such an event, it might have been too late, with the person already having bought or sold a property. Social media now plays a major role in people's lives, so take advantage of it as a tool to generate business.

NOTE:

I will dive deeper into social media strategies in Chapter 14: Social Media.

Groups

In 2021, some past clients reached out to me about helping them buy a second home in Ft. Lauderdale, Florida. Since I wasn't licensed in Florida, I told them I couldn't assist personally but asked if they'd be open to me referring them to a great agent in the area.

At the time, I didn't know a Realtor in Ft. Lauderdale, but not wanting to miss out on an opportunity for extra income, I set out to find a qualified Realtor to help.

I was part of a few Realtor referral networks on Facebook, so I immediately posted: "Hi everyone, I'm looking for an awesome Realtor in Ft. Lauderdale, Florida to help buyer clients of mine. If you work in the area or know a Realtor who does, please let me know." Within minutes, I received DMs from agents working in the area, and my post lit up with comments from agents offering their services or recommending someone else. After Googling the names I received, I narrowed it down to three agents I thought could be a good fit. I set up calls with all three, and after speaking to them, I found one I really liked. A day later, I introduced my client to the agent, and three months later, I received a referral check for over $5,000.

Referral groups on Facebook and LinkedIn can be great places to generate extra business with minimal effort. Most groups are open to any Realtor, but some require approval to join. To help you get started, here are a few Facebook groups worth considering:

- Lab Coat Agents
- The Real Estate Agent Group
- National Association of Realtors YPN

> **TIP:**
> Make checking these groups a part of your daily office routine.

Referrals also work both ways. Agents in these groups may refer clients moving to your market, so being active and setting up notifications for referral posts is key to getting the most out of these groups.

> **NOTE:**
> I'll dive deeper into how to utilize Realtor referrals in the next chapter.

| Open Houses

In the summer of 2010, I was still struggling to generate business and getting desperate. I had been trying various strategies to drum up clients, but nothing had materialized yet. My database hadn't come around to using me or sending referrals, and the few rentals I'd done came from my cousin. While I appreciated the business from my cousin, I knew I had to find a way to get my own clients.

One day, while sitting in the office, I overheard a veteran agent in a nearby cubicle talking on the phone about a new listing he'd just put on the market. The property was a three-bedroom, two-bath condominium, recently updated and priced at $450,000. As soon as I heard the price, my ears perked up. At that point, I had rarely set foot in a listing at that price, let alone sold one. After he finished his call, I heard him sigh heavily, as if no one was around, and say, "Ugh, I don't want to sit an open house."

A few minutes later, he walked past my cubicle and gave me a half-hearted smile. As he kept walking, I blurted out, "I'll sit the open house." Hearing me, he stopped in his tracks, turned around, and looked at me for a few seconds before saying, "OK." Then, he turned back and kept walking.

That Sunday, I arrived at the listing a few hours early to prepare for my first open house. The night before, I did extensive research on the property and the area, so I could confidently speak to visitors and show I was knowledgeable. I placed the open house directional signs (borrowed from the listing agent) at street corners that would generate the most foot traffic. I spent the rest of the time setting up—putting out marketing materials, preparing the sign-in sheet, turning on all the lights, reviewing my notes, and walking through the property to practice giving a tour.

Over the next few hours, only four groups came through, but I did my best to provide each group with an excellent experience. By the end, I had gathered contact information from two people who didn't have agents, and I planned to follow up with them in hopes of converting them into clients.

Though my first open house had low turnout, I continued sitting at the listing every week until the agent sold it. During that time, I picked up three buyer clients—one of whom purchased a home a few years later.

When you're just starting out, you may not have a listing of your own for a while, but don't let that stop you from sitting open houses for other agents. Most veteran agents are happy to let someone else sit at their open houses because it's a win-win. Their listing gets more exposure, and you get an opportunity to meet potential buyers. Just make sure to choose listings that align with the type of client you want to work with. For example, if your ideal client is a first-time homebuyer looking for a $250,000 home, focus on sitting listings within that price range. You'll need to demonstrate knowledge and experience in that market to win clients. Sitting at high-end properties might make it harder to convince those clients to consider you, as they may expect more experience with luxury listings.

> **TIP:**
>
> Search the MLS for listings that agents in your office have so you know whom to ask about sitting open houses.

Focusing on what will generate business quickly helps you gain experience and build momentum early in your career, leading to greater opportunities later on.

> **TIP:**
>
> Keep an open house kit in your car, stocked with everything you need to host one. Include: blank paper, tape, scissors, permanent markers, pens, business cards, and any marketing materials about yourself.

Realtor Referrals

One day, I was speaking with an agent I had known for a long time. I was introduced to her by my cousin when I first entered the industry, and we had crossed paths many times since. During our conversation, she mentioned that she had stopped actively selling a few years ago and was now earning around $50,000 a year solely from referral fees. While I had sent and received numerous referrals throughout my career, I had never heard of anyone generating that much income from them. Curious, I asked her how she was doing it. She explained that over the course of her career, she had built up a referral network of Realtors across the country. Anytime someone needed a Realtor in Chicago, she would refer them to her partner. If someone contacted her about buying or selling elsewhere, she would introduce them to a Realtor she knew in that city.

Even if you're just starting your career, you can use the same method my colleague did. Earlier in the chapter, I mentioned using Realtor referral groups on social media to generate business. While these groups are useful for finding agents in cities where your clients are moving, you can also use them to build a referral network across the country (or even internationally). Start by making a list of the cities you want to target, and reach out to Realtors in those areas to establish referral partnerships. Most agents are open to this type of arrangement because it benefits both parties. While you may not be able to rely solely on referral income at first, it's still a great way to earn extra income that you might not have otherwise.

> **NOTE:**
> If you work for a nationwide company, you can likely tap into its internal network to find Realtors in any location.

> **NOTE:**
> Referrals are typically paid as a percentage of an agent's commission. For example, if you're referred a buyer with a 25% referral agreement and your commission at closing is $4,000, your office will send the referring agent's office a check for $1,000 (25%). Your commission payout will then be based on the remaining $3,000.

Networking Events

In 2016, I was working in my office on a spring day when I received a call from a friend. He told me he was planning to attend a networking event that evening and asked if I would join him. Although I rarely attended events like these, I could tell from his voice that he really hoped I'd say yes, so I decided to go with him.

The event was being held at the Merchandise Mart, a massive 25-story building along the Chicago River, home to hundreds of companies and a regular host for networking events.

After spending 15 minutes trying to find the room where the event was being held, I finally found my friend waiting for me outside. We walked in together, registered at the front table, put on our name tags, and grabbed a pre-made drink from a nearby table before the emcee called everyone to take their seats.

The guest speaker for the event was reality TV personality and MasterChef Graham Elliot. For the next hour, the moderator asked the Chef various questions about his time on the show, his life afterward, and how he got into the culinary field. Once the Q&A ended, Chef Elliot stepped off the stage and headed to a designated table where he would be signing copies of his book, available for purchase. My friend and I enjoyed what the Chef had to say, but we were more interested in mingling with the fifty or so people in the audience. Over the next hour, we made an effort to speak with as many people as possible.

By the end of the night, I had collected a dozen business cards and a few potential prospects. The next day, I followed up with everyone via email and added them to my CRM. Nine months later, I helped two of the people I met at the event—one bought a property in the city, and the other rented an apartment around the corner from the Merchandise Mart.

Networking events have been around for a long time, and thanks to the internet, it's now easier than ever to connect with a large group of people at once. No matter where you live, there's likely an event nearby. Websites like Meetup.com and Eventbrite.com are full of events happening every day of the week, all year long. These sites are easy to navigate, allowing you to search for events that match your interests, whether business-related or personal.

Preparation is Key

Before attending a networking event, there are a few things to keep in mind to help you maximize your time there:

☑ **Let others do the talking, and you focus on listening**

When engaged in a conversation, make sure you're fully present and paying attention to what the other person is saying.

> **TIP:**
> Ask follow-up questions based on their responses and only interject when necessary.

☑ **Come prepared with interesting stories to tell**

Studies show that people remember stories and the individuals who tell them.

> **TIP:**
> Practice your stories at home to ensure you deliver them with maximum impact.

✓ **Bring plenty of business cards (or use a digital business card app)**

Make it a point to give your card to everyone you speak with and ask for theirs in return.

> **TIP:**
>
> Add everyone you meet to your CRM.

✓ **Send a follow-up email the next morning to everyone you spoke with**

Reintroduce yourself and remind them that you can assist with anything real estate-related.

> **TIP:**
>
> Reference something specific from your conversation to help them remember you.

> **TIP:**
>
> To help remember people's names, make notes in your phone immediately after speaking with them, including their name and key points from the conversation.

Go Solo

When attending networking events, consider going alone. Flying solo allows you to focus on making as many connections as possible without distractions or the temptation to stick with a familiar face. Without a partner, you'll be more motivated to speak to new people and make the most of the event.

Non-Realtor Partner

If you prefer attending with someone, consider bringing a friend who is not a Realtor. Ideally, you want to be the only Realtor in the room to avoid competition for potential clients. Choose someone who is great at starting conversations and engaging with people. Once inside, split up the room—each of you working a different side. Set a specific time and place to meet later to share who you've met. This way, you can strategize about who you should connect with and avoid wasting time by covering the same ground. Having a shared connection (your partner) can also help ease the conversation with new people.

Cold Calling

When I was running my brokerage, I had a veteran agent who was a skilled Realtor but never stuck with anything he started. Every time we spoke, he was trying something new, hoping he'd strike gold eventually. One day, I arrived at the office around 9:30 AM and found the agent sitting in the conference room. It was clear he'd been there for a while—his laptop was set up, his notepad open, papers scattered across the table, and a large cup of iced coffee half-finished. When he saw me, I walked over and asked what he was up to.

He told me he was cold calling for sale by owners, expired listings, and canceled listings. Over the next five minutes, he walked me through his plan, showed me his scripts and rebuttals, and shared his daily goals. After hearing all this, I told him that if he was serious about cold calling, he'd need to commit to doing it consistently to achieve the results he hoped for. He assured me he would, so I wished him good luck and went to my office.

For the next two weeks, the agent came in every morning, following the same routine. He would set up and start calling at 8:30 AM, continuing until 10:30 AM. At the end of week two, I checked in with him, and he said he had made a few connections and booked one listing appointment. Although he was disappointed that he hadn't gotten more appointments, I encouraged him to keep going, reminding him that seeing some results was better than none.

By week three, he came in Monday through Wednesday and Friday but skipped Thursday. In week four, he showed up two days, in week five just one, and by week six, he had stopped coming in altogether. The next time I saw him, I asked why he stopped cold calling. He said it wasn't working, so he was going to try something else.

I know plenty of agents who have built very successful businesses through cold calling. It's an excellent way to prospect for new business—if you know what you're doing and, most importantly, if you're fully committed to doing it. Commitment is key because cold calling is a numbers game. The more people you call, the better your chances of generating business. As my agent learned, it's not something you can do for a short time and expect consistent results.

If you decide to cold call, aim to do it at least five days a week for a few hours and give it time—at least six months—before deciding whether or not to continue. The high level of commitment required to be successful at cold calling isn't for everyone. Before you dive in, speak with Realtors who cold call regularly and do your research.

NOTE:

There are laws regarding whom you can call and the methods you can use. Before making any calls, ensure you understand and comply with state and federal regulations.

| Door Knocking

In August of 2022, I was invited to be part of a panel discussion at a major real estate company's broker-owner retreat in Austin, Texas. The organizers asked us to share insights on how we built and managed our brokerages. On the morning of the discussion, I arrived at the conference a little early to meet the other panelists and chat with some of the attendees.

Shortly before 10 AM, the moderator called me and the other three panelists to the stage. For the next hour, we discussed various topics, from recruiting agents to the tools we used to streamline our businesses.

Near the end of the discussion, an attendee asked what advice we would give to an agent who had just moved to a new area and needed to build their business from scratch. The first panelist recommended speaking with agents in their new office to learn about the market and doing independent research. The second panelist suggested using social media to tap into local Facebook Groups to introduce themselves. When it was my turn, I said, "Go door knocking."

Seeing the surprise on the faces of the audience, I explained that an agent in a new area—or a new agent entering the market—has no brand awareness and may not know anyone. To compete with established agents, they'll need to do something those agents aren't doing. Since door knocking is no longer common, it gives agents a chance to get their name out quickly and build personal relationships with local residents.

Done properly, door knocking is still an effective way to generate business, though few agents invest time in it. The key to success is planning, preparation, and consistency. Here are a few steps to follow if you decide to door knock:

- **Find a neighborhood** you want to work in, ideally one with a few hundred houses.
- **Print a map of the area** using Google Maps, showing all the houses. Use this map as your guide to track which houses you've visited and the outcomes. For example, if someone answered the door, mark a check. If no one answered, mark an X. If you got a lead, you could use a smiley face, and if they weren't interested, a frowny face. Create a key for yourself to stay organized.
- **Research the area** and know your statistics, such as average market times, sales prices, and the list-to-sale price ratio.
- **Create and print marketing materials** to hand out to anyone who answers the door.
- **Print door hangers** to leave at houses where no one answers.

> **TIP:**
> Have a simple script ready for anyone who opens the door. It should capture their attention and make them want to continue the conversation with you.

Farming

My cousin lives in a 340-unit condominium building that spans an entire city block in Chicago's West Loop neighborhood. She's lived there for as long as I can remember, and I'd been to the massive building many times before joining her team.

Whenever I visited, she would introduce me to people who lived in the building. Whether we were in the elevator or walking down the hall, my cousin seemed to know everyone. I never thought much of it until I joined her team and started asking how she knew so many people. I understood she had lived there for a long time, but the building was so large that I couldn't comprehend how so many people knew her.

She explained that for years, she had a plastic flier holder in the lobby with her branding on it, containing a back-to-back market summary. One side featured recent sales in the building, units that had accepted offers, and those still available, while the other side contained information about her. She also sent monthly postcards to every unit, using various marketing strategies such as comparing renting versus buying in the building. Additionally, she and her partner were highly involved in the building, running the recycling drive, helping plan holiday events, and serving on the building's board, which manages important decisions for maintenance and operations. Through these efforts, she became the go-to Realtor in the building, responsible for the majority of the sales there.

Farming, like working your database, aims to create name (or brand) recognition among the people you market to so they think of you for all their real estate needs. The difference is that with farming, you're targeting a concentrated area such as a neighborhood or a large building. To farm effectively, it takes more than just sending a few postcards and hoping for business. It requires a combined effort of various strategies, as my cousin demonstrated. While farming takes time and patience, when done properly, it can pay off.

| Consistency

In my fourth year in the industry, I began working with buyer clients after primarily handling rental clients. It had been four years since the 2009 crash, and the market was starting to recover. Traditional buyers—those purchasing with mortgages—were returning to the market. Earlier that year, I picked up two buyers: one directly from my database and the other a referral.

I had recently gotten an offer accepted for one of the buyers and was about to do the same for the other. Although they weren't high-priced deals, I felt my business was finally turning a corner. One day, as I sat in my office, a real estate coach I knew walked in and asked how I was doing. Trying not to sound too excited, I told her I was about to get my second offer accepted and was close to having all my clients under contract. I expected her to congratulate me and boost my ego, but instead, she looked at me and said, "Good. Now go get more clients," and walked away.

Stunned by her response, I sat at my computer, processing what had just happened. After a few minutes, I understood the lesson she was trying to teach me: getting a few offers was no reason to stop. I needed to keep prospecting because prospecting never stops.

Being consistent starts with your schedule. Block out time every day to dedicate to prospecting—whether it's 30 minutes, an hour, or however much time you can commit. Then, decide what activities you'll do each day, such as calling your database, following up with leads, or sending out your monthly newsletter. Also, find ways to remind yourself to keep prospecting outside of your dedicated time. For example, one year when I was selling, I set my phone wallpaper to say "PROSPECT ALWAYS!" in white lettering on a black background. Seeing that every day helped me keep prospecting top of mind.

There are many ways to prospect, and the trick is to find what you enjoy doing and commit to it. Real estate, like any sales job, is a contact sport. The more people you contact, the better your chances of generating business. The best way to do this is to be consistent and prospect every day.

❚ The First 100 Days

When I was running my brokerage, my partner and I focused much of our recruiting efforts on new agents. We understood that it would take time for these agents to start generating income for the company, but we were confident that the education and mentorship we provided would help them become successful Realtors quickly. As part of joining us, each agent was required to complete our six-week mentorship program, which was designed to kickstart their business while also creating opportunities for growth.

As we launched the program, many new agents expressed feeling overwhelmed by everything they had to do when starting their real estate careers. They often felt there wasn't enough time to focus on generating business amidst all the setup tasks. This prompted us to dig deeper to understand the challenges they were facing. What we found was that the initial phase—setting up their business, acclimating to the brokerage, and trying to learn as much as possible—was a lot to handle. This left little room for prospecting or business development.

Knowing firsthand how critical the first 100 days are for a Realtor, we spoke with each agent about prioritizing tasks so they wouldn't fall behind on prospecting from day one. By putting things in perspective, they were able to shift their focus to the most important tasks.

The first 100 days of your career are crucial in laying the foundation for future success. While it's important to get tasks like headshots and email signatures done, these shouldn't take precedence over the activities that will help you learn and generate business.

Instead, prioritize tasks such as:
- Building your database
- Developing a marketing plan for your database
- Creating new connections
- Utilizing social media to build brand awareness
- Sitting at open houses
- Shadowing experienced agents
- Attending networking events

The rest of the tasks can be done in your free time, after you've focused on the activities that will directly impact your growth.

Important to Remember

Personalities

- **Type A:** High achievers, competitive, ambitious, and organized.
- **Type B:** Relaxed, consistent, and steady.
- **Type C:** Similar to Type A but with a focus on perfectionism.
- **Type D:** Can lean towards negativity but are warm, peaceful, and sensitive to others' emotions.

Be Likable

- People gravitate towards likable individuals because they build trust and rapport.
- **Smile:** A smile communicates friendliness and approachability.
- **Listen:** Focus on others' words and use them as a connection point.
- **Find Common Ground:** People are drawn to those with shared interests.
- **Mirroring:** Mimic the other person's body language and speech patterns.
- **Be Authentic:** Likable people come from a place of security, not insecurity.

Ideal Client

- Knowing the type of client you want to work with helps you attract them, but consistent effort is needed to maintain and grow your client base.

A.B.P (Always Be Prospecting)

- Prospecting should be an ongoing activity, not confined to a specific time of day.

Your Database

- Prospecting your database is both effective and easy to generate business.

Social Media

- People often post major life events (babies, jobs, relocations). Use these as opportunities to offer your services.

Groups

- Utilize referral groups on platforms like Facebook and LinkedIn to generate business with minimal effort.

Open Houses

- Sit open houses for other agents if you don't have your own listings to capture unrepresented buyers.

Realtor Referrals

- Build a referral network across the country (or world) to tap into when needed.

✓ Networking Events

- Get in front of a large group of people.
- **Preparation is Key:**
    - Let others do the talking and focus on listening.
    - Come prepared with interesting stories.
    - Carry plenty of business cards or use a digital business card app.
    - Follow up with an email the next morning to everyone you met.
- **Go Solo:** Maximize connections by attending alone to avoid distractions.
- **Non-Realtor Partner:** If attending with someone, bring a non-Realtor and work different areas of the room.

✓ Cold Calling

- Cold calling requires regular effort and at least six months to assess its effectiveness.

✓ Door Knocking

- Success in door knocking comes from planning, preparation, and consistency.

✓ Farming

- Marketing to a specific area or building through multiple strategies to create brand recognition as the go-to Realtor.

✓ Consistency

- Start by creating a daily schedule dedicated to prospecting.

✓ The First 100 Days

- The first 100 days are crucial for setting up long-term success. Focus on:
    - Building your database
    - Developing a marketing plan
    - Creating new connections
    - Leveraging social media to create brand awareness
    - Sitting open houses
    - Shadowing experienced agents
    - Attending networking events

NOTES

Chapter 12
Leads

In early 2016, I was sitting in my office working when my phone started buzzing on the table beside me. Glancing at the caller ID, I saw it was a Realtor friend I hadn't spoken to in a while. I answered, and after a few minutes of catching up, he told me that he had recently started investing in certain zip codes on Zillow and was getting around five to ten leads a week. Having just left a team that did the same, I assumed he was calling for advice or to get my opinion on something, but that wasn't the case.

He explained that over the past few days, he had been receiving leads at a higher price point (around $400,000) and only wanted to focus on those. He didn't want to waste time on lower-priced leads and asked if I was interested in one he had received for a buyer looking at properties around $75,000. Although the price point was lower, I agreed to take the lead and see what I could do. A few minutes after our call, I received an email from him with the lead's information.

I immediately called the number, but no one answered, so I left a voicemail and followed up with a text and email. A few hours later, having heard nothing back, I tried again, but still no response. I kept following up over the next few days, eventually spacing out my attempts so it wouldn't seem like I was spamming them. After my sixth attempt, I started to think they weren't interested and decided I'd just add them to my monthly newsletter in hopes of connecting later. Then, a few days later, I received a text from a random number. I checked it, and it was the lead. They apologized for not responding sooner, explaining that they'd had a family emergency and were now ready to talk. We texted back and forth a few more times and scheduled a meeting for a few days later.

When I met Alex (name changed for confidentiality), he wasn't what I had expected. I had assumed I'd be meeting a young first-time homebuyer, but instead, Alex was an older gentleman looking to buy an investment property with his retirement funds so that his son could live in it and pay rent to him. We spoke for over an hour, and by the end of our conversation, Alex had a clear idea of what to expect from the buying process, and I had a better understanding of what he was looking for.

With a budget of around $75,000, Alex didn't have many options, but I found him a condominium in the south suburbs that was exactly what he and his son were looking for. Since then, Alex has purchased five other rental properties with my help, and his son has also bought his first home through me. Altogether, they have purchased over $3,500,000 worth of real estate with me.

Lesson Learned

It's easy to want to disregard leads that aren't at higher price points, no matter where they come from. The idea of working with someone and not being well-compensated for your efforts can be hard to accept. However, you never know where one connection might lead. I've spoken to many leads who initially started searching at lower price points, only to end up closing on properties much higher in value. I've also worked with clients who bought at a lower price initially, but over time, purchased and sold multiple properties with me—often at higher price points—while also referring me to others.

I've met many Realtors who refuse to engage with leads below a certain price point. Fortunately, their reluctance creates opportunities for those willing to take on these leads.

TIP:

To generate more business, ask veteran Realtors if you can work with any lower-priced leads they receive, in exchange for a referral fee. Just be sure that you retain the client after closing.

Never make assumptions based on the search price you see on third-party sites. Often, that price doesn't reflect what the client is truly comfortable spending. Instead, have a conversation with the lead to discover their real preferences before drawing any conclusions.

At the same time, don't expect people to respond the first time you contact them. Nowadays, most people won't answer or respond to unfamiliar numbers or people they don't know. That's why it's essential to follow up multiple times and have a plan in place to do so.

If I had told my friend I wasn't interested in the lead or had stopped following up after a few attempts, I never would have met Alex and would have missed out on thousands of dollars in income.

▎ What is a Lead?

When I started my career, I didn't see a real lead for two years. I was working as part of my cousin's team, and any lead I received was one of her clients she had me assist. The first time I was introduced to an actual lead was when I took my first lead shift at my second brokerage.

After my cousin and I joined the new office, I signed up for the first available lead shift three days later, from 4:00–8:00 PM on a Friday night. I arrived at the office a few hours before my shift to work on other tasks, including meeting with my Managing Broker about what I should be doing during the shift. Finally, at 3:59 PM, I sat down at the designated computer, set everything up, and logged into the system. The system was designed to notify me with a pop-up whenever a lead was added to my contact list. For the next five minutes, I sat with my phone in hand, ready to make a call, but no leads came in. Thinking something might be wrong with the program, I refreshed the screen, but still didn't see any new contacts. This pattern continued for the next hour and a half as I repeatedly refreshed the screen, hoping to magically make a lead appear.

I had envisioned names pouring into my contact list, but the reality was the exact opposite. As 6:00 PM approached, I started to feel like I would never receive a lead. Finally, I got a notification. I immediately clicked on the pop-up, which brought me to the lead's information. The name read "Johnny Doe," the phone number was 123-456-7890, and the email was "notinterested@aol.com." After laughing to myself at the fake information, I lowered my expectations for the rest of the evening. By the end of my shift, I had received seven legitimate leads. Although I wasn't able to get in touch with any of them, I was excited to have seven new people to follow up with.

A real estate lead (also called a prospect) is someone who has shown interest in buying, leasing, or investing in a property and is typically not working with a Realtor but might be open to representation. Depending on where the lead comes from (a third-party site, company site, referral, or someone who found you online), these individuals usually provide some basic information—name, email, phone number, and occasionally, details about what they are looking for.

| Warm vs. Cold

There are two types of leads you need to be aware of: warm leads and cold leads. Both can generate business, but they are very different.

Warm Leads

Warm leads are people you know (or who know you), such as individuals in your database, family, friends, or past colleagues. Since these people are familiar with you, they are more likely to use your services or refer you to others. Warm leads are much easier to convert into clients because they already trust you.

Cold Leads

On the flip side, a cold lead is someone you don't know. These leads typically come from sources such as your company, third-party sites, or advertising you do. Since these individuals don't know you, it takes much more effort to convince them to use your services.

TIP:

To generate business faster, focus most of your efforts on generating warm leads.

Sources of Leads

One summer, later in my career, I attended a mixer hosted by my association's YPN (Young Professional Network). I had been going to these events almost every year since entering the industry because they're a great way to establish new relationships while strengthening existing ones.

TIP:

Don't talk about yourself at events—make the conversation about the other person by asking questions and actively listening to what they say.

While waiting at the bar to be served, I struck up a conversation with a woman who was also waiting. We made small talk about how long it was taking, and after introducing ourselves, we started discussing the market and how the year was going. She mentioned having a great start to the year, so I asked where she was getting her clients from. Expecting the usual responses (past clients, referrals, social media, etc.), I was completely surprised when she told me that most of her clients come from waiting in line for the women's bathroom. She explained that women's bathroom lines are typically long, so she starts conversations with the women around her. By the time they reach the bathroom, she's established a rapport and gets their information to add to her CRM.

Leads can come from anywhere—even places you might never think of—but there are a few common sources, each with its own positives and negatives.

Database

Your database is the best lead source available because these are people who know and trust you. While it may consist mostly of friends and family at first, as you add past clients to it, referrals will significantly increase.

The Positives and Negatives of Database Leads	
Positives	**Negatives**
✔ Warm leads	✔ Family and friends might not want to use you due to knowing their financial situation*
✔ Easier to convert	
✔ Flexible spending—achieve results with minimal investment	✔ It might take time to see results while building brand recognition
✔ More likely to give you opportunities early in your career	✔ More pressure to perform since you know them personally

*Family and friends will typically refer you, even if they don't feel comfortable using your services themselves.

Referral Programs

Referral programs generate leads through programs that do the work for you. Sites like Redfin, Realtor.com, and Referral Exchange offer agents leads in exchange for a percentage of their commission upon closing. There are many referral sites to choose from, including niche ones like Gay Realty Network and Homes for Heroes. A Google search will show you available programs to consider.

The Positives and Negatives of Referral Programs	
Positives	**Negatives**
☑ Typically no upfront costs	☑ Usually take 30% or more of your commission as a referral fee
☑ Leads are sent with no effort on your part	☑ Reliant on the program rather than your own efforts
☑ Many programs allow customization of the types of leads you receive	☑ Cold leads, harder to convert
	☑ Usually require experience to be eligible to sign up

Company-Generated Leads

Some companies offer opportunities for agents to receive leads, which may come from the company website, walk-ins, or call-ins. These leads are typically distributed through a round-robin system.

The Positives and Negatives of Company-Generated Leads	
Positives	**Negatives**
☑ No upfront costs	☑ Takes a larger percentage of your commission than your standard split with the company
☑ Leads are sent with no effort on your part	☑ Cold leads, harder to convert
☑ Leads are exclusively yours to work	☑ No control over the type of lead you receive

Third-Party Sites

When consumers search for properties online, they are typically drawn to the most common sites (Zillow.com, Realtor.com, Homes.com). These sites have invested billions of dollars into their platforms to encourage frequent use. In return, they offer Realtors the chance to pay for "impressions" in specific zip codes, which sends the agent leads when a consumer searching in that zip code clicks on the site's numerous call-to-action buttons.

NOTE:

Paying for leads on third-party sites can be very expensive, so make sure to do thorough research before committing any money.

The Positives and Negatives of Third Party Leads	
Positives	**Negatives**
✅ Leads are sent with no effort on your end	✅ Expensive
✅ You can typically select the zip codes from which to receive leads	✅ Cold leads, harder to convert
	✅ Leads may be sent to multiple agents simultaneously
✅ Highly searched sites generate more leads	✅ Lower-quality leads

TIP:

Partner with a or other industry professional to help cover some of the costs.

Social Media

When your friends and followers see your posts regularly, it can prompt them to DM (direct message) you with real estate questions or inquiries about entering the market. These messages can turn into clients. Since people spend over two hours on social media daily, the more you post, the more likely it is that people will reach out to you.

TIP:

Social media leads are organic, not from paid advertising.

The Positives and Negatives of Social Media Leads	
Positives	**Negatives**
✅ Free	✅ Requires a lot of effort
✅ Warm leads	✅ Results may take time while building brand recognition
✅ Easier to convert	
✅ Almost everyone is on social media	✅ More pressure to perform since you know the leads personally

Advertising

Paying for ads remains relevant, even in our changing world. While traditional ads like those in newspapers or on bus benches are less effective, platforms like Facebook, Instagram,

YouTube, and Google offer powerful alternatives. A well-crafted ad campaign can quickly get your brand in front of more people.

The Positives and Negatives of Advertising Leads	
Positives	**Negatives**
✓ Can reach a larger audience	✓ Expensive
✓ Can target ads to specific types of clients	✓ Cold leads, harder to convert
✓ Analytics allow for adjustments to campaigns	✓ Lower-quality leads

Cold Calling

While people are often reluctant to answer calls from unfamiliar numbers, cold calling still has a place in lead generation. Many successful Realtors continue to use cold calling as their primary method for acquiring new clients. If done consistently and properly, it can yield significant results.

The Positives and Negatives of Cold Calling Leads	
Positives	**Negatives**
✓ Direct communication with potential clients	✓ Expensive if purchasing a cold calling program
✓ Can target specific demographics or geographic areas	✓ Cold leads, harder to convert
✓ Cold calling program analytics allow for adjustments to calling strategies	✓ Leads are typically contacted by multiple agents

Anywhere

Leads are not restricted to the sources mentioned above—anyone you meet, anywhere, can be a lead. Whether it's standing in line for the women's bathroom or chatting at a backyard BBQ, anyone you talk to can potentially turn into a client.

The Positives and Negatives of Cold Calling Leads	
Positives	**Negatives**
✓ Unlimited number of leads available	✓ No consistency
✓ In person contact	✓ Requires you to be proactive at all times
✓ Easier to convert in person	✓ Most people are not ready to buy or sell when you meet them

Focus on Getting the Meeting

After sitting a few lead shifts, I began accumulating a long list of leads in my contacts. My routine was to call the person right away, follow up the next day, and then let the automated follow-up system in the program continue reaching out. One of the most common types of leads I received was people asking for more information on a property. When these inquiries came in, I'd call the lead, and if someone answered, I'd reference the property address and ask how I could help. Most were just curious about the property, but some were interested in seeing it.

At that stage in my career, I was not yet skilled at converting leads. Eager to set up showings, I would schedule them in the hopes that if the lead showed up (many didn't), I could convince them to work with me. It wasn't until later that I realized this was not the best approach.

When you haven't established a relationship before showing a property, you're just someone opening a door. The lead is focused on the property, not you. Instead, your goal should always be to set up a meeting with the lead as soon as possible. The quicker you secure a meeting, the better your chances of converting them into a client.

> **NOTE:**
> According to NAR, 71% of buyers interviewed only one real estate agent during their home search.[1]

This is because the meeting is where the real sale happens. Many Realtors think they sell real estate for a living, but what they're actually selling is themselves. Anytime an agent meets with a lead, they're essentially trying to convince that person to choose them over other agents in the market.

Before showing a property to a lead, ask them to meet you somewhere first, so you can walk them through the buying process and answer any questions they have. After you've established a relationship, then show the property. If a lead is serious about buying, they will be open to meeting with you.

> **TIP:**
> Do not show the property first and then attempt to meet afterward. Once the showing is over, there's a strong chance they will cancel the meeting.

Time Matters

In my first month on my second team, the team leader began sending me leads he received from paying for impressions on third-party sites. His method was to forward me the emails he received from one of the sites he was investing in. The emails contained the information the consumer provided when filling out the site's form, along with details about the property or properties they were inquiring about.

The first few leads I received were mostly junk—people had entered fake information. For the few real leads I did receive, I couldn't get any response. After a week of this, I was frustrated with how the leads had turned out. So, when I saw an email notification pop up on my phone while I was at lunch, I decided to finish my meal before calling them back. About 20 minutes later, I dialed the lead's number, and to my surprise, the person answered. After introducing myself, I asked how I could help. They thanked me for the call but said they had already spoken to a Realtor 20 minutes earlier and planned to meet with them the next day. They added that if things didn't work out with that agent, they would reach out to me.

Bummed but not overly concerned, I set a reminder to check in with the buyer in a week. When I followed up, they told me they had seen several places with the other agent the previous weekend and had their offer accepted on a $450,000 house on the northwest side of the city. This time, when the call ended, I was devastated, knowing I had lost out on a potential $11,000 commission. From that moment, I vowed never to delay following up with a lead again.

Throughout my career, I've had to leave many events to follow up immediately with a lead. I've walked out of hockey games, baseball games, football games, family parties, movies, dinners with friends, dinners with my wife, family time at the zoo, and family time at museums, just to name a few. Knowing that most buyers will only interview one agent, being the first to contact them is vital. Even though consumers are less likely to answer calls from unknown numbers, some still do—and missing that opportunity isn't worth the risk.

| Ask Questions

My partner and I spent a lot of time ensuring people could find our brokerage when searching for real estate online. One of the main things we did was optimize our Google Business profile so that when people searched for Chicago real estate, we would appear near the top of the results. As a result, we received one to two leads a week, which we always passed on to our agents.

One of the agents I mentored was new and just getting his business off the ground. We met virtually every Friday to review his week, discuss different aspects of his business, and tackle any challenges he faced. One week, I sent him an online lead early in the week and asked him to work it. When we met a few days later, I asked how it went. He told me he had spoken to the lead but wasn't able to set up a meeting and didn't know what the lead was looking for. Hearing this, I asked him what questions he had asked during the conversation. He said he had asked if the person was working with an agent, and when they said no, he asked what their price point was. From there, the conversation fizzled out, and he never followed up.

What my agent did is common among new agents who aren't yet familiar with how to speak to a lead. When you talk to a lead, you need to build rapport as quickly as possible. The best way to do this is by asking questions—not just about the property they're looking for, but about themselves as well. The goal is to get them to share as much as possible so they feel comfortable with you and are more likely to meet with you. By starting with a price point question, my agent unintentionally gave the impression that he was only concerned about money rather than the person. While knowing someone's price range is important, it's a question that should come later—after you've established rapport and have a clearer understanding of what they're looking to buy.

TIP:

Start by asking personal questions to establish common ground with the lead. For example, "Have you lived in (your city) long?" or "What do you like about the city?"

| Have a Follow-Up Plan

In my first week with my second team, the team leader showed me his system for following up with leads and suggested I follow it as well. He was having a lot of success with it, so I decided to implement his approach. The system was simple: when I received a lead, I would call them immediately. If I couldn't reach them, I would leave a voicemail, send a text, and send an email. If I hadn't heard back after a few hours, I'd repeat the process. I would then follow up once a day with a call, text, and email for the next two days. If I still hadn't made contact after day three, I would discard the lead. Using this follow-up plan, I converted around 12% of the leads I received.

NOTE:

When I was receiving leads, the sites we invested in (Zillow, Trulia, Homes.com) were just gaining momentum, and the leads were much stronger and cheaper than they are today.

About halfway through my third year with the team, I noticed it was becoming harder to get responses from leads compared to the past. After some research, I found that consumer habits had changed. People were more aware of spam calls and messages, making them more likely to ignore my calls and delete my texts and emails. At the same time, I also discovered that 80% of Realtors, just like me, stopped following up on a lead after only three days. This statistic made me realize there was a huge opportunity for any Realtor willing to keep following up.

I decided to develop a more strategic plan that extended well beyond three days. The new plan involved significantly more follow-ups (15 total) spread over 75 days. As a result, my conversion rate increased from 12% to 24.8%, which equated to four or five additional transactions per year.

> **NOTE:**
> I only considered a lead "converted" if they met with me.

In today's world, people receive between 65–80 notifications on their devices each day. Getting their attention isn't easy. The only way to do it is by having a follow-up plan that includes numerous touchpoints and executing it consistently.

> **TIP:**
> When creating your follow-up plan, provide value to the leads you're following up with. Offer them something they can't easily find on a third-party site to demonstrate your expertise and capture their attention. For example, you could mention a new park being planned near a property they're interested in.

| Tracking

The first month I extended my follow-up efforts beyond three days, I realized that keeping track of all my follow-ups was becoming more challenging. Previously, when I only had to do three follow-ups, I was able to track everything using a simple Google Document. I had a table with four columns: one for the lead's information and three others for the dates I followed up with them. This system worked at the beginning of my new method, but as I started handling five to ten leads at a time, fitting everything into three columns no longer made sense. I knew I needed a better way to track leads, so I created a Google Sheet with my entire follow-up program laid out, along with a section for lead information. Once I did that, I never had an issue again.

Tracking leads is vital to understanding how your follow-up system is performing. When you implement your follow-up plan, make sure you also have a method for tracking it. Whether it's a spreadsheet or your CRM, analyze the data regularly and make adjustments as needed to improve your response and conversion rates.

| Never Let Go!

On a Wednesday in early February 2016, I was sitting in a large ballroom, listening to a presentation about the current state of the housing market. I was surrounded by Realtors, mortgage professionals, and attorneys, all paying close attention in hopes of gathering insights to share with their clients. About a quarter of the way through the event, I noticed an email notification pop up on my phone. The sender's name looked familiar.

February 4th, 2016, 10:46 AM
From: Steve XXXXXXX
Subject: Can You Help Us Buy a Condo?

Hi Mike, I doubt you remember me. You contacted me a few years ago when I was looking at properties on Zillow. My wife and I were just browsing at the time and weren't serious about buying. I've been receiving your monthly newsletters for a while now and was wondering if you'd be interested in helping us buy our first home.

Hope to hear from you soon!

Steve and Mary XXXXXXX
Steve: 312.XXX.XXXX

Sent from my iPhone

After reading the email, I quickly maneuvered past the three people blocking my row and exited through the large double doors. Once I was in the hallway, I immediately dialed Steve's number, hoping to catch him before he walked away from his phone. On the fourth ring, Steve answered. Over the next five minutes, we chatted briefly about his wife and current situation and set up a time to meet a few days later to discuss things in more detail.

Two days later, I met Steve and Mary on a cloudy afternoon at a Starbucks in Chicago's River North neighborhood. After some small talk, I pulled out my iPad and walked them through my buyer's presentation. They listened attentively as I spoke about my credentials, the buying process, associated costs, and other important details. Once I finished, I answered a few of their questions, and we discussed what they were looking for in a property. They had been renting but had saved enough for a downpayment and were now looking to purchase a two-bedroom, two-bath condominium in the city. I took notes in my iPad's notes app, asking questions to further refine what they were seeking.

After our meeting, I connected them with a mortgage lender I trusted so they could get pre-approved before we began the property search. Seven weeks later, they closed on their new home. Since then, Steve and Mary have bought and sold two additional properties with me and referred three of their friends and family members.

When I first received Steve's initial lead notification from Zillow years prior, I did what most agents know to do: I called him right away. He didn't answer, so I also texted and emailed him. I repeated this process for several days, but he never responded to any of my attempts. Realizing he likely wasn't ready to buy, I stopped calling and texting—but I made sure to add him to my monthly newsletter, so he would continue hearing from me. This simple act turned out to be a key factor in acquiring one of my best clients.

Whenever I couldn't get a hold of a lead, I would always add them to my monthly newsletter so they would continue to receive updates from me. From my experience, when someone clicks something on a third-party site, they may not be ready to buy or sell right away. However, that doesn't mean they won't be ready in the future. It just might not be the right time at that moment. Adding leads to my newsletter has generated millions in sales for me over the course of my career. So, make sure you do the same—or have another plan in place to ensure you never let a lead go.

| Timelines Do Not Matter

In my second year at my second brokerage, I didn't have any appointments set up for a Saturday morning, so I signed up to sit a leads shift from 8 AM to 12 PM. When I arrived at the office, I saw an agent I had never met before sitting at the second leads computer. I introduced myself and took my seat at the first computer. For the next two hours, not many leads came in for either of us. Sitting for so long with nothing to do was starting to wear on me, and I was beginning to zone out when I heard the other agent's voice. He was on the phone, introducing himself to a lead he had just received. Curious about how he handled leads, I listened in, hoping to pick up a few tips.

The agent spoke with the lead for a couple of minutes until he learned that the lead wasn't planning to buy for at least another year or two. As soon as he heard this, his tone changed completely, and he seemed to lose interest. He asked the lead to hold on for a moment, rolled back in his chair, and popped his head over the divider between us to ask if I wanted the lead. I was surprised he would give it up so quickly, but I didn't question him and said yes. He told the lead he had another agent who could help them and handed me the phone. I spoke with the lead for a few minutes, and we set up a meeting for the following week.

> ## NOTE:
> It doesn't matter if a lead is looking to buy or sell now or in the future—always try to set up a meeting with them immediately to establish a relationship, so when they are ready, they choose you.

I met with the lead and his wife a week later. I walked them through my buyer's presentation and learned more about what they were looking for at that time. They weren't ready to buy yet because they had just signed a new lease, but they believed they would be ready when the lease expired the following year. After our meeting, I added them to my database and continued to follow up with them monthly. When their lease was up 12 months later, they decided they still weren't ready to buy and signed another year-long lease. Nine months after renewing their lease, they told me they were finally ready, and three months later, we closed on a three-bedroom, two-and-a-half-bath townhome on the north side of Chicago.

If the other agent had kept the lead, he could have had clients who eventually bought, sold their townhome five years later to upgrade to a more expensive home, purchased an investment property, and even bought a summer home in another state—potentially generating a referral commission.

It is rare to speak with a lead who is ready to buy or sell immediately. Most leads tend to have longer timelines, but that is no reason to discard them. Instead, add them to your database and follow up with them regularly. You never know when they will be ready to buy, and as you do this with more leads, you will build a pipeline of future business that will pay off as your career progresses.

Important to Remember

✔ What is a Lead?

A real estate lead (also called a prospect) is a person who has shown interest in buying, leasing, or investing in a property. Typically, they are not currently working with a Realtor but might be open to being represented.

✔ Be Likable

- **Warm Leads:** Warm leads are people you know (or who know you), such as those in your database, family, friends, or past colleagues.

- **Cold Leads:** A cold lead is someone you do not know. These leads usually come from sources like your company, third-party sites, or advertising.

✔ Sources of Leads

- **Database:** Your database is the best lead source available because these are people who know and trust you, making them warm leads.

- **Referral Programs:** Sites like Redfin, Realtor.com, and Referral Exchange generate leads for agents who agree to give up a portion of their commission once the lead closes.

- **Company-Generated:** Leads provided by your brokerage.

- **Third-Party Sites:** Platforms like Zillow.com, Realtor.com, and Homes.com allow agents to spend money on "impressions" in specific zip codes, generating leads when a consumer takes an action.

- **Social Media:** Regular posts on social media can entice friends and followers to direct message you when they have real estate questions or are considering entering the market.

- **Advertising:** Advertising on platforms such as Facebook, Instagram, YouTube, or Google can help generate leads.

- **Cold Calling:** Calling potential clients (For Sale By Owners, Expired and Canceled Listings) to offer your services.

- **Anywhere:** A lead can come from anywhere—be mindful that anyone you speak to could potentially become a client.

✔ Focus on Getting the Meeting

Realtors may think they sell real estate, but in reality, they sell themselves. The meeting is where the real sale happens.

✔ Time Matters

Most buyers and sellers will only interview one agent, so being the first to contact them is crucial. This often means stopping everything you're doing to respond quickly.

✅ Ask Questions

Asking questions about both the person and their property needs is the best way to build rapport quickly with a lead. The goal is to get them to share as much information as possible so that, when you meet, you are prepared to sell them on your services.

✅ Have a Follow-Up Plan

In today's world, people receive between 65–80 notifications on their devices daily. To capture their attention, you need a detailed follow-up plan with multiple touchpoints, and you must execute that plan consistently.

✅ Tracking

Tracking your leads is essential for understanding how your follow-up system is working. Use a spreadsheet or CRM to track leads, and analyze the data regularly to make necessary adjustments that can increase your response and conversion rates.

✅ Never Let Go!

If a lead doesn't respond, don't discard them. Add them to your database and follow up with them regularly.

✅ Timelines Do Not Matter

It's rare that a lead will be ready to buy or sell immediately. Most leads have longer timelines, but that's no reason to discard them. Add them to your database and continue following up regularly.

NOTES

Chapter 13
Branding

I could feel the occasional chilly breeze on my exposed legs as I stood on the porch of a west-side two-unit graystone building, waiting for my cousin's buyers to arrive. A wave of discomfort washed over me, and I tried to ignore it by focusing on the trees across the street, their leaves just beginning to change colors. This worked for a few seconds, but each time a breeze blew by, the unease returned. Trying to distract myself further, I glanced at the listing information sheet in my hand, reading over the details to familiarize myself with the property I was about to show. This was my first showing, but my discomfort had little to do with that. Instead, my mind was fixated on what I was wearing.

Coming from corporate America, I was used to wearing a dress shirt, slacks, and formal shoes every day, as my company mandated "business attire." The dress code was an unspoken hierarchy: the higher-ups always wore tailored suits with perfectly pressed shirts that looked fresh from the dry cleaner. Managers dressed in slacks and long-sleeve collared shirts, which appeared to have been ironed at home. Then, there were workers at my level—most of us wore khakis with a mix of long-sleeve shirts or polos, often wrinkled, likely worn a few times between washes.

The office itself was a mix of different groups, each run by a manager with their own interpretation of the dress code. Unfortunately, my group took it as seriously as a Catholic school uniform policy. I had been reprimanded more than once for having my shirt untucked. The only reprieve came on casual Fridays, designed to boost morale. Even then, though I could wear jeans, I still had to tuck in my dress shirt, which always felt awkward. As a result, I rarely participated in the "morale-boosting" attire change.

Now, in my new career, standing in front of a $300,000 property, I was seriously second-guessing my choice of outfit. Taking cues from my cousin's typical attire, I had decided to wear khaki cargo shorts, an untucked dark orange polo, and dark brown leather flip-flops that morning. As I stood there, I caught a glimpse of my reflection in the glass front door. My eyes trailed down to my exposed legs and feet, and I didn't feel right.

Just then, out of the corner of my eye, I noticed a black Mercedes pull up in front of the property, snapping me back to reality. Turning around, I took a deep breath, preparing to greet the buyers, all the while trying to ignore the nagging thought that I looked more suited for a beach bar than for a real estate showing.

Lesson Learned

When I joined my cousin's team, I had no idea what I was supposed to wear. There isn't a formal dress code for Realtors, so, not knowing any better, I followed her lead and dressed the way she did. At the time, it made sense to me since I was on her team. What I didn't understand then was that how my cousin dressed was part of who she is and her brand. Having been a Realtor long before I came around, she had built her business by being herself, and her clients understood and accepted this.

It didn't take me long to realize that while my cousin's brand was perfect for her, it wasn't for me. That day on the steps of the two-unit property taught me that I needed to be myself, not someone else. From that day forward, I made sure to dress in what I considered a more professional way, which allowed me to feel comfortable.

Everything you do is a direct reflection of your brand, so make sure what people see (and hear) is exactly how you want your brand to be perceived.

Before I explain how to build a brand, it's important to first understand what a brand is and why having one is essential.

❙ What is a Brand?

In 1983, Howard Schultz was on a business trip to Milan, Italy, when he walked into an Italian coffeehouse. He was immediately struck by how different it was compared to where he got coffee back in the States. He noticed how it was designed for people to relax, to be a place that wasn't home or work. He also saw that the menu offered a wide variety of coffee drinks—cappuccinos, macchiatos, caffè lattes, espressos—along with gourmet food items like croissants and pastries. Lastly, he recognized that the person taking his order wasn't just a cashier but an artist, with their canvas being a porcelain cup and their paint, roasted beans steeped in hot water.

When Schultz returned to Seattle, Washington, he decided to use this new understanding of Italian coffeehouses to transform his coffee bean shop into what we know today as Starbucks.

When you think of Starbucks, what comes to mind? Is it just a place to get coffee? You can get coffee anywhere, so why do people spend more for a cup at Starbucks when they could get the same thing at Dunkin'? It's because Starbucks is much more than just a place to get coffee. When people walk into a Starbucks, they experience a relaxed ambiance, they see others studying or working, they notice the extensive list of specialty drinks behind the counter, and they are greeted by friendly baristas—not just cashiers. The Starbucks brand encompasses all of these elements, which is why over 10 million people visit its 35,000+ locations daily.

When most people think of a brand, they typically focus on a logo or its colors, but these are just a few aspects of a brand. A brand goes much deeper. It is the distinct set of feelings, perceptions, attitudes, and associations people have when they think about a person or company. It is every element of a person or company, wrapped together and positioned in people's minds—for better or worse. In other words, a brand is a personality, and how people view that personality will dictate whether they trust and engage with it.

| Why Building Your Brand is Important

In 2019, the film studio 20th Century Fox released Ford vs Ferrari, starring Matt Damon and Christian Bale. The movie tells the story of the battle between the two car manufacturers to win the famous 24 Hours of Le Mans race in the mid-1960s. Ferrari, widely regarded as one of the top manufacturers of the time, had won the race four of the last five years, and Ford was determined to build a race car from scratch to dethrone them.

Early in the movie, there's a scene at the Ford company headquarters where the President, Henry Ford II, played by Tracy Letts, listens to a pitch from the head of marketing, Lee Iacocca, played by Jon Bernthal. Iacocca tries to explain that Ford needs to think differently—they need to think like Ferrari. Upon hearing the pitch, Executive Vice President Leo Beebe, played by Josh Lucas, laughs and says, "Ferrari makes fewer cars in a year than we make in a day. We spend more on toilet paper than they do on their entire output." Iacocca immediately responds, stating that Enzo Ferrari, the President of Ferrari, will go down as the greatest car manufacturer of all time because of what his cars stand for, not because of how many they make. Iacocca adds that Ferrari wins at Le Mans, and people want a piece of that victory.

This scene is important to the plot but also highlights the power of the Ferrari brand at the time. Ferrari was seen as more than just another car company. Their success on the racetrack made their cars highly desirable for the affluent, with Ferraris viewed as works of art. The iconic prancing horse logo became synonymous with success. Despite producing only 300+ cars for sale, Ferrari's cars sold for significantly more than most others, including Ford.

Today, the Ferrari brand is considered one of the most recognizable, desirable, and trusted brands in the world. Ferrari cars represent a lifestyle that millions aspire to but is out of reach for the average consumer due to the high price tag. Even with more competition and prices now in the millions, Ferrari continues to dominate as one of the top-selling luxury brands globally, with annual revenues in the billions.

In 2024, The Wall Street Journal summed up Ferrari's reputation: "Ferrari has been synonymous with opulence, meticulous craftsmanship, and ridiculously fast cars for nearly a century."

While you may not be selling high-end cars, you are selling yourself—your brand. Every time you meet with a buyer or seller, you're trying to convince them to choose your services over the many other Realtors in the market. Having a brand that people trust will help you win more business because clients will know what kind of service to expect when working with you. Additionally, strong brand recognition will lead to repeat business and referrals, ultimately increasing your sales and income. Finally, when you're ready to expand, having a recognizable brand will help you recruit talented individuals and retain them—both of which are crucial for building a successful team.

Builds Trust

Established in 2004, The RepTrak Company owns the world's largest reputation benchmarking database, collecting over 1 million company ratings annually. These ratings are used by CEOs, boards, and executives in more than 60 countries worldwide. Each year, RepTrak releases its ranking of the 100 most reputable brands in the world.

To narrow down to the top 100, the Boston-based data analysis firm polls more than 50,000 people from the world's 15 largest economies. For a company to qualify, it must have a global revenue of over $2 billion, break a familiarity threshold of 20%, and achieve a reputation score—factoring in elements like products and services, innovation, workplace, governance, citizenship, leadership, and financial performance—above the median score of 67.3.

In 2021, Global RepTrak released its top 100. Leading the pack was toymaker Lego Group, with a high score of 80.4. Lego was followed closely by Rolex, which scored 79.6, and Ferrari, which came in at 78.8.[1]

People trust Ferrari because of its performance, prestige, design, heritage, and collectability. This trust draws people to the brand globally. Buyers know exactly what they're investing in and understand that the millions they spend are worth every penny.

When you work with clients, you are building trust. The effort you put into helping them and the guidance you provide will leave them with a positive (or negative) perception of you and your brand. This trust is what will lead them to refer you to others and return to you in the future. Similarly, when people search for you online, they'll see your positive reviews and know that you are someone trustworthy to contact.

Generates Revenue

Returning to the Ford vs Ferrari movie reference in the introduction of this section, when Lee Iacocca says, "people want some of that victory," he's referring to consumers who buy Ford vehicles. His next line, "Now, what if the Ford badge meant victory? And meant it where it counts: with the first group of seventeen-year-olds in history with money in their pockets?" is meant to explain to Mr. Ford that winning on the racetrack would result in sales for Ford with the next generation of car buyers.

This idea was rooted in Ferrari's success. Their dominance on the track led consumers to associate Ferrari with winning, driving up the desire to own a Ferrari. Iacocca had the same vision for Ford—he understood that if Ford could win Le Mans, the brand would become more desirable, leading to increased sales and revenue.

It's easy to assume that Ferrari's revenue comes mostly from selling cars, but that's only part of the picture. Today, a significant portion of their revenue comes from merchandise. Ferrari generates around $4 billion in annual revenue, with $2 billion of that coming from merchandise. Their products range from model cars, branded caps, and flags to high-end luxury fashion items, such as a $4,000 leather trench coat.

As mentioned earlier, when you have a brand that people know and trust, it becomes easier for them to refer your business and continue using your services. Both of these activities are key drivers of revenue for a Realtor. The more referrals and repeat business you receive, the more revenue you generate. This also applies to people searching for a Realtor online—when they find your profile, the first thing they'll check is your reviews. Once they see that you are a highly-reviewed agent, they'll be more likely to reach out, resulting in even more revenue for you.

| How to Build Your Brand

In 1962, former University of Oregon track-and-field athlete Phil Knight, in search of a better running shoe, toured the Onitsuka (now Asics) factory in Japan. He was impressed by the company's quality and efficient production. This trip led to a deal for Knight to distribute the Onitsuka Tiger, the company's signature shoe, in the United States. After a few years, however, Knight believed he could design a better shoe than the one he was selling. In 1964, he and his University of Oregon track-and-field coach, Bill Bowerman, founded Blue Ribbon Sports and created their version of the Onitsuka Tiger—the iconic Tiger Cortez in 1967.

The shoe was a success, and the company, now turning a profit, began to expand. Around the same time, the relationship with the Japanese company began to deteriorate, eventually leading to a split. This separation convinced Knight that it was time to rebrand his company, and in 1971, Nike was born.

With continued growth over the next few years, Nike was ready to take the next big step. In 1976, they hired John Brown and Partners as their first advertising agency. The following year, the agency created the "There is no finish line" campaign. By 1980, Nike had captured 50% of the U.S. athletic shoe market, and the company went public in December of that year.

Unfortunately, the next four years saw Nike struggle. In 1984, in an attempt to revitalize its floundering basketball shoe division, Nike made a bold move: they spent their entire marketing budget to sign NBA rookie Michael Jordan. Jordan signed a five-year, $2.5 million contract to promote the Air Jordan, a black-and-red basketball shoe that initially sold for $65 (equivalent to $192 in 2023). Within the first two months of the shoe's release, Nike sold $70 million worth of Air Jordans. By the end of 1985, Nike reported revenues in excess of $100 million.

Since then, the Nike brand has grown into one of the most recognizable in the world. Their philosophy of aligning the brand with athletes, rather than just their products, has solidified Nike in the minds of consumers. At the same time, the company has never lost sight of its core values as an athletic brand—not a fashion company.

Building a brand is much more than designing a logo. It's about fully understanding who you are and what you stand for. Once you've grasped this, all the other components of your brand will naturally complement it.

Who Are You?

In his last semester of business school, Phil Knight wrote a paper titled, "Can Japanese Sports Shoes Do to German Sports Shoes What Japanese Cameras Did to German Cameras?" Knight spent weeks on the assignment, essentially moving into the school library and devouring everything he could find about importing, exporting, and starting a company. What began as a simple paper turned into an all-out obsession. Yet, it didn't immediately lead him to create Nike.

After graduating from business school at 24, Phil Knight didn't want to take the conventional route of working for a major corporation. He wanted to create something of his own. As a former runner for the University of Oregon track and field team, he knew running was central to his identity, so he decided to focus on the most important equipment for a runner: shoes.

Fifty years later, although Nike has expanded into apparel, equipment, and accessories, shoes remain at the core of its business. The desire to create the best shoes for athletes is still the company's main focus. This authenticity—staying true to its values—is what makes Nike one of the most recognizable brands on the planet.

When you begin creating your brand, first ask yourself: Who are you? What are the things that make you, you? What is your identity? It's crucial to understand this before doing anything else, as your brand will be a direct reflection of you. In today's world, people seek authenticity. They can easily spot a fake, and once they do, they'll no longer want to associate with that brand. By being authentic, you'll avoid the trap of trying to be something you're not. Just as Nike never strayed from its core values, you should stay true to yours when building your brand.

Once you have a clear understanding of your brand's identity, the next step is designing the attributes that people will see and associate with it.

Colors

When I was running my brokerage, one of my agents asked for help with her branding. She had recently completed our mentorship program and was struggling to put everything we'd discussed about branding into practice. When we met, I had her tell me more about herself so we could identify her brand identity. Then, we moved on to the color she wanted to use for her brand.

The agent explained that her favorite color was hot pink, and she wanted it to be the primary color of her brand. Knowing that hot pink is not a traditional color in Realtor marketing, I suggested that before making a final decision, she should spend some time applying the color to everything she planned to use for branding (social media posts, postcards, business cards, property flyers, etc.) to see if she liked how it looked.

A week later, we met again, and her opinion had changed. She explained that while hot pink looked good on some materials, it didn't work as well on others. Specifically, she mentioned that it clashed with items that included a lot of brown—common in real estate marketing (roofs, bushes, trees, siding, etc.). As a result, she decided that hot pink wasn't the right choice. Instead, she chose a light shade of red, which she felt worked well across all her future marketing materials.

> **TIP:**
> Before deciding on a brand color, apply it to everything you plan to use for branding to ensure it looks good across all platforms.

When choosing your brand's color, it's ideal to stick with one primary color. This keeps things simple and ensures your branding remains consistent.

> **NOTE:**
> If you want more than one color, a secondary color is okay, but try to limit your palette to no more than two colors.

For most of its history, Nike has used red and white as its main brand colors, and many of the world's most popular brands keep their color schemes simple as well. For example, Apple's logo is chrome, Tesla's logo is red, Netflix's name is red, and Spotify's logo is bright green.

To create brand awareness (more on this later in the chapter), your branding needs to be consistent. Make sure you choose a color that not only works but also represents you.

Fonts

Fonts are often overlooked when designing a brand. We see them everywhere, but we don't usually stop to think about which font is being used. However, fonts play a significant role in shaping a brand's identity. If you study successful brands, you'll notice they typically use one or two fonts for everything. For instance, Nike uses a modified version of Futura Bold Condensed Oblique for its logo and Nero Ultra Wide Display for branding, packaging, posters, social media, and titles. Apple uses a modified version of the Myriad font called Myriad Set in all its marketing materials.

The reason these brands use the same one or two fonts is for consistency (I'll touch more on consistency later in this chapter). By using the same fonts across all platforms, they increase the chances of consumers remembering their brand because of the familiarity created through repetition.

Fonts should be simple and easy to read. You want people to be able to understand them without any effort. This means you should choose fonts that are clear and straightforward, not overly stylized. Just like with your color choices, test your font on your future marketing materials—your email signature, property details on a flyer, and social media posts. See what looks best and use that font consistently across everything you do.

> **NOTE:**
> Aim for one primary font. If you prefer to use more, choose a primary font for your main branding elements (such as your name and logo) and a secondary font for marketing materials (like property details on a flyer). The website www.dafont.com offers a wide variety of free fonts for download.

Logos

After founding Nike, Phil Knight needed a logo to match the company's name. He was adamant that it should be simple, fluid, and convey motion and speed. Nike reached out to Carolyn Davidson, a design student at Portland State University, to create sketches. Over the following weeks, Davidson presented several options to Knight and two other executives. They ultimately chose the design now recognized worldwide as the Swoosh, inspired by the wings of the Greek goddess Nike.

Nike officially trademarked the logo on June 18, 1971. By June 1972, at the U.S. Track and Field Olympic Trials in Eugene, Oregon, Nike's first official track shoe, the Nike Cortez, was released, sporting the new Swoosh. Today, it is one of the most recognizable and valuable logos in the world, worth over $100 billion.

Having a logo is not a necessity, but it's something I highly recommend. A logo helps consumers identify you; it's a symbol people will use to recognize your brand. Since your logo represents you, it's best to have it professionally designed to ensure it embodies everything your brand stands for.

> **NOTE:**
> A common mistake I see is agents feeling they need to tie real estate imagery into their logos—using houses or keys often makes the logo look forced. The best logos I've seen are simple, sometimes just using an agent's initials in a clever way. When thinking about your logo, start by experimenting with your initials. Also, make sure to incorporate your brand's color and font.

While designing the branding meeting for my brokerage's mentorship program, I needed a way to explain logo simplicity. Reflecting on all the Nike Swooshes I doodled in high school, I coined the term "doodable"—meaning something that can be easily drawn by anyone. The Nike Swoosh is the perfect example of a doodable logo. Even someone with no graphic design skills, like me, can draw it.

Your logo should be simple enough that people can remember it quickly. The human brain consumes over 34GB of information daily, and our minds aren't wired to process complex information accurately. The more complicated your logo is, the less likely people will remember it!

Slogans

In the 1980s, as fitness trends swept the U.S., Reebok, one of Nike's main competitors, focused its campaigns on aerobics. In response, Nike launched what it called a "tough, take-no-prisoners ad campaign." The goal was to appeal to all Americans, regardless of age, gender, or fitness level. Nike wanted to position its sneakers as fashion statements, not just fitness gear, so they hired the advertising firm Wieden+Kennedy to craft a slogan that was both "universal and intensely personal."

At a 1988 agency meeting, co-founder Dan Wieden introduced the slogan "Just Do It," which he credits as being inspired by death row inmate Gary Gilmore's last words: "Let's do it."

The Just Do It campaign launched in 1988 across various media—merchandise, billboards, print ads, and even graffiti art. The campaign was a huge success, using diverse ethnicities, races, and notable athletes to make Nike relatable to both everyday consumers and professional athletes. The slogan helped associate Nike with success, sportsmanship, and achievement, and consumers began linking their purchases with the prospect of achieving greatness.

Though a slogan isn't necessary, it can make your brand more memorable and open up additional marketing opportunities, just as it did for Nike.

Just like your other brand elements, your slogan should be simple. Try to limit it to just a few words that clearly convey your brand's essence. Too many words complicate the message and clutter your marketing materials. For example, when I opened my brokerage, my partner came up with the slogan: "An agent-centric real estate company with full marketing and commission autonomy." While it described our brokerage well, it was long and didn't look good on any of our marketing materials. After my partner left, I simplified it to: "A Brokerage Without Limitations." The new slogan captured the same idea in seven fewer words and fit perfectly across all our materials.

When designing your slogan, keep it concise and direct. Anyone reading it should immediately understand what your brand represents.

> **TIP:**
>
> Test your slogan on friends or colleagues to get honest feedback. If they don't understand what your brand represents after reading it, rework it until they do.

Consistency

Going back to the Nike Swoosh—since its introduction in 1972, Nike has consistently featured the logo in all of its advertising. Whether it's on a billboard, in a TV commercial, a social media ad, or something they sponsor, the Swoosh is always present. The logo is also displayed on every product Nike creates. This consistency has established Nike as a familiar and trusted brand, known for delivering high quality.

Nike isn't the only company to prioritize consistency for brand recognition. Apple, Tesla, and Louis Vuitton also make a point of displaying their logos prominently on everything they produce and in all their marketing. These companies know they need to get their brand in front of as many people as possible, as often as possible, and they do so consistently.

As a Realtor, competition for clients is fierce. Most markets are saturated with hundreds, if not thousands, of agents all competing for the same clients. Your branding is essential to setting yourself apart, and consistency is how you stay top-of-mind with consumers.

> **TIP:**
>
> All aspects of your brand need to work together to have the greatest impact. Your marketing, social media, and even smaller details like your email signature should be consistent with your branding. The more often people see the same message from you, the better the chance they'll remember it and reach out when they need your services.

▌ Creating Brand Awareness

In 2003, American entrepreneurs Martin Eberhard and Marc Tarpenning set out to develop an electric sports car. Eberhard stated that he wanted to build "a car manufacturer that is also a technology company," with its core technologies being "the battery, the computer software, and the proprietary motor." To undertake such a massive endeavor, they needed funding to bring their vision to life. In February 2004, the company raised $7.5 million (equivalent to $12 million in 2023), including $6.5 million (equivalent to $10 million in 2023) from Elon Musk, who had received $100 million after selling his interest in PayPal two years earlier. Musk quickly became chairman of the board and the largest shareholder of Tesla.

Tesla's strategy was to begin with a premium sports car aimed at early adopters and then expand into more mainstream vehicles, including sedans and affordable compacts.

However, they were entering a crowded, well-established industry with a new and unconventional product. By 2008, when Tesla Motors released its first car—the all-electric Roadster—the only other notable electric vehicle on the market was the Toyota Prius, which had been released in 2000. While the Prius found some success, it could not match the dominance of gas-powered cars. Tesla's challenge was convincing the public that electric cars could compete with and even surpass gas cars in performance and efficiency.

By January 2009, Tesla had delivered 147 cars, and after Eberhard and Tarpenning stepped down, Musk became CEO. Under Musk's leadership, Tesla experienced explosive growth with the introduction of new vehicles, the expansion to other countries, and the development of additional products. What many people don't realize is that Tesla achieved this without spending anything on traditional marketing. In fact, 2023 was the first year the company paid for marketing.

So, how did Tesla build such massive brand awareness without traditional advertising? While having an eccentric CEO with a massive social media following certainly helped, Tesla's success came from more than just tweets. They focused on word-of-mouth marketing, telling a compelling story about the company and its benefits, and leveraging social media to highlight their products and events. These efforts have paid off, positioning Tesla as the go-to brand when people think of electric cars. Today, Tesla is worth over $500 billion and produces nearly 2 million cars annually.

Just as Tesla entered a crowded market, so are you. You're competing with countless other Realtors in your area, all striving to be the first name that comes to mind when people think about real estate. This is no small feat when you consider how much branding we're exposed to every day. According to speaker and bestselling author Grant Cardone, we encounter over 10,000 pieces of branding daily. From the clothes we wear to the cars we drive, branding is everywhere, making it challenging for smaller brands to capture attention.

However, the modern world offers numerous opportunities to create brand awareness without breaking the bank. It requires effort and time, but it's entirely possible to establish yourself as the Realtor people think of first.

Word-of-Mouth

As I mentioned earlier, Tesla didn't spend any money on marketing until 2023, yet it still grew to become one of the largest companies in the world. Instead, Tesla focused on creating a strong community of passionate customers and turning them into brand ambassadors by providing excellent user support. This led to a large community of people who would speak on the company's behalf through word-of-mouth. Tesla also used a referral system for years to spread the word, offering prizes to owners who referred others and incentivizing them to share their vehicle purchase decisions openly.

I experienced this firsthand in 2017 when a friend of mine leased a Model S and took me for a ride. During the drive, I got a 30-minute sales pitch from my friend while experiencing an amazing product. After that, I was sold.

Word-of-mouth marketing is one of the most powerful forms of marketing because it's grounded in trust. Unlike traditional advertising, which is often met with skepticism, recommendations from friends or family carry personal credibility. Research shows that people are significantly more likely to use a service when referred by someone they trust.

To be successful in generating word-of-mouth marketing, authenticity is key. It's about building genuine relationships and providing exceptional service that stands out. You need to offer an experience that clients are naturally willing to talk about when real estate comes up in conversation. By doing so, your clients become your advocates, spreading the word to their networks.

Word-of-mouth is more than just a marketing tactic—it's a crucial part of a comprehensive marketing strategy in the digital era. It's something you need to focus on to generate business.

TIP:

After closing a deal with a client, ask them to share their experience with you on social media and tag you, or ask them to post their recommendation on third-party sites like Zillow or Realtor.com.

Tell Your Story

Tesla's journey from a small electric car manufacturer to a global leader in sustainable energy is a testament to the power of strategic storytelling. The company has effectively used narratives to engage with its audience and shape its brand image, selling a vision of a cleaner, more sustainable future.

One of the key aspects of Tesla's storytelling strategy is its consistent emphasis on innovation. Each product launch or major development is accompanied by a compelling narrative that goes beyond technical specifications. Tesla doesn't just introduce a new car; it tells a story of progress, sustainability, and a commitment to pushing the boundaries of what's possible. This storytelling has earned Tesla a loyal following that eagerly anticipates each new innovation, driving the company's growth.

Brand storytelling is crucial because it helps evoke emotions within your audience and establishes a connection. Consumers want to build relationships and engage with brands. A good storytelling strategy allows you to foster a sense of community with your audience, humanizing your brand and helping to build more authentic connections.

Storytelling can set you apart from competitors and make you more memorable, which in turn helps convert your audience into clients. By sharing your journey, you allow people to relate to and connect with you on a personal level. This connection builds trust, which can lead to referrals and repeat business. Sharing stories that are relatable, inspiring, and consistent helps your brand create lasting relationships with your audience.

> **NOTE:**
> It's important to communicate your brand values through storytelling so that your customers can recognize and resonate with them.

Social Media

Tesla's social media success has played a vital role in building a global community of electric vehicle enthusiasts and renewable energy advocates. By sharing engaging content, highlighting user-generated stories, and promoting sustainability initiatives, Tesla has created a loyal fan base that actively participates in online discussions and shares the company's vision for a cleaner future.

Part of Tesla's social media strategy includes posting educational content to connect with its target audience. For example, in a March 9, 2023, post on Instagram, Tesla highlighted the evolution of its iconic Falcon Wing doors, using a "before and after" theme to show the journey of innovation—from the initial concept to the sleek design used today. At the same time, the company utilized YouTube to engage viewers through long-form, informative content. These videos give people a closer look at Tesla's innovative products and features, as well as behind-the-scenes glimpses into the company's operations.

Tesla's commitment to social media as a primary marketing strategy has reduced its reliance on traditional advertising while establishing a more direct line of communication with its audience. This approach has fostered trust and transparency—essential components for building strong customer relationships.

Social media should be one of the primary tools you use to market yourself. These platforms allow you to spread your message to an unlimited number of people for free, making them a crucial part of your marketing plan.

> **NOTE:**
> I'll go into more detail about how to leverage social media for your business in the next chapter.

Marketing

In 2023, General Motors spent $3.6 billion on global advertising and promotions, which translates to $580 in spending for each of the more than 6 million cars the company sold.[2] In contrast, Tesla spent $6.4 million on ads in 2023—an enormous leap from the $0 spent the previous year, but still a fraction of what other carmakers invest. Although Elon Musk has repeatedly expressed his dislike for traditional advertising, he acknowledged that market conditions sometimes dictate a change in approach. Due to slower sales, Musk authorized the marketing department to allocate money for ads on platforms like YouTube, Facebook, Instagram, and X.

Despite this shift, Tesla stayed true to its core principles. Consistent with its prior approach to "marketing," the paid ads continued to focus on building an emotional connection with the audience and strengthening the company's brand presence. There's no doubt that a well-strategized marketing campaign can benefit your brand. The key is to ensure you're spending wisely. As a newer Realtor, you may not have a large marketing budget, so it's important to allocate your funds where they will have the most impact. One common mistake Realtors make is spending their entire marketing budget on social media ads, thinking it will fast-track their business. Unfortunately, the small amounts they can allocate are often overshadowed by the millions of dollars big companies spend, leaving their ads buried and ineffective.

If you decide to spend money on marketing, focus on targeting your existing database. These are the people most likely to hire and refer you because they already know and trust you. In other words, they are "low-hanging fruit"—warmer leads compared to cold Facebook or Instagram prospects who may only click on an ad because it caught their eye.

Once you've built your brand and started spreading the word, the last—and most important—task is to protect it.

| Protect It

On October 2, 1996, at the age of 25, Lance Armstrong was diagnosed with stage three (advanced) testicular cancer. The cancer had spread to his lymph nodes, lungs, brain, and abdomen. On October 3, in an Austin, Texas hospital, Armstrong underwent surgery to remove the diseased testicle. When his doctor was later asked in an interview what he thought Armstrong's chances of survival were, he said, "Almost none," though he had told Armstrong at the time that his chances were 20 to 50%—mainly to give him hope.

After his surgery, Armstrong decided to continue treatment at Indiana University Medical Center in Indianapolis. The standard treatment for his cancer was a "cocktail" of drugs and chemotherapy. Following further treatments and surgery, Armstrong completed his final chemotherapy session on December 13, 1996, and by February 1997, he was declared cancer-free.

On July 25, 1999, Armstrong became the second American to win the Tour de France, cycling's most prestigious race, and the first to win for an American team. He would go on to win the race a record seven consecutive times.

Throughout his career, Armstrong had been accused of doping multiple times, but he consistently denied the allegations. Various tests cleared him of any wrongdoing, and he maintained his innocence. However, in April 2010, his teammate Floyd Landis sent an email to a USA Cycling official, admitting that he and other former teammates—including Armstrong—were guilty of doping. The following month, a U.S. federal grand jury investigation into Armstrong's doping allegations began. The U.S. Anti-Doping Agency (USADA) later revealed damaging evidence against Armstrong, and in January 2013, during a televised interview with Oprah Winfrey, Armstrong admitted to using performance-enhancing drugs from the mid-1990s through 2005.

Before Armstrong's admission, he was viewed as an American hero, someone who had overcome incredible odds to triumph. People rallied around his story and invested in his charitable foundation, Livestrong. But after his interview with Oprah, his narrative changed forever, and he is now remembered differently in the public's mind.

When Armstrong was winning the Tour de France, his brand was something people wanted to be associated with. He was frequently interviewed on TV and even made cameos in films, such as the 2004 comedy Dodgeball: A True Underdog Story. However, everything changed after his doping admission. His brand took a massive hit, and to this day, he is still struggling to rebuild it.

Unfortunately, we live in a world where people make decisions based on the negative things they see and read, often overlooking the positives. For example, if you've ever ordered something from Amazon, you probably checked the reviews before making a final decision. Did you focus on the positive reviews, or did you go straight to the negative ones? My guess is you looked at the negative reviews first (I know I do). You wanted to see if the negative feedback was significant enough to dissuade you from purchasing the item. The same applies to Realtors—when people look you up, they will search for any negative information to decide whether or not they want to work with you.

It is crucial to always protect your brand, ensuring that you don't give anyone a reason not to use your services. Clean up your social media accounts and remove anything that could leave a bad impression (e.g., college party photos). Be mindful of what you say and how you say it, and avoid situations where you could be recorded and posted on social media. As I mentioned earlier, everything you do is a direct reflection of your brand—whether it's posting on social media, attending a baseball game, or even at a family gathering. Your brand is always on display. This also applies to how you dress, speak, and carry yourself. One wrong move can ruin everything you've built.

"It takes 20 years to build a reputation and 5 minutes to ruin it."

—Warren Buffett

Important to Remember

✓ What is a Brand?

A brand is the distinct set of feelings, perceptions, attitudes, and associations people have when they think about a person or company.

✓ Why Building Your Brand is Important

- Having a trusted brand will help you win more business. Brand recognition generates repeat business and referrals. A recognizable brand also helps you recruit and retain talented people.
- **Builds Trust:** The effort and guidance you provide leave clients with a favorable view of you and your brand.
- **Generates Revenue:** When your brand is known and trusted, clients are more likely to refer business to you and work with you again.

✓ How to Build Your Brand

- Building a brand is more than designing a logo—it's about fully understanding who you are and what you stand for.
- **First, ask:** Who Are You?
- **Colors:** Choose one primary color. If needed, add at most one secondary color.
- **Fonts:** Select one simple, easy-to-read font.
- Explore fonts on www.dafont.com for free options.
- **Logos:** Make it "doodable"—simple enough for anyone to draw easily.
- **Slogans:** Keep it short and simple with as few words as possible.
- **Consistency:** Ensure all brand elements work together to create a strong impact on consumers.

✓ Creating Brand Awareness

- Focus on becoming the first Realtor people think of when real estate comes to mind.
- **Word-of-mouth:** Offer exceptional experiences that clients naturally talk about when discussing real estate.
- **Tell Your Story:** Share your personal story to help people connect with you and build trust.
- **Social Media:** Leverage social media to spread your brand and message to the world.
- **Marketing:** Direct your marketing efforts toward your existing database until you're financially ready to expand elsewhere.

✅ Protect It

Everything you do is a direct reflection of your brand, which is constantly on display. Always protect it.

NOTES

Chapter 14
Social Media

I had been staring at my phone for over an hour, trying to figure out what to post on social media. Initially, I planned to post a picture of myself with an inspirational quote, but I couldn't take a photo I felt comfortable sharing. Next, I attempted to create a post about my company, but before hitting the post button, I deleted it because the text didn't seem good enough. Finally, I thought I had come up with the perfect post—something about my twin boys—but after writing the caption, I couldn't find any photos I liked. Frustrated beyond measure, I threw my phone on the desk and decided to work on something else.

A few minutes later, determined to post something, I picked up my phone to try again. But my mind went completely blank, and after staring at the screen for so long, it eventually turned black. At a loss for ideas, I opened Google and typed in "what to post on social media." In less than a second, a full page of links popped up, offering suggestions. I started scrolling, hoping something would catch my attention. I clicked on a few links and read through the ideas, but nothing stood out as interesting enough. After trying several different search terms, I finally gave up.

Realizing I had wasted an hour and a half with nothing to show for it, I felt defeated. Knowing how important social media is to a Realtor's business, I opened Instagram and began scrolling aimlessly to see what other people were posting. I came across a few posts that looked amazing, but I had no idea how those people created them, and I wasn't ready to start figuring it out. I kept scrolling until I saw a post from a Realtor I knew. His post was simple enough for me to try and replicate. The picture showed him sitting at his desk, looking focused on something in front of him. To make it more dramatic, he added a black-and-white filter. Above the image, he had written, "Can't outwork me! #workhard."

Excited to finally have an idea of what to post, I started looking through the photos on my phone, hoping to find one similar to the agent's. After scrolling back a few years, I found one that was close enough. Feeling a sense of relief, I immediately opened Instagram and tapped the plus button at the bottom of the app. In the next section, I searched for the photo I had found earlier. After scrolling through hundreds of images, I finally found it and clicked "next," which took me to the filter options.

What I thought would be a quick task turned out to be more difficult than I had imagined. I tried various filters but couldn't decide whether to go with black and white or something more colorful. I eventually settled on black and white, inspired by the agent's post. In the caption section, I typed the same text the agent had used, changing the hashtag slightly to say #hardwork, just to be a little different.

Finally, I was ready to click the share button when I noticed something off in the background of the picture. Thinking I could fix it with a different filter, I went back to the filter options and began experimenting again. After a few minutes, I still couldn't find one that worked. Frustrated, I opened my gallery again to search for another photo. Fifteen minutes later, still without a suitable image, I closed my phone and told myself I'd post something later. I never did.

Lesson Learned

Posting on social media had always been a challenge for me. No matter how many articles I read about its importance for a Realtor's business, every time I went to post something, I would freeze up. It was as if my mind hit the off switch the moment I tried to post, only to flip back on as soon as I decided not to. I can recall multiple instances when I had a post all set and ready to go, but I deleted it because something about it didn't feel right. It wasn't until later in my career, once I understood how social media worked, that I finally became comfortable posting regularly.

Social media is more than just sharing pictures of your dinner or dog—it's about letting the world into your life. It brings people closer to you without having to meet them in person. The opportunity this creates for a Realtor's business is incredible. From marketing to building connections, social media is an essential tool if you want to succeed quickly in real estate.

If you're like I was and feel nervous about using social media, don't worry—I'll walk you through it in detail so you'll fully understand what you need to do. Before we dive in, let's explore why using social media is so vital to a Realtor's business in today's world.

| Before Social Media

Let's rewind to the time before MySpace Tom became everyone's first friend. Before the internet became mainstream in the early '90s, Realtors had to rely on expensive and time-consuming marketing strategies. To generate business, agents would spend money on things like bus bench ads, billboards, newspaper listings, and direct mail campaigns. They would also cold-call from the Yellow Pages, knock on doors, and hold open houses. While some of these tactics are still used today, they now serve as supplements to an agent's marketing strategy, rather than the primary approach.

Fast forward to today, where the internet fits in your pocket and social media platforms account for much of our daily interactions. With the tap of a button, you can broadcast your message to the world for free! The power of social media can be life-changing for both you and your business—if you use it consistently and, more importantly, correctly.

Although much of using social media effectively involves creating great content on a regular basis, that's not all there is to it. There are several key factors you need to focus on; without them, no matter what you post, it won't have the impact you're hoping for.

▌ Maximize Your Profiles

We live in a "Tinder world" where people make judgments in the blink of an eye, and with the swipe of a finger, can erase the thought of someone for eternity. If you've ever used a dating app, you understand how this process works. The same can be said for social media profiles. When someone is referred to you or finds you online, they will likely Google you before deciding whether to reach out. This decision often hinges on what they see on your social media profiles. Since social media sites rank high on Google searches due to their SEO (Search Engine Optimization), your profiles are often the first impression you make. If they don't appear professional, there's a good chance that person will look elsewhere for assistance.

Your profiles are a direct reflection of you. They should represent how you want the world to perceive you and your brand.

Profile Photos

The first thing people see is your profile photo, so it's important to start there. Your photo says a lot about you, and people will immediately form opinions, good or bad, based on what they see. Ideally, you should use a professional headshot, as this gives you the best chance of holding someone's attention. If you can't afford a professional photographer, ask a colleague or friend to take one with your phone. Modern smartphone cameras are high-definition, so your photo will still look great.

When choosing a photo, aim for one that makes you look approachable and inviting. Smiling in your picture is more likely to create a positive impression compared to a serious or neutral expression.

Banners

If the platform you're using offers a banner option (e.g., Facebook, LinkedIn, YouTube), take the time to ensure it's clear, sized correctly, and visually appealing. The banner is likely the second thing people will notice after your profile picture, so make sure it represents your business and brand appropriately. In addition to your branding and logo, consider including relevant information like your website address, phone number, and email. You can easily create a professional-looking banner for free using tools like Canva (www.Canva.com).

Bios

After viewing your photo, the next thing people will check is your bio. Make sure every platform you use has a well-written, detailed bio. Sites like Instagram, Facebook, and TikTok have limited bio sections, so you'll need to maximize the character count to present yourself effectively. LinkedIn, on the other hand, offers a short bio at the top and a larger

"About" section where you can go into more detail. I'll cover LinkedIn more in-depth later in this chapter.

In all your bios, be sure to include key information such as your title, any notable achievements (e.g. Top Producing Agent), how people can contact you, your website URL, and perhaps something personal that reflects your passions. Your bio doesn't need to be overly formal, but it also shouldn't include anything inappropriate.

TIP:

For Instagram, writing your bio directly in the app can be tricky since it's not designed for formatting, such as starting new lines. To get around this, write your bio in the Notes app on your phone, then copy and paste it into Instagram. This also makes it easier to add emojis.

As humans, we gravitate toward people we can relate to. Imagine being at a party where you spot two random people across the room—one wearing your favorite sports team's hat and the other not. Who are you more likely to approach? The same principle applies when we look at people's profiles: if we see something in common, we're more inclined to connect. That's why it's important to fill out your profile with as much information as you're comfortable sharing. Include details like where you went to school, previous workplaces, and even favorite quotes. You never know when someone might relate to something on your profile and reach out because of it.

❙ Clean Up Your Profiles

The next thing I want you to understand is that we live in a world where people love to dig deep and find what's wrong or focus on the negative. For example, think about when someone recommends a restaurant to you. What's the first thing you do? You probably Google the restaurant's name and click on sites like Yelp to check out the reviews. But are you looking for the good reviews? Likely not. Just like on Amazon, you're searching for the bad reviews, looking for anything negative to see if it's something you can live with or not. Essentially, you're looking for reasons not to go to that restaurant. Only after reading those reviews will you decide whether to make a reservation or find another place with better ratings.

This is exactly what consumers will do when someone refers them to you, or when they find your name online while searching for a Realtor. As I mentioned earlier, they'll Google your name, and your social media profiles will likely appear near the top of the first page. Then they'll start clicking, judging you based on what they find. If they see lots of photos of you drinking, videos of you doing questionable things, or a profile that looks incomplete and unprofessional, that could be enough for them to decide not to reach out to you.

So, take the time to clean up all your social media profiles immediately by deleting anything that could be viewed negatively (if you're worried about losing pictures, save them somewhere else first). After that, make sure to fill in any missing information on your profiles.

A word of advice: when you're cleaning up your pages, go all the way back to the beginning of your profiles. I understand that some of you may have created your accounts a long time ago and think people won't scroll back that far, but people do like to dig—so why take the chance? Just like in the restaurant example, people are looking for reasons not to hire you, and a photo of you doing something inappropriate, even from years ago, could be all they need to pass on you.

| Focus on the Right Platforms

As I mentioned in Chapter 11: Prospecting, your clients will most likely be people who are similar to you. For this reason, it's important to focus on the platform(s) where your target audience spends their time. Deciding which platform(s) to use depends largely on your generation, as each one has its favored social media spaces. Below are the platforms each generation tends to frequent:

- **Gen Z:** Instagram, TikTok, Snapchat, and to a lesser extent, Facebook (Meta)
- **Millennials:** Facebook and Instagram
- **Baby Boomers:** Facebook

> **NOTE:**
>
> There is a micro-generation called **Zillennials** (people born between 1990 and 2000) who bridge the gap between Millennials and Gen Z. This group primarily uses Instagram, with a heavy focus on the Stories feature.

These are the platforms where you should spend the bulk of your time. However, you should also dedicate time to one of the most underutilized yet vital platforms for showcasing your professionalism: **LinkedIn.**

LinkedIn

Although LinkedIn isn't typically viewed as a social media site like those listed above, it's a platform you absolutely need to be on. Why? First, it ranks very high in SEO and will likely show up on the first page of a Google search when someone looks up your name. Second, it essentially acts as your digital business card, reflecting your professional image.

Your LinkedIn profile should be polished and as detailed as possible. Include information such as your job history (experience), education, skills, recommendations, publications, honors & awards, charitable organizations you belong to, and personal interests. Additionally, take advantage of the "About" section to write a comprehensive biography.

> **TIP:**
>
> When writing your bio, consider using a storytelling format. A narrative about your journey is far more captivating than a simple paragraph of facts.

When posting on LinkedIn, make sure your content is professional and relevant to your industry. This isn't the place for personal photos or casual posts. Share things like articles or blogs you've written or found valuable, interviews or podcasts you've been featured in, awards you've won, or educational articles related to real estate. The LinkedIn algorithm favors educational content, so aim to post informative and insightful materials regularly.

The most important thing to remember about LinkedIn is that it's a professional platform, and people expect to see professionalism. Anything that falls short of that standard will be quickly discredited.

| How the Algorithms Work

If you've ever wondered why you keep seeing the same things repeatedly on your social media feeds, it's not by accident. Every platform's algorithm is designed to learn what you want to see and to show it to you. Algorithms are essentially forms of Artificial Intelligence (AI). They study how you interact with the site and how people interact with you, tailoring content based on what they think you'll enjoy. For example, if you like or comment on a friend's or follower's posts, you'll start seeing more of their content, and vice versa—if they engage with your posts, they'll see more of yours. These sites are built to create a seamless user experience, keeping you engaged for longer periods. The longer you stay on a platform like Facebook, Instagram, TikTok, LinkedIn, or YouTube, the more ads you see—and the more ads you see, the more money the platform makes from advertisers.

That's why, whenever a new feature or app grows in popularity, other platforms quickly adopt similar features. For example, when TikTok gained traction with short-form videos, Facebook and Instagram introduced Reels, and YouTube followed with Shorts. Similarly, Facebook and Instagram developed Stories to compete with Snapchat.

Now that you understand how these platforms work, how can you use this to your advantage? The answer is simpler than you might think. To take advantage of the algorithms, you have to "play their game." Every day, spend time liking and commenting on as many posts as possible. As you engage with other people's content, keep posting your own. The algorithm will show your content to those whose posts you've interacted with, as it assumes they'll be interested in your content too. As they like and comment on your posts, their followers may see your profile suggested as someone to follow—allowing you to grow your audience and reach more people!

> **TIP:**
>
> Facebook shows you whose birthday it is each day, so make sure to wish everyone a Happy Birthday!

Multiple Algorithms

Another key point is that each platform has multiple features, and each feature has its own algorithm. For example, standard wall posts have a different algorithm than Reels or Stories. To fully "play the game," you'll need to engage with content from each feature of the platform. This means spending time commenting and liking posts from each section and also posting content across all features.

> **TIP:**
>
> Facebook owns Instagram, so you can link the two. When you post on Instagram, it will automatically share to your Facebook wall. However, this only applies to regular posts and Stories; you'll need to upload Reels separately to each platform.

| What to Post

The goal of social media isn't to "go viral"—anyone can do that by posting something ridiculous or controversial. The true goal is to grow your audience and market to them so your brand expands and generates more business. The best way to achieve this is by understanding what types of posts perform best and consistently posting them to make sure the algorithms work in your favor.

Let's start with one of the biggest mistakes I see Realtors make: only posting business-related content on platforms other than LinkedIn (which, as I mentioned earlier, should primarily focus on business). If you want to lose your audience's attention quickly, only post about your business. Business posts are, in essence, boring, and no one is browsing social media to be bored. This means you need to focus on personal posts and sprinkle in some business content. Personal posts always perform better because they are more relatable. For example, when someone shares a picture of their pet, most people can relate because they likely have a pet too. However, not many people can relate to hosting an open house.

To maximize the algorithms, you must post a mix of both personal and business content. There's nothing wrong with posting about new listings, open houses, or recent closings, but make sure to emphasize posts that your audience can relate to and that showcase who you are as a person. Because personal posts typically get more interaction (likes, comments, and shares), the algorithms love them. Not only will they show these posts to your audience more frequently, but they'll also boost your business posts in turn.

If you're looking for specific business-related post ideas, here's a list of some of the best ones to include in your strategy. These types of posts tend to get the most engagement and should be part of your social media arsenal:

- Videos

- Pictures

- Surveys

- Polls

- Questions

- Reposting old content (don't assume everyone saw the original post)

- "Then and Now" posts

- "Before and After" posts

- Posts related to current trends or viral topics

TIP:

Go live on your preferred platforms to share your knowledge and show off your personality—this helps people get to know and trust you better.

I especially want to highlight surveys, polls, and questions. These are three of the algorithm's favorite post types. They tend to get lots of engagement because they naturally encourage interaction.

NOTE:

Interactive content (polls, surveys, questions) can boost audience engagement by over 50% compared to static content.

Since the algorithms don't differentiate between these and regular posts, they see the high level of engagement and show these posts more often, which in turn boosts the visibility of your other content. Make sure to incorporate these into your weekly content plan.

TIP:

You can also combine business and personal content into one post, which is a great way to kill two birds with one stone—and it's easier than you think. For example, if you love reading, you could take a selfie of yourself sitting on a couch in a home where you're hosting an open house, with the caption, "I could get lost in my favorite book in this great room! Come check it out at my open house from 10:00-12:00!" This highlights your love for reading, which is relatable for many people, while also reminding them that you're in real estate.

| Post Consistently

As I mentioned earlier, social media platforms are designed to keep us engaged for as long as possible. To achieve this, they prioritize showing fresh content, regularly refreshing our feeds. This means new posts will appear at the top, and as more people post, older content gets buried. If you have many friends and followers, you've probably experienced this when trying to find a post you saw earlier in the day, only to have to scroll endlessly to locate it.

At the same time, according to Forbes, 78% of people in the U.S. use their phones exclusively to access social media.[1] Our phones are practically extensions of our hands, so it makes sense we'd prefer to browse social media on our phones rather than on a computer. But we consume content differently on a phone. Due to the way these apps are designed, we tend to scroll quickly, only stopping when something catches our eye. If you only post occasionally, your content is more likely to be passed over as people quickly scroll through post after post.

In today's fast-paced world, capturing people's attention isn't easy. To increase the chances that your content will be seen by as many people as possible, you need to post a lot—and do so consistently.

Content Calendar

Earlier in this chapter, I mentioned that posting consistently has always been a challenge for me. I bet I'm not alone in this. Posting on a regular basis can be a daunting task for many people, which is why, like me, they end up not posting at all. Knowing this was a challenge, I had to find a solution to help me post more regularly: creating a content calendar.

A content calendar allows you to plan ahead for the week (or longer), so you know exactly what, where, and when to post. Every Sunday night, I would sit down and type out my planned posts for the upcoming week using a simple Google Sheet spreadsheet. I included details such as the text for each post, what picture(s) or video I planned to use, and which platform I would post it on.

One added benefit of using a content calendar is that it helps you track what you've posted. I never deleted my old calendars, so I could always refer back to them when needed. Instead, I created a new calendar each month. This system helped me determine if enough time had passed to repost something or avoid posting similar content too close together.

Sample Content Calendar

SITE	MONDAY	TUESDAY	WEDNESDAY	THURSDAY	FRIDAY	SATURDAY	SUNDAY
INSTAGRAM							
FACEBOOK							
TIK TOK							
LINKEDIN							

> **TIP:**
>
> One thing I never did but wish I had was to track engagement on each post. If I had reviewed the previous week's posts and added their statistics to the spreadsheet, it would have helped me understand which posts performed best with my audience. I could have then doubled down on those types of posts, giving my audience more of what they wanted.

Although a content calendar is a great way to ensure you're posting regularly, you can't rely solely on it. Your audience also wants to see more relatable, organic, non-business-related posts. I recommend using the content calendar for business-related posts and sharing personal content as it happens. I'll discuss what to post in more detail later in this chapter.

| Review Content Regularly

Reviewing content regularly is something I often see agents overlook, but it's one of the most important steps in using social media effectively. The world and people's tastes are constantly changing, and as things change, we can't keep doing the same things and expect the same results. For example, throughout most of the 2010s, people enjoyed seeing photo-based posts, with less focus on video. Now, that has flipped, and video posts outperform photo posts. If an agent continues to rely solely on photos, they risk losing audience engagement and missing out on opportunities.

If you're just starting with social media for your business or are struggling to use it effectively, take some time to test what resonates with your audience. Experiment with different types of posts, post at various times, and diversify your content using a content calendar to track everything. Then, take note of what gains the most traction. This will help you determine what your audience prefers so you can focus on that moving forward.

Set a regular reminder to review your content and make adjustments where necessary. The more you can stay ahead of trends, the more effective your social media strategy will be.

Hashtags

The hashtag, or pound sign (#), was first used on Twitter in 2007 by Chris Messina, a product designer and Twitter employee at the time. Messina suggested using the pound sign to group tweets around a common topic, such as a conference, and to provide context for shortened URLs or unclear tweets. He tweeted, "How do you feel about using # (pound) for groups. As in #barcamp [msg]?" Twitter eventually adopted the idea, and hashtags spread to all other major social media platforms.

Hashtags help users find content by acting as tags that categorize posts. For example, a Realtor might use #justlisted or #justsold when posting a photo of a new listing or sale. Hashtags boost engagement by attracting attention to posts and encouraging interaction. They also provide additional context, making messages clearer and more engaging. For Realtors, using a mix of popular and niche hashtags can connect you with potential customers who are actively searching for real estate services.

Whenever you post, include a few relevant hashtags to help people understand your content and increase its visibility.

> **NOTE:**
>
> Each platform has a preferred number of hashtags:
>
> **Instagram:** 3–5
>
> **Facebook:** 2–3
>
> **TikTok:** 3-5
>
> **LinkedIn:** 3
>
> **X (formerly Twitter):** 2

Business Page vs. Personal Page

In November 2007, at a Facebook event attended by hundreds of marketers, CEO Mark Zuckerberg introduced Facebook Business Pages. The original intent of these pages was for brands to have their own space on Facebook and to amplify their presence with ads. Since its introduction, the Business Page has evolved into a tool that anyone with a business can use, regardless of whether they plan to run ads. However, many agents still struggle with the decision of whether or not to set one up. If you're considering creating your own Business Page, there are a few factors you'll want to consider.

One of the main challenges with creating a Business Page is getting people to follow it. As of 2021, there were over 200 million small businesses with a Facebook Business Page[2], and that number has grown exponentially since. If you're like me, you likely receive several requests each week to follow different businesses' pages. And, like me, many of those requests probably get lost among the constant notifications these platforms send us daily.

Getting people to follow your page is no easy task and takes time, but it's crucial—if someone doesn't follow your page, they won't see your content. Additionally, Business Pages have their own algorithms, so you'll need to actively seek engagement on your page for the algorithm to show your content to your followers. Finally, as we discussed earlier, personal posts tend to perform better than business posts, making it even harder to get engagement on a page that's primarily business-related.

On the other hand, there are significant advantages to using your personal page for both business and personal content. The main advantage is that your personal page likely already has a large, organically built audience from years of being on the platform. You don't need to build a new audience from scratch like you would with a Business Page. Additionally, because your followers are people who know or are interested in you, they're already inclined to engage with your content. Furthermore, since you've been on these platforms for a long time, the algorithms are already optimized to show your content to your audience. These factors make it easier to market yourself to a large number of people, allowing you to grow your brand and business more quickly.

Ultimately, you'll need to decide which approach is best for your business. Take the time to carefully consider your options so you can make a decision that aligns with your goals and doesn't waste your time on something that won't benefit you.

Facebook/Instagram Ads

Aside from starting a team, there's another reason to set up a Business Page: if you plan to run ads on Facebook and/or Instagram. To run ads on these platforms, you're required to have a Business Page. The good news is that you don't need to spend much time creating an elaborate page. You can take a few minutes to set up a generic one. When running ads, you won't necessarily direct users to your Business Page—you can direct them to a contact form, landing page, or anywhere else that captures their information or provides more details about your services. Of course, you can direct them to your Business Page if you prefer, but it's often more effective to send them to a location where you can engage with them directly or offer additional value.

| Stories

Stories are a feature on Facebook and Instagram created to compete with Snapchat and TikTok. They are essentially short clips or pictures, and you can find them at the top of both apps—making them the first thing people see when they log in. Stories are a great way to quickly put out more content since they don't require much effort and are ideal for sharing real-time updates. For example, if you're about to show a property, you can do a quick Story about it with descriptive text overlays, fun GIFs, effects, and music.

The main difference between a Story and a regular post is that Stories only last for 24 hours before disappearing forever. However, you can post multiple Stories in a day, and people can scroll through all of them at once. I recommend using Stories to give people a glimpse into your personal life and what it's like to be a Realtor.

Keep in mind that the algorithms we discussed earlier apply only to posts on your walls. Stories have their own algorithm, which works similarly. To get your Stories seen by more people, you need to engage with other people's Stories by commenting and liking them.

NOTE:

On Instagram, you can save a Story as a Highlight after you post it. **Highlights** appear as icons under your profile information and allow you to organize your saved Stories for others to review anytime. You can set up as many Highlights as you like, but typically five is an ideal number since most people check social media on their phones, and five is the maximum number viewable at one time without swiping left.

| YouTube

In the past, consumers would visit websites, read online reviews, and check out blogs to learn about a product or brand. Today, with video content so widely available on social media, consumers rely more on videos during their research phase. According to HubSpot Blogs research, 66% of consumers have watched video content (such as product demos, reviews, FAQs, unboxings, etc.) to learn about a brand or product.[3]

Although video is accessible on most platforms, YouTube remains the top destination for video content. This is primarily because it is designed specifically for video consumption. If you plan to create videos for your business, setting up a YouTube channel is a smart move.

YouTube Algorithm

The YouTube algorithm works similarly to other social media sites, taking into account likes and comments, but with two key differences: it relies more heavily on views and watch time. The more views your videos receive and the longer people watch them, the more the algorithm will promote them to others who may be interested, based on their viewing preferences. For example, if you watched a Mr. Beast video, the next time you visit the site, you'll not only be recommended more Mr. Beast videos but also other similar videos with high views and watch time.

To use YouTube effectively, you need to encourage people to watch your videos. This can take time, but sharing your video links and incorporating them into your marketing strategy can help you build your subscriber base more quickly.

> **NOTE:**
>
> Unlike other platforms, you don't need to post on YouTube as frequently. Posting once a week or every other week is sufficient.

Just be sure to plan your content carefully, just as you would with other social media platforms, so you always have a strategy for what you post.

> **TIP:**
>
> Study the most popular channels to see how they structure their videos, and try to emulate them. Nowadays, people prefer quick cuts and dynamic editing to keep the content exciting, rather than someone talking into a microphone for extended periods.

Shorts

Much like how Facebook and Instagram introduced Stories to compete with TikTok, YouTube created **Shorts.** Shorts are videos up to 60 seconds long, ideal for capturing real-time moments or using exciting segments from your longer videos. Shorts have their own algorithm, so you'll need to treat them as a separate entity, just as you would with Stories.

▌ X (Formerly Known as Twitter)

It's hard to categorize exactly what type of platform X is. Is it a social media site or an informational site? I tend to lean toward the latter. If you've spent any time on X, you've likely noticed how fast information moves. This constant influx of information can make it hard to process everything. With a character limit of 280, X is designed for absorbing small pieces of information quickly. While it's perfect for staying informed in real-time, it's not as ideal for marketing yourself.

The most effective way to use X is as a resource to stay up-to-date on current events. This allows you to speak knowledgeably on timely topics, which can help you connect with people and establish relationships faster.

To get the most out of X, tailor it to your interests by following the people, topics, and companies that align with the information you want to stay informed about.

> **TIP:**
>
> Even though X isn't the best platform for generating business, people may still look you up there. X appears on the first page of Google search results when people search your name, so make sure your profile looks polished and free of anything that might deter potential clients.

Social media has forever changed the way Realtors do business. With just one tap on your phone, you can send a message out to millions of people—an incredible opportunity that's also free. Realtors of the past could never have imagined this. So, don't miss the chance to leverage these powerful platforms. Build and clean up your profiles, create a content plan, and start using social media to grow your brand and your business!

Important to Remember

✅ Before Social Media

Before the internet became mainstream in the early '90s, Realtors had to engage in expensive and time-consuming marketing. Now, with just a tap, you can share your message with the world for free!

✅ Maximize Your Profiles

- Your profiles are essentially your virtual business cards.
- **Profile Photo:** Choose a personable and inviting photo.
- **Banners:** Make sure your banner represents your business and brand professionally.
- **Bios:** Ensure every platform has a well-written, detailed bio.

✅ Clean Up Your Profiles

People often look for negatives when deciding to use a service. Make sure your profiles are free from anything that could deter potential clients.

✅ Focus on the Right Platforms

- **Gen Z:** Instagram, TikTok, Snapchat, and (to a lesser extent) Facebook
- **Millennials:** Facebook and Instagram
- **Baby Boomers:** Facebook
- **LinkedIn:** A professional platform that acts as your digital business card. Keep it polished and focus on business-related content.

✅ How the Algorithms Work

- Algorithms are essentially AI that studies how you interact with platforms and tailor content based on your preferences.
- **Multiple Algorithms:** Each feature on a platform (e.g., Stories, posts) has its own algorithm.

✅ What to Post

- Types of posts that drive engagement:
  - Videos
  - Pictures

- Surveys
- Polls
- Questions
- Repost old content
- Then and now posts
- Before and after posts
- Posts related to hot or viral trends

Post Consistently

- People scroll quickly—if you're not posting regularly, your content may get lost.
- **Content Calendar:** Plan your posts ahead of time to know what, when, and where to post.

Review Content Regularly

- Regularly review and adjust your content to stay ahead of trends and keep your social media effective.

Hashtags

- Hashtags boost engagement by attracting attention, clarifying messages, and helping you reach target audiences.

Business Page vs. Personal Page

- Each has its own algorithm.
- Your personal page already has an audience, while a business page requires time to build.
- Running Facebook/Instagram ads requires a business page.

Stories

- Stories last for only 24 hours and have their own algorithm, similar to regular posts.

YouTube

- YouTube is the top platform for video content.
- **YouTube Algorithm:** Relies more heavily on views and watch time than likes and comments.
- **Shorts:** Videos up to 60 seconds are ideal for real-time moments or exciting segments of longer videos. Shorts have their own algorithm.

X (Formerly Known as Twitter)

- More of an informational site.
- Use it to stay updated on real-time events and engage in a variety of conversations.

NOTES

PART
03
Grow »

Chapter 15
Building a Team

One late night in 2022, while working at my brokerage, an agent who was also staying late approached me and asked if I had a few minutes to talk. This agent had been with my brokerage for four years and often sought my advice, so I expected him to ask about a challenging sale. Instead, he mentioned he was considering starting a team and had been interviewing candidates for an assistant position. He had recently interviewed someone he thought would be a good fit and wanted my opinion on her.

Knowing how much production he handled annually, I asked why he felt the need for an assistant. He launched into a long-winded explanation about feeling overwhelmed and thought hiring an assistant would relieve him of some tasks, allowing him to focus on more important things. Unsatisfied with his reasoning, I pressed further, asking what exactly he felt overwhelmed by. Caught off guard, he paused to gather his thoughts before mentioning paperwork, answering emails, and showings, then struggled to think of anything else before stopping.

Sensing that he was looking for a quick fix to a problem of his own making, I spent the next 30 minutes chatting with him about how he ran his business to get a clearer picture of his challenges. By the end of our conversation, I had made several simple suggestions he could implement to make his business more efficient. This way, when he was truly ready to expand, his future hire could seamlessly integrate into his operations.

The agent left that evening, and I felt confident he was in a good place moving forward. A few weeks later, I arrived at the office to find him sitting in the conference room with someone I didn't recognize. Not thinking much of it, I went to my office to start my day. About ten minutes later, there was a knock on my door. The agent stood in the doorway with the person from earlier, introducing her as his new assistant. He expressed excitement about what she could bring to his business. Though I didn't agree with his decision, it was his business, and if he believed this was the best course of action, I wanted to support him. I welcomed her to the company.

A few months passed before the agent called me with a question about a challenging sale. After helping him resolve the issue, I asked how things were going with his new assistant. He admitted she wasn't a good fit for his business, explaining that she ended up taking too much of his time, so he had to let her go.

Lesson Learned

I've often had conversations with Realtors considering expanding their business, only to discover they haven't taken the time to assess whether they're truly ready for growth. Many Realtors are drawn to the idea of starting a team because they believe it will solve all their business problems. What they fail to realize is that if their business isn't structured for expansion, bringing on another person can create even more issues. To build a successful team, you must already be running an organized and efficient business. Otherwise, anyone you bring in is likely to exacerbate the problems rather than solve them.

The decision to expand is not one to take lightly. Expanding too early, before you're ready, can undo much of the hard work you've put into your business and set you back. On the other hand, expanding at the right time can elevate your business to new heights and allow you to grow beyond your current limitations.

Throughout this book, I've given you the tools to build a successful real estate business. If you follow my advice, maintain relentless determination, possess a true desire to succeed as a Realtor, and exercise patience, you will one day find yourself at the crossroads of deciding whether or not to start a team.

> **NOTE:**
> Before starting a team, ensure you fully understand how teams are treated at your brokerage, particularly how commissions and fees are handled.

| Positives and Negatives of Starting a Team

Throughout my career, I've been part of multiple teams and have also had several teams working within my company. These experiences have allowed me to witness firsthand how different team leaders manage the balance between overseeing a team and maintaining their own book of business. I've seen that with a well-organized and well-managed team, growth is achievable. However, without structure, a team can struggle. Additionally, I've observed the significant impact that hiring the right—or wrong—people can have on a team's success.

While being part of and observing these teams, I spent considerable time speaking with the team leaders to understand their experiences. Drawing on what I saw and what these leaders shared, I've compiled a list of key positives and negatives of running a team. These are essential factors to consider before deciding whether to start a team of your own.

The Positives and Negatives of Starting a Team	
Positives	**Negatives**
✅ Greater market growth potential	✅ Training team members can be time-consuming
✅ Increased income opportunities	✅ Addressing conflicts and disagreements between team members
✅ Enhanced brand visibility and growth	✅ Recruiting high-quality team members is challenging and time-consuming
✅ Ability to delegate unwanted tasks	

- ✅ Inspiration and creativity from working with like-minded individuals
- ✅ More personal recognition within the industry
- ✅ Greater focus on growth opportunities
- ✅ Opportunities to share knowledge and mentor others

- ✅ Managing multiple moving parts of the business can become overwhelming
- ✅ Navigating different personalities isn't easy
- ✅ Dealing with the difficult task of firing team members
- ✅ Additional costs associated with starting and maintaining a team

After considering these factors, if you decide to start a team, the first step is to evaluate how your business is currently structured. Ask yourself if your business is organized in a way that allows anyone you hire to seamlessly step in and take over certain tasks. If not, you need to begin by reviewing your business and taking the time to streamline its operations. Growth is only effective if every element is designed to support it.

| Systems

The primary reason teams fail is due to a lack of organization. I've spoken to many agents who were part of failed teams, and what I've found is that these teams failed because the team leader thought they were ready to expand but didn't account for the fact that their business wasn't structured to allow others to take over any part of it. These leaders essentially run every aspect of their business in a way only they can manage, not in a way that anyone else could easily step into. When teams operate like this, it's common for the leader to become frustrated with team members and reclaim the tasks they had delegated, believing that their team isn't meeting expectations. In truth, the team leader's expectations are unrealistic because the business isn't designed for others to function within it.

> **TIP:**
>
> When designing your systems, keep others in mind. Make them simple and easy to follow. Checklists are an excellent tool for this.

The most successful teams are those with systems in place that anyone can operate, independent of the team leader. This means that no matter who joins the team, they can step in and know exactly what to do because the business is structured to support them. There are a few essential systems that need to be in place before you're ready to expand. Many of these have been covered in greater detail earlier in the book, so refer back to those sections if needed. Each system should be written out clearly and in detail, not only to ensure it can be easily taught to a new team member, but also so that anyone can refer back to it at any time for guidance on prospecting, managing leads, social media, working with buyers, and handling new listings.

List of Systems to Have in Place

- ☑ Onboarding new members
- ☑ Offboarding team members who leave
- ☑ Prospecting for new clients (see Chapter 11: Prospecting)
- ☑ Converting leads (see Chapter 12: Leads)
- ☑ Using social media (see Chapter 14: Social Media)
- ☑ Working with new buyers (see Chapter 9: Buyers)
- ☑ Working with new listings (see Chapter 10: Listings)

TIP:

Onboarding and offboarding systems are essentially checklists of tasks that need to be completed when a team member joins or leaves. For example, onboarding might include scheduling new headshots for the team member and reviewing team policies and procedures. Offboarding might involve removing the individual from the team website and deactivating their access to any team programs.

Team Leader Responsibilities

A team leader is essentially the CEO of the team, and like CEOs of major corporations, you will be responsible for managing the team while overseeing all aspects of the business. This means everything goes through you. For example, if a team member is unsure how to handle a negotiation, they will likely turn to you for guidance. If the marketing director is uncertain about posting something they created, they will seek your opinion first. Additionally, if a team member makes a mistake, such as showing a property without prior approval from a tenant, you'll be the one responsible for addressing the issue both with the client and the agent involved.

As CEO, you'll wear many hats simultaneously, and in many cases, you'll also need to continue selling as well. Given the extent of these responsibilities, it's crucial to fully understand your role before adding the CEO title to your business card.

The list of responsibilities for a team leader is extensive, but to give you a better understanding, here are a few key ones:

- ☑ Training and mentoring, especially for newer agents
- ☑ Recruiting top talent (A-players)
- ☑ Problem-solving and resolving issues as they arise
- ☑ Developing and implementing marketing strategies
- ☑ Managing expenses and budgets
- ☑ Setting goals and planning for the future
- ☑ Overseeing daily operations

> **NOTE:**
> As the team leader, you are also the face of the business. How you conduct yourself reflects on the entire team and sets the standard that your team members will follow.

Team Structure

How you structure your team will largely depend on your vision for its growth. This includes defining the roles and responsibilities of each team member. For instance, if you're handling both buyers and listings but prefer to focus on listings, you might consider hiring a buyer's agent. Their role would be to show properties to buyers and attend inspections while you concentrate on handling negotiations. As your business evolves, you might want to shift your focus solely to luxury listings. In that case, your next hire could be a listing agent who handles all lower-priced listings, attends inspections and appraisals, and conducts final walk-throughs for properties under a certain price point.

When determining your team's structure, it can be helpful to create a visual diagram. Start with yourself at the top (CEO), then list each team member's role beneath you, along with their corresponding responsibilities.

Below is an example of a top-producing team and the responsibilities if each member.

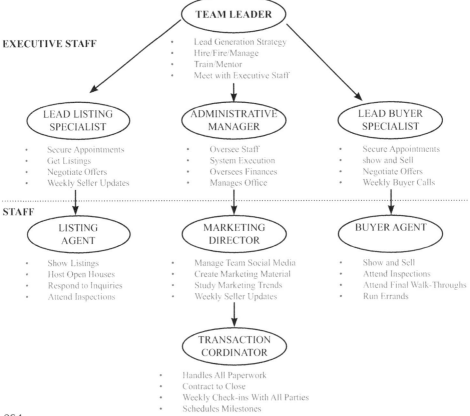

▌ Team Pay Structures and Responsibilities

Choosing the right pay structure for each team member depends on their role, as not all roles are compensated the same way. With many options available, it's important to base your decision on what's best for your business while ensuring the structure remains competitive in your market.

TIP:

Ask other team leaders in your market about their pay structures. This helps ensure your compensation plan is competitive and attracts top talent.

Buyer and Listing Agents

Realtors who are full-time members of the team are typically either independent contractors paid on a commission basis or salaried employees. Some teams even offer a hybrid of both models.

Commission-based Realtors are generally paid a percentage of each sale they participate in. For example, a buyer's agent representing one of the team's buyers will earn a portion of the commission based on their agreement with the team. Commission-based agents are typically paid by the brokerage and receive a 1099 at tax time.

NOTE:

Some teams differentiate commission splits based on whether the agent or the team generated the client. For instance, if an agent brings in their own client, they might receive 75% of the commission (75% agent/25% team). If the client came from the team, the split could be 50/50.

Salaried Realtors, on the other hand, are usually paid bi-weekly, similar to employees of large corporations. Taxes are deducted from their checks, and the team provides them with a W-2 at tax time.

NOTE:

Ensure your agents know who is responsible for covering any required fees, such as Realtor association fees or brokerage fees.

Staff

Staff members can either be paid hourly or on salary. If you opt for hourly pay, staff are treated as independent contractors and may receive a 1099 at tax time. Salaried staff are treated similarly to salaried agents, with taxes withheld and a W-2 provided.

> **NOTE:**
> The IRS requires businesses to issue a 1099 if they pay a contractor at least $600 in a year.

Bonuses

One of the key responsibilities of a team leader is motivating team members, and monetary bonuses are a powerful incentive. Many teams offer performance-based bonuses, which can be awarded to individuals or the entire team. For example, you might offer a listing agent a bonus for securing a certain number of listings or reward the whole team if they meet an overall production goal.

Bonuses don't always have to be monetary. Some teams offer gift cards, vacations, or watches as rewards. If you choose to implement a bonus structure, ensure it not only motivates your team but also aligns with the short- and long-term goals of your business. It's essential to avoid frustration or disappointment among team members if bonus structures change or don't meet initial expectations.

> **NOTE:**
> Before implementing a bonus system, consult with your accountant to understand how the bonuses you're considering will be taxed.

À La Carte Items

In addition to regular compensation, many teams offer ways for members to earn extra money by taking on tasks outside their main responsibilities. These tasks typically have a set fee, ranging from $25 to a few hundred dollars. For example, picking up a lockbox from a listing might earn $25, while meeting a photographer at a property might bring in $100.

If you choose to include these tasks as part of your team's compensation plan, be transparent about the value of each task and how team members will be paid.

> **TIP:**
> Use a tracking system, such as Google Sheets, to monitor completed À La Carte items so you can ensure timely and accurate payments.

| First Hire

The first person you hire is arguably the most important, as your business—essentially you—is likely operating at full capacity. Without additional support, taking on more business could negatively impact the level of service you provide your clients.

When forming your team, focus on hiring to address your biggest need first. This allows you to delegate time-consuming tasks, freeing you up to concentrate on growth-oriented activities. For example, if you're juggling both buyer and listing clients, your first hire might be a buyer's agent who can manage all buyer transactions, allowing you to focus on listings. Buyers generally require more time and energy, so this would give you the bandwidth to focus on the other areas of your business. Alternatively, if you're overwhelmed with administrative tasks and struggling to maintain your service quality, hiring an assistant can relieve you of these duties, giving you more time to focus on your clients.

Whichever role you decide to fill first, ensure it's someone who can take your team to the next level.

❙ A Players

"A small team of A+ players can run circles around a giant team of B and C players."

—Steve Jobs

Steve Jobs, during his lifetime, ran two of the most successful companies in history— Apple and Pixar. At the core of both companies was a belief that to achieve remarkable things, a business must be built on remarkable people. Although Steve is no longer with us, this philosophy has persisted, allowing both companies to continue thriving without him. From my conversations with numerous team leaders, one common mistake when starting their teams was hiring someone convenient, regardless of qualifications. Eager to get their teams going, they often brought on whoever was available, rather than taking the time to find a highly qualified person. This approach led to frustrations and hurt their businesses instead of helping them grow.

When building your team, follow Steve Jobs' example and focus on hiring A players. Take your time, and ensure anyone you bring on strengthens your business, not weakens it.

How to Find A Players

Finding A players isn't easy—if it were, every team would be full of them. While starting your search in the real estate industry is a natural step, don't overlook someone simply because they don't have a real estate license. If you believe someone would improve your team, consider asking them to join. For example, if you meet a car salesperson with exceptional selling skills, you might approach them about becoming a buyer's agent. If they're interested, they can work toward getting licensed before officially joining your team.

> **NOTE:**
> If you hire someone without a license, be prepared to mentor them, as they will need significant guidance in the beginning.

Talent can be found anywhere, so once you're ready to start building your team, always keep an eye out for A players.

After identifying a potential candidate, set up a meeting to get to know them better before making any commitments. A solid vetting process will help you distinguish between true A players and those who may fall into the B or C categories.

Buyer's Agent

A buyer's agent's role is to manage the team leader's buyers while also continuing to service their own clients. They are typically one of the first hires a team leader makes, as buyers tend to be more time-consuming, and delegating them to a buyer's agent frees up the team leader to focus on other responsibilities.

The specific responsibilities of a buyer's agent can vary depending on how you plan to utilize them and their qualifications. For example, if you hire an experienced agent, you might feel comfortable allowing them to work with buyers from start to finish. However, if you hire a newer agent, you may start by assigning them limited tasks, such as showing properties and attending inspections and final walk-throughs, until they gain more experience. Since these are your buyer clients, it's important to be comfortable with the level of responsibility you delegate.

Buyer's Agent Responsibilities
- Showing properties to buyers
- Creating Comparative Market Analyses (CMAs)
- Negotiating offers
- Attending home inspections
- Attending final walk-throughs
- Attending contractor walk-throughs

From my experience, there are certain qualities that distinguish a good buyer's agent from a great one, regardless of experience. Below is a list of qualities to look for when hiring a buyer's agent:

Qualities of a Great Buyer's Agent
- Highly motivated
- Excellent communication skills
- Exceptional customer service
- Patience

- ✔ Willingness to learn
- ✔ Strong organizational skills
- ✔ Team player
- ✔ **Bonus:** Market knowledge and real estate experience

❙ Listing Agent

Hiring a listing agent can be more challenging, as agents who handle a lot of listings often prefer to work independently or start their own teams. More often than not, listing agents are either existing team members who are promoted or experienced buyer's agents from outside the team who have managed a few listings. Additionally, listing agents are typically one of the last hires team leaders make, as most team leaders prefer to handle listings themselves until the team has grown to a point where they can fully step back from this role and focus on scaling the business.

The responsibilities of a listing agent can vary based on how you plan to utilize them and their qualifications. Given the heavier marketing component involved in listings, it's essential to delegate carefully.

Listing Agent Responsibilities
- ✔ Creating Comparative Market Analyses (CMAs)
- ✔ Marketing properties
- ✔ Inputting listings into the MLS
- ✔ Scheduling showings
- ✔ Negotiating offers
- ✔ Attending home inspections
- ✔ Attending final walk-throughs
- ✔ Attending contractor walk-throughs

Similar to buyer's agents, certain qualities distinguish great listing agents from the rest, regardless of experience. Here's a list of qualities to seek when hiring a listing agent:

Qualities of a Great Listing Agent
- ✔ Highly motivated
- ✔ Excellent communication skills
- ✔ Exceptional customer service
- ✔ Patience
- ✔ Willingness to learn
- ✔ Strong organizational skills
- ✔ Team player
- ✔ Marketing expertise
- ✔ **Bonus:** Market knowledge and real estate experience

Assistant

An assistant ensures that the team operates efficiently by handling administrative and clerical tasks, as well as providing support for both the team leader and other team members. In many teams, the assistant acts as the gatekeeper for the team leader, managing routine tasks like answering emails, scheduling meetings, and handling paperwork. This allows the team leader to focus on more critical responsibilities.

> **NOTE:**
> Some team leaders hire assistants solely for themselves, without having them support other team members.

When it's time to hire an assistant, focus on someone who can take on a significant amount of responsibility and embodies the qualities listed below. A great assistant can be a key factor in the success (or failure) of your team.

Assistant Responsibilities
- Answering the team leader's emails
- Managing the team's main phone line
- Scheduling meetings for the team leader
- Scheduling team meetings
- Ordering office supplies
- Managing the team's budget and expenses=

The best assistants I've worked with possessed the following qualities. Finding individuals with these skills will help elevate your team to the next level.

Qualities of a Great Assistant
- Strong communication skills
- Excellent interpersonal skills
- Time management abilities
- Organizational skills
- Attention to detail
- Adaptability
- Problem-solving capabilities
- **Bonus:** Relevant experience

Marketing Director

A marketing director controls the overall messaging and brand of the team. This person oversees all marketing efforts, from sending e-blasts to posting on social media. The significance of this position cannot be overstated, as consumers are 2.5 times more likely to choose a brand they recognize over a lesser-known competitor. Additionally, 64% of consumers consider brand reputation and awareness when deciding which products to purchase.[1]

When hiring a marketing director, seek someone who can take your vision for the team's brand and make it a reality. The best marketing directors I've worked with understood this and were not afraid to push creative boundaries to achieve greatness.

When you're ready to fill this role, hire someone you believe is capable of helping you realize your vision.

Marketing Director Responsibilities
- Producing and posting team-related social media content
- Generating and sending e-blast marketing campaigns
- Creating marketing materials
- Developing the team's branding message
- Designing and implementing advertising campaigns
- Conducting competitor research
- Managing the team's brand identity

A great marketing director can elevate both the individual team members and the team as a whole. From my experience, the most successful marketing directors possess the following qualities:

Qualities of a Great Marketing Director
- Proficient in graphic design
- Marketing expertise
- Attention to detail
- Teamwork skills
- Ability to plan marketing strategies
- Creativity
- Analytical skills
- Project management abilities
- **Bonus:** Relevant experience

> **NOTE:**
>
> Our world changes quickly, so make it a priority to have regular meetings with your marketing director to stay up to date on current trends and remain relevant in consumers' minds.

Transaction Coordinator

A transaction coordinator focuses on the administrative side of real estate transactions, ensuring that all parties—Realtors, buyers, and sellers—are satisfied with the process. Their tasks are centered on coordination, communication, and organization.

The purpose of a transaction coordinator is to alleviate administrative duties from team members, allowing them to focus on building relationships and generating new business. Hiring a transaction coordinator at the right time can accelerate your team's growth. Make sure the candidate you choose can handle all of the responsibilities effortlessly.

Transaction Coordinator Responsibilities

- Inputting listings into the MLS
- Updating buyers and sellers on the status of their transactions
- Handling paperwork (getting listing documents and contracts signed, sending out signed contracts)
- Communicating with all parties involved (lenders, attorneys, title companies, cooperating agents, etc.)
- Monitoring contingency deadlines
- Coordinating showings on team listings
- Coordinating property inspections
- Coordinating final walk-throughs
- Coordinating contractor walk-throughs
- Obtaining client testimonials

The best transaction coordinators I've worked with were able to manage multiple transactions simultaneously without missing a beat. This ability, along with the qualities listed below, is essential for a team's growth.

Qualities of a Great Transaction Coordinator

- High organizational skills
- Strong communication skills
- Excellent customer service
- Attention to detail
- Proficiency in IT
- System-oriented thinking
- Flexibility and adaptability
- **Bonus:** Relevant experience

▌ Client Concierge

A client concierge, distinct from a transaction coordinator, is primarily responsible for nurturing client relationships before, during, and after transactions. Their role is to ensure that clients are highly satisfied, so they will not only remember to work with the team again but also refer other potential clients in the meantime.

A client concierge is typically not one of the first hires for a team. This position usually becomes relevant after the team has established itself and has the resources to allocate for it. That being said, this role can be instrumental to the long-term success of the team, as referrals and repeat business are crucial for sustained growth.

Client Concierge Responsibilities

- ☑ Nurturing and maintaining client relationships
- ☑ Scheduling initial consultations
- ☑ Sending welcome and congratulatory emails, cards, and gifts to new and past clients
- ☑ Providing clients with relevant information (e.g., local details about the area surrounding a recently closed home)
- ☑ Planning client appreciation events

The best client concierges I've worked with were naturally outgoing and exceptionally friendly, making everyone they interacted with feel comfortable and valued. When hiring for this position, look for individuals who make you feel the same way.

Qualities of a Great Client Concierge

- ☑ Strong customer service and relationship-building skills
- ☑ Excellent communication skills
- ☑ Outgoing personality
- ☑ Takes initiative
- ☑ Strong organizational abilities
- ☑ Patience
- ☑ **Bonus:** Relevant experience
- ☑ **Bonus:** Multi-lingual

NOTE:

As your team grows and more members join, it's important to periodically reevaluate each team member's role to ensure they are in the best position for both themselves and the team.

Important to Remember

- ☑ **Positives and Negatives of Starting a Team**
  - • Positives
    - ▫ Larger market growth potential
    - ▫ More income potential
    - ▫ Larger brand growth and visibility potential
    - ▫ Delegation of unwanted responsibilities

- ▫ Being around like-minded people spurs inspiration and creativity
- ▫ More personal recognition from the industry
- ▫ Ability to focus more on growth opportunities
- ▫ Opportunity to share knowledge and mentor others
- Negatives
  - ▫ Training team members can be time-consuming
  - ▫ Addressing every conflict and disagreement that arises from team members
  - ▫ Recruiting quality team members takes time as they are not easy to find and persuade
  - ▫ Managing a lot of moving parts of the business can be overwhelming at times
  - ▫ Managing different personalities is not easy
  - ▫ Having to fire a team member
  - ▫ Additional costs required to start and run a team

✅ Systems

- List of systems to have in place
  - ▫ Onboarding new members
  - ▫ Off-boarding team members who leave
  - ▫ Prospecting for new clients
  - ▫ How to convert leads
  - ▫ Using social media
  - ▫ Working with a new buyer
  - ▫ Working with a new listing

✅ Team Leader Responsibilities

- List of Team Leader Responsibilities
  - ▫ Training and mentorship (especially for newer agents)
  - ▫ Recruiting A players
  - ▫ Problem-solving issues
  - ▫ Develop and implement marketing strategies
  - ▫ Managing expenses and budget
  - ▫ Goal setting and planning
  - ▫ Oversee daily operations

✅ Team Structure

- How you structure your team will largely depend on the vision for it. This includes deciding on the roles and responsibilities of each team member.

- When deciding how to structure your team, it is effective to create a visual of it by making a diagram. Start with you at the top (CEO), then under you list each member's role and their responsibilities for that role.

✓ Pay Structures

- Buyer and Listing Agents
  - Realtors who are full-time members of the team are typically considered either independent contractors and are fully commission-based or treated as employees and are paid a salary (although it is also possible to be a hybrid of both).
- Staff
  - Staff are typically paid either by the hour or as a salaried employee.
- Bonuses
  - Many teams will offer performance-based incentives to their team members.
  - Bonuses can be offered on an individual basis or for the team as a whole.
- À La Carte Items
  - Can pay team members for doing tasks outside of their main responsibilities i.e. picking up a lockbox, sitting an inspection on a team listing, or showing a team listing.

✓ First Hire

- Focus on hiring for your biggest need first.

✓ A Players

- Take your time and make sure anyone you decide to hire will strengthen your business and not weaken it.
- How to Find A Players
  - Start within the industry but don't discount a person because they don't have a real estate license.
  - Talent can be found anywhere so always be on the lookout.

✓ Buyer's Agent

- Buyer's Agent Responsibilities
  - Showing buyers properties
  - Creating Comparative Market Analysis (CMAs)
  - Negotiating offers made
  - Attending home inspections
  - Attending the final walk-through
  - Attending contractor walk-throughs
- Qualities of a Great Buyer's Agent
  - Highly motivated
  - Excellent communication skills
  - Provides exceptional customer service
  - Patience
  - Willingness to learn
  - Organized

   □ Team player
   □ BONUS: Market knowledge and real estate experience

✅ Listing Agent

- Listing Agent Responsibilities
  - □ Creating Comparative Market Analysis (CMAs)
  - □ Marketing properties
  - □ Inputting listings into MLS
  - □ Scheduling showing requests
  - □ Negotiating offer received
  - □ Attend home inspections
  - □ Attend the final walk-through
  - □ Attend contractor walk-throughs
- Qualities of a Great Listing Agent
  - □ Highly motivated
  - □ Excellent communication skills
  - □ Provides exceptional customer service
  - □ Patience
  - □ Willingness to learn
  - □ Organized
  - □ Team player
  - □ Marketing knowledge
  - □ BONUS: Market knowledge and real estate experience

✅ Assistant

- Assistant Responsibilities
  - □ Answering the team leader's emails
  - □ Answering the team's main phone line
  - □ Scheduling team leader's meetings
  - □ Scheduling team meetings
  - □ Ordering office supplies
  - □ Managing the team's budget and expenses
- Qualities of a Great Assistant
  - □ Strong communication skills
  - □ Interpersonal skills
  - □ Time management skills
  - □ Strong organizational skills
  - □ Attention to detail
  - □ Adaptability
  - □ Problem-solving
  - □ BONUS: Relative experience

✔ Marketing Director

- Marketing Director Responsibilities
  - Producing and posting team-related social media content
  - Generating and sending e-blast marketing campaigns
  - Creating various marketing materials
  - Developing team branding message
  - Designing and implementing advertising campaigns
  - Conducting competitor research
  - Brand management
- Qualities of a Great Marketing Director
  - Proficient in graphic design
  - Marketing background
  - Attention to detail
  - Teamwork
  - Marketing planning
  - Creativity
  - Analytical skills
  - Project management
  - BONUS: Relative experience

✔ Transaction Coordinator

- Transaction Coordinator Responsibilities
  - Inputting listings into the MLS
  - Updating sellers and buyers on the status of the transaction
  - Handling the team's paperwork (getting listing documents signed, getting contracts signed, and sending signed contracts out to all parties involved)
  - Communicating with all parties involved with the transaction (lender, attorney, title company, cooperating agent, etc.)
  - Monitoring contingency deadlines
  - Coordinating showings on team listings
  - Coordinating property inspections
  - Coordinating final walk-throughs
  - Coordinating contractor walk-throughs
  - Obtaining client testimonials
- Qualities of a Great Transaction Coordinator
  - High organizational skills
  - Strong communication skills
  - Customer service skills
  - Meticulous attention to detail
  - IT skills
  - System oriented
  - Flexible and adaptable
  - BONUS: Relative experience

✅ Client Concierge

- Client Concierge Responsibilities
  - Nurturing and maintaining client relationships
  - Scheduling initial consultations
  - Sending welcome and congratulatory emails, cards, etc. to new and past clients
  - Providing relevant information to clients (local information on the surrounding area near a home the client closed on)
  - Planning of client appreciation events
- Qualities of a Great Client Concierge
  - Customer service/relations
  - Strong communication skills
  - Outgoing personality
  - Takes initiative
  - Organizational skills
  - Patient
  - BONUS: Relative experience
  - BONUS: Multi-lingual

NOTES

Recommended Tools

In 2009, when I entered the industry and joined my cousin's team, I was immediately introduced to how beneficial recent advances in technology can be for someone starting a business. My cousin, who called herself a "paperless agent," was always searching for new technology to run her business more efficiently. She introduced me to e-signature programs, which had become legal in 2001, and showed me how to use a tablet to search the MLS in real-time with clients. She also demonstrated how the right applications on your phone can enable you to run your business from anywhere. During my time working with her, I was constantly exposed to emerging technology, which was advancing rapidly at that time.

Throughout my career, I continued to follow my cousin's example, consistently seeking out new technologies to benefit my business and clients. I'm not alone in this; all successful Realtors rely on a set of tools that help them stay organized, simplify processes for their clients, and allow them to work from anywhere in the world.

To help you get started, I've listed the tools I regularly use and how I apply them. These tools allowed me to manage both my business and brokerage simultaneously, all while still having time for family and friends.

NOTE:

It took me a while to find which tools worked best for me, so I encourage you to experiment with your own. Only you know how you work best, and it's important to find the tools that fit your style to ensure you're as efficient as possible in your day-to-day business.

Google Drive

Google Drive is the main tool I use (and still use). It offers an array of powerful tools, all for free! All you need is a Gmail account to access them. Once you've signed up, click the nine-dot square in the upper right corner, and you'll see all the applications available to you. These apps can be used online or downloaded individually on any device. They also sync across devices, allowing for seamless use. For example, if I add a note to Google Keep on my phone, I'll immediately see that note on my computer's Keep application.

Here are a few Google Drive applications I use regularly:

Calendar

Realtors live and die by their calendars—it's essential to learn how to manage it, or it will manage you. Google Calendar is incredibly easy to use, and it syncs across all your devices, so you can access it anywhere. Plus, it sends you reminders for appointments, which is extremely helpful when you have a million things happening at once.

Keep

This application is great for taking notes or making checklists. I have multiple checklist templates built, including my new listing checklist, new buyer checklist, and after-closing checklist. I also use it for my daily to-do lists, keeping everything—business or personal—organized in one place.

Docs (similar to Microsoft Word)

I use Docs for everything I would typically use Word for. For example, I draft all my listing descriptions on Docs before adding them to the MLS. I also have a showing schedule template that I share with clients after scheduling their property viewings.

Sheets (similar to Microsoft Excel)

For anything I would normally use Excel for, I turn to Sheets. It functions just like Excel with the same formulas and formats but in an online version. One of its primary uses for me is tracking my transactions year after year.

DropBox

DropBox is where I store all my documents, both business and personal. It's reasonably priced, offering tons of storage space. As a cloud-based program, it allows access to your files on any device as long as you download the application.

Evernote

Evernote is similar to Google Keep but more advanced. It's fantastic for tracking checklists or anything you need to keep organized. It's free to use on two devices, but once you add a third, there's a charge. I use Evernote to track showings on my listings and the feedback I receive. I also maintain my office to-do list, including tasks like following up with leads and finding properties for buyers.

> **NOTE:**
> One key difference between Evernote and Google Keep is that Evernote's checkboxes don't automatically cross out or remove items once checked. This makes it ideal for recurring tasks you complete daily.

Keynote

Keynote is a presentation app similar to Microsoft PowerPoint. I use it on my iPad for buyer and listing presentations, updating them quarterly to reflect current market conditions.

> **NOTE:**
> Google Slides, part of Google Drive, is another presentation app similar to PowerPoint.

DocuSign

DocuSign is an e-signature program that can be used on your desktop or downloaded as an app on your smart device. Although there's an annual fee, it's incredibly user-friendly and saves the hassle of printing documents for client signatures. As e-signatures have become the norm, it makes sense to have this tool in your arsenal.

> **NOTE:**
> Another popular e-signature program is DotLoop. Both offer similar features, so explore each to determine which fits your business best.

Canva

Canva.com is a free online tool, perfect for anyone without a graphic design background. Whether you're designing logos, social media posts, presentations, or even editing videos, Canva is versatile and easy to use. I highly recommend getting familiar with this tool and using it often.

Mailchimp

Mailchimp is an ideal program for sending e-blasts to your database and other Realtors, such as monthly newsletters or marketing campaigns. It's easy to use with pre-made templates or customizable options, and it allows you to segment contacts for targeted outreach. The free version accommodates a certain number of contacts before requiring payment to add more.

▌ iMovie

iMovie is a user-friendly video editing tool. It's simple to use for basic video editing, allowing you to add sounds, titles, pictures, clips, and transitions. It's perfect for quick video projects without requiring complex editing skills.

NOTE:

iMovie is only available on Apple devices. If you don't use Apple, consider alternatives like Camtasia or Adobe Premiere Pro.

▌ Additional Tools to Consider

Here are a few other tools that are worth considering for your business:

- A CRM program for contact management and marketing (Wise Agent)
- A social media management tool (HootSuite)
- Video conferencing software (Zoom)

Recommended Readings

For many of the world's most successful people, reading is not just a hobby—it's a way of life. From business leaders and political figures to celebrities and everyday individuals, the most successful people are often avid readers.

However, successful people don't read just anything. They are selective, choosing to be educated over entertained. They view books as gateways to learning and knowledge. According to Tom Corley, author of Rich Habits: The Daily Success Habits of Wealthy Individuals, wealthy people (with an annual income of $160,000 or more and a liquid net worth of $3.2 million-plus) read for self-improvement, education, and success. In contrast, those with lower incomes (annual income of $35,000 or less and a liquid net worth of $5,000 or less) primarily read for entertainment.

Reading for self-improvement was advice given to me by an older friend when I was in my early twenties. Until then, I would occasionally read, but it was mostly magazines, not books. After my friend explained how regular reading benefited him, I saw the success he was achieving and decided to follow his lead. Since then, I've read hundreds of books, making reading a part of my daily evening routine.

To increase your chances of success in business and life, it's essential to dedicate time each day to reading material that will benefit you. I've found that a combination of informational newsletters and educational books provides the knowledge needed to set yourself apart and create the life you desire.

Reading has helped me build a life where I can provide for my family while doing what I love—and it can do the same for you!

Newsletter Suggestions

Newsletters help you stay informed, inspired, and connected with what's happening in the world. They're curated by experts in various fields, so you don't have to spend hours searching the web for impactful content. Digesting this information can help you converse on a wide range of topics, allowing you to build rapport quickly.

Here are some newsletters I recommend:

Briefcase

A weekly newsletter for real estate entrepreneurs, sharing insights on how trends and events impact the real estate industry.

The Close

Designed for Realtors, teams, and brokerages, this newsletter provides actionable, strategic insights on real estate marketing, lead generation, technology, and team-building from industry professionals.

Inman Agent Edge

This newsletter equips you with tools and techniques to grow and scale your real estate business, featuring intel from industry pros and reporting from a talented editorial team.

Housing Wire News

A daily newsletter offering a comprehensive view of housing news, trends, and analytical data sent every business day.

Morning Brew

Delivers quick, insightful updates about the business world every day, covering topics from Wall Street to Silicon Valley.

The Hustle

Provides witty and insightful analysis of tech and business trends, offering a humorous take on current events.

Entrepreneur Daily

Sent every morning from Monday to Saturday, this newsletter highlights top business news, inspiring stories, advice, and exclusive reporting from Entrepreneur magazine.

> **TIP:**
> Make reading these newsletters part of your morning routine, so you can utilize the information throughout the rest of your day.

▌Book Suggestions

To help you get started with reading (or to offer suggestions if you're already an avid reader), I've included ten books that have greatly impacted my business and life. I've read each of these multiple times and plan to continue rereading them throughout my life.

> **TIP:**
> If you're unsure what book to read next, consider what you need most at that moment and find a book that addresses that area.

The Miracle Morning for Real Estate Agents | Hal Elrod

This book is written as a story, taking you through the journey of a fictional top-producing agent and his top-producing mortgage professional wife as they manage their businesses and lives. It provides guidance on structuring your days to set yourself up for success when no one is telling you where to be and when.

> **NOTE:**
> Early in my career, I struggled with structuring my days. This book gave me the blueprint I needed, and after following it, I became a much more organized person.

Limitless | Jim Kwik

Jim Kwik, a world-renowned brain coach, shares science-based practices and field-tested tips to accelerate self-learning, communication, memory, focus, recall, and speed reading, leading to extraordinary results.

> **NOTE:**
> Our minds are incredibly powerful, yet few people know how to harness their full potential. This book showed me how to unlock the capabilities of my own mind.

Atomic Habits | James Clear

James Clear, an expert on habit formation, offers a proven framework for improving daily habits. He reveals practical strategies for forming good habits, breaking bad ones, and mastering the small behaviors that lead to remarkable outcomes.

> **NOTE:**
> We are the product of our habits. After reading this book, I identified and changed a few bad habits I didn't even realize I had, which made a huge difference in my daily life.

How to Win Friends and Influence People | Dale Carnegie

Carnegie's time-tested advice has helped countless individuals achieve success in their business and personal lives. This book will teach you how to:

- ☑ Make people like you
- ☑ Win people over to your way of thinking
- ☑ Change people's behavior without arousing resentment

> **NOTE:**
>
> Building relationships is crucial for success, and this book taught me how to communicate effectively and gain others' understanding by being likable.

You're Not Listening | Kate Murphy

Murphy explores why people aren't listening, the consequences of this, and how we can reverse the trend. She breaks down the psychology, neuroscience, and sociology of listening and introduces us to exceptional listeners, such as CIA agents, focus group moderators, and bartenders.

> **NOTE:**
>
> Listening is a vital skill for Realtors, but many don't know how to do it well. This book showed me how to listen more effectively to truly understand what people are trying to convey.

Think and Grow Rich | Napoleon Hill

While money and material things are important, Hill explains that the greatest riches come from lasting friendships, loving family relationships, and inner harmony. Applying the philosophies in this book will prepare you to attract and enjoy both material and spiritual success.

> **NOTE:**
>
> This book helped me understand how some of the most successful people throughout history built their fortunes and achieved peace of mind.

Unlimited Power | Tony Robbins

Tony Robbins teaches that your mindset determines what you can and can't achieve. He offers techniques to reprogram your mind, improve your health, strengthen relationships, and become a persuasive communicator.

> **NOTE:**
>
> So much of being a successful Realtor is about mindset. Tony helped me understand how self-talk and reactions to the world around me can make a huge impact on both my life and the lives of others.

The Seven Levels of Communication | Michael Maher

This book explores strategies to help readers build relationships and generate referrals. Each chapter is filled with actionable tools and techniques for business and personal success.

> **NOTE:**
> Referrals are a major part of a Realtor's business. This book helped me understand how to build and maintain relationships so people remember me when they need my services.

Crushing It! | Gary Vaynerchuk

Gary Vaynerchuk breaks down every major social media platform and offers tactical advice on how to amplify your personal brand. Whether you're a professional or just starting out, this book provides practical insights on leveraging social media to grow your brand.

> **NOTE:**
> I read this book to learn how to use social media to increase my brand recognition.

The Millionaire Real Estate Agent | Gary Keller

This book offers a plan to transform a real estate sales job into a million-dollar business. Gary Keller outlines the models needed for success and provides a step-by-step guide to implementing them.

> **NOTE:**
> This book taught me how to think like a top producer and helped me take my business to the level where I could make a million dollars. It's a must-read for anyone ready to expand their career.

| Additional Recommendations

Here are a few more books that complement the ones mentioned above. Together, they offer many layers of knowledge to help you create the life you envision:

- ✅ Rich Dad Poor Dad | Robert Kiyosaki
- ✅ Money: Master the Game | Tony Robbins
- ✅ Think Like a Monk | Jay Shetty
- ✅ Never Eat Alone | Keith Ferrazzi
- ✅ The Power of Habit | Charles Duhigg

- Unshakable | Tony Robbins
- Smarter Faster Better | Charles Duhigg
- When | Daniel Pink

| Suggested Autobiographies

We can learn a lot from those who came before us. Their mindset, work ethic, and mistakes provide valuable lessons. Here are a few autobiographies that offer insight into what it takes to be great:

- Steve Jobs | Walter Isaacson
- Michael Jordan: The Life | Roland Lazenby
- Elon Musk | Ashlee Vance
- Shoe Dog | Phil Knight
- Total Recall: My Unbelievably True Life Story | Arnold Schwarzenegger

Afterword

Ever since I was a young kid, I've felt that I was meant for something bigger. I didn't know what it was, so I followed the path my parents preferred. I graduated from college and got a job at a major corporation. After two years, I knew it wasn't for me, so I did something I had never done before—I quit.

When I left corporate America, I had no idea what I wanted to do with my life. I just knew I never wanted to be an employee again. When I discovered real estate, I immediately fell in love with the industry. The idea that my success was directly related to my efforts, coupled with the opportunity to help people make one of the most important decisions of their lives, was exactly what I was looking for.

Being a goal-driven person, I entered the industry determined to win a top producer award. Though it took me almost a decade, in 2018, I won top producer awards for both total sales production and the number of properties sold. But as soon as I achieved this, the drive I had for being a Realtor vanished. I had accomplished everything I wanted on the sales side, so I needed a new focus. I turned my attention to growing the brokerage I had started a few years earlier. In under a decade, with the help of my partner, we expanded the brokerage to 66 agents, two offices, and annual real estate sales of $200 million. As much as I loved what we were doing, deep down I felt I had taken it as far as I wanted. By mid-2023, I made the decision to sell, and officially sold the business in February 2024.

Throughout most of 2023, I felt lost. From the moment the clock struck midnight on December 31, 2022, something didn't feel right. I spent the year exploring different methods to figure out what was off. I started seeing a therapist, took up meditating every evening, and even changed my workout routine. But it wasn't until early November that everything became clear.

One weekend, while my wife and kids were out of the house, the weight of feeling lost overwhelmed me. I decided to meditate, knowing I wouldn't be interrupted. Sitting on a few cushions in my downstairs living room, I let my mind drift. I entered a deep meditative state, one I had never experienced before. That's when everything became clear, and I understood exactly what I was meant to do.

For my entire career, I had noticed how little education was available for newer Realtors. I often sought out agents who needed help and offered my advice. This desire to help others led to the creation of my brokerage, which was built on providing new agents with the education I and so many others had missed when we started. These thoughts coalesced during my meditation, forming a vision to transform the real estate industry—starting with this book.

I wrote the first version of this book quickly in late 2022. After receiving feedback, I realized it wasn't very good. So, I started revising it until business and personal responsibilities forced me to put it down in March 2023. It wasn't until eight months later, after my vision, that I picked it up again. This time, I knew exactly why I needed to write it. It couldn't just be any ordinary book; to transform a 100-year-old industry, it needed to be designed and written in a way that readers would remember the content and apply it easily.

Every detail of this book was thought out to have the greatest impact on you—from the order of the chapters and how they're laid out, to the stories, examples, tips, and additional sections. I also want you to know that none of this book was written using artificial intelligence. I believe the greatest impact comes from learning from others, not machines. The only time I used AI was to help generate ideas when I was stuck on a topic. The actual words, however, come from my knowledge, experience, and research.

After reading this book, I hope you'll have the confidence, knowledge, and tools to build the business and life you desire. At the same time, I hope you understand the importance of your role in helping people make the most significant financial decision of their lives. I encourage you to take this role seriously, so we can change how consumers view Realtors and elevate the respect for our profession.

In conclusion, I want to leave you with a few pieces of wisdom that have greatly benefited me throughout my life:

- Your time is limited. Be selective about how you spend it, and don't waste a second. Time is the one commodity you can't buy more of.
- Seek knowledge from everywhere, all the time.
- Appreciate your relationships, work to strengthen them, and create new ones.
- Don't ignore your health. You only get one body, and how you treat it has a significant impact on your life and the lives of those around you.
- Strive to be better every single day—don't let yourself get complacent.
- Never settle for less; always pursue more.
- Most importantly, treat your clients as you would want to be treated and provide them with the highest level of service possible.

Thank you for sharing part of your life with me.

I wish you nothing but the best.

Acknowledgments

Of all the chapters in this book, this one is the most challenging for me. How can I possibly thank all the people in my life who have played a role in helping me become the person I am today? This question echoed in my mind as I struggled to find the words. In the end, I realized I can't possibly thank everyone individually, so I will keep it to a few. To everyone I don't mention, thank you for being a part of my journey. Whether you were in my life for a short time or longer, I appreciate all of you!

I want to start with my wife. I've rewritten this part countless times because I'm not sure how I can put into words what you mean to me. I am so grateful that we found each other in this life. You are my perfect complement, the one person who truly understands me. You challenge me every day to be better and guide me through the unknowns. Most of all, you love and support me unconditionally. I love you with all my heart, and I am beyond blessed to have you by my side on this journey. I love you!

To my boys, thank you for your love and for being my daily reminder that while work is important, being present in the moment with you is priceless. I love you both so much!

To my parents, thank you for everything you've done for me. For the sacrifices you made to give me the childhood I had and for your continued support as I grew older. I love you!

To my brother, thank you for all the experiences we've shared and for being my best friend growing up. Love you, bro!

To my guy Alejandro, I appreciate our partnership and the time we've spent working together. Your different perspective has helped me see things I might not have otherwise. Thank you for all your support.

Being a Realtor is not something one can do alone. It takes the support of many to build a successful career. To all my colleagues in the real estate industry, I am deeply grateful to each and every one of you. Thank you for your generosity with your time and for all the guidance you've provided along the way.

Finally, to you, the reader—thank you! Not only for purchasing this book but, more importantly, for reading and applying it. Your trust in my words means everything to me, and I hope this book helps you as much as writing it helped me.

About the Author

In August 2009, Michael Opyd left a comfortable corporate job and plunged headfirst into real estate with only $2,000 to his name and no plan B. He entered the industry during the Great Recession, one of the toughest markets in the country's history. The early years were lean—Michael managed to help only a handful of people find rentals and didn't make his first sale until his third year. To make ends meet, he took on odd jobs for veteran Realtors, who paid him in cash, and attended broker's opens (open houses for Realtors) on Tuesdays, which provided lunch and gift cards to stretch his meals throughout the week.

Michael's first brokerage was poorly managed, offering no formal education, and his managing broker wasn't interested in mentoring new agents. Left to his own devices, Michael took matters into his own hands. He dedicated his early years to self-education, shadowing veteran agents on appointments, asking countless questions, reading everything he could, and attending every educational event he could afford.

After switching to a brokerage that offered more education, training, and mentorship, Michael's business started to gain traction. During this time, he was elected to the Chicago Association of Realtors Young Professional Network board for two consecutive terms, serving alongside many of Chicago's top up-and-coming Realtors, some of whom have become top producers and brokerage owners.

Though it took a few years for Michael to close his first sale, once he did, his production increased year after year. To date, he has sold nearly $75 million in real estate without any assistance. In 2018, Michael was recognized by the Chicago Association of Realtors as a top producer in both total sales and total number of transactions.

Recognizing the lack of education for new Realtors, Michael opened his own brokerage in Chicago's West Loop in 2016. His brokerage was built on the foundation of providing new agents with the education and tools necessary for success. To support this mission, Michael and his partner developed a six-week mentorship program covering everything from mental preparation for the challenges of real estate to working with clients and building a brand. Nearly 50 agents graduated from the program, averaging 5.6 sales in the 12 months following completion—well above the national average of 1-2 for new Realtors. Before selling the company in February 2024, the brokerage had two offices, 66 agents, and closed nearly $200 million in sales annually.

Michael's unique perspective on the real estate industry has led to his being featured in numerous online articles, including Forbes, Inman, US News, Investopedia, The Chicago Tribune, and The Chicago Sun-Times. He has also been featured multiple times in Chicago Agent Magazine, both on the cover and as a contributor, and in Chicago Real Producers Magazine.

Michael's true passion lies in educating Realtors. From his early days mentoring new agents, he realized that helping people in the industry is his calling. Having experienced the challenges firsthand, Michael is dedicated to ensuring that new Realtors receive the proper education and support they need to thrive, so they don't have to face the same struggles he did when starting out.

| Connect with Michael Opyd:

- Instagram: @michaelopyd
- Facebook: @michaelopyd
- LinkedIn: @michaelopyd
- TikTok: @michaelopyd
- YouTube: @michaelopyd

Index

Chapter 12 | Leads

Chapter 13 | Branding

Chapter 14 | Social Media

Chapter 15 | Starting a Team

What did you think of The Education of a Real Estate Agent? I hope this book helped you to build the business you desire and lead you on a path to achieve all you want in life!

I have one small favor to ask before you go, could you please leave me a review on Amazon? It would mean the world to me to hear what you thought (good or bad). Just scan the QR code below to leave it. Thank you again for purchasing my book!

Also, make sure to pick up the workbook that compliments this workbook! You can purchase It below.

PURCHASE IT HERE

Finally, make sure to check out my website **www.michaelopyd.com** I have FREE downloadable resources to help your business and while your there please make sure to sign up for my weekly educational newsletter!

Made in United States
North Haven, CT
27 March 2025

67274367R00163